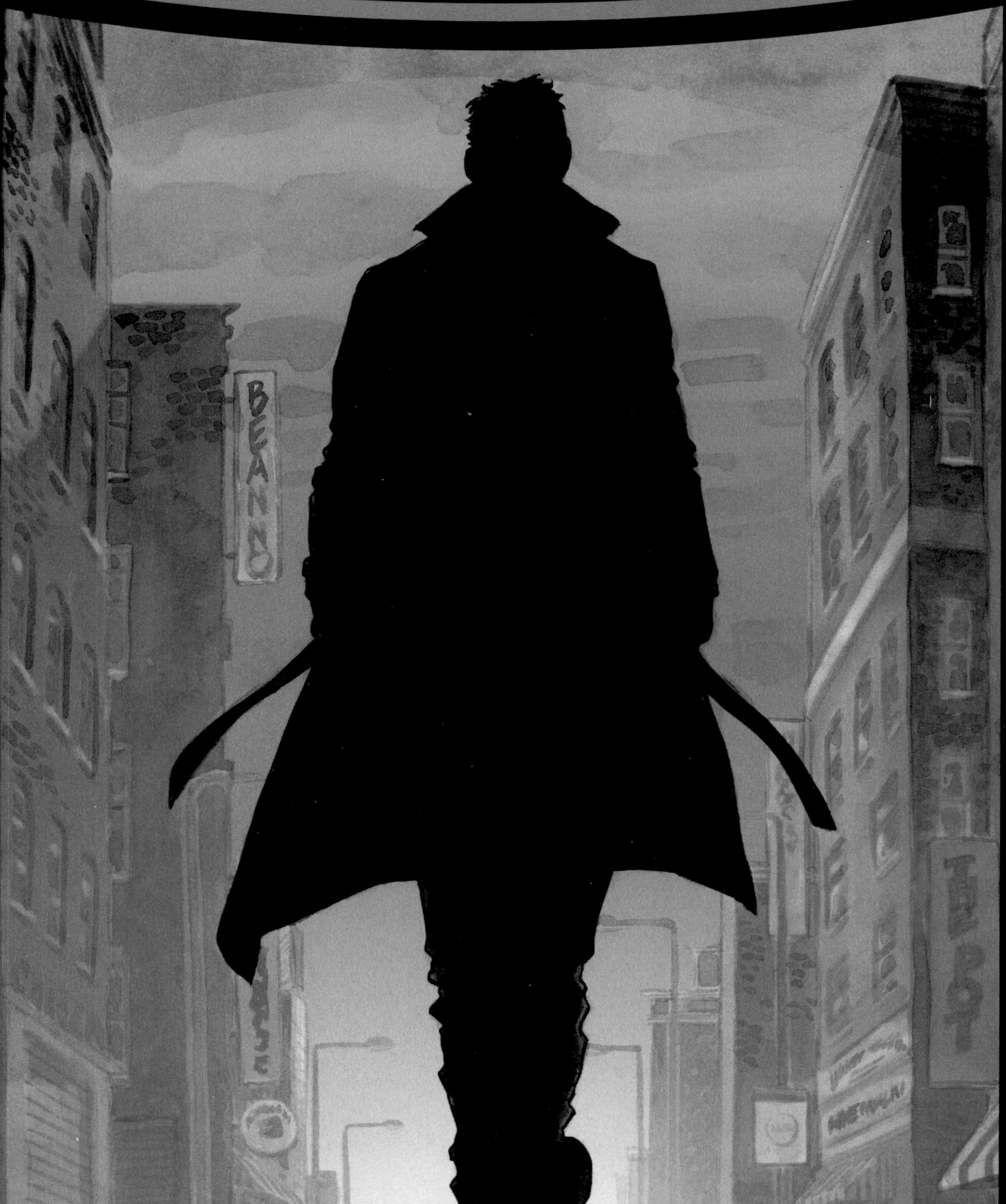

THE HELLBLAZER

VOL. 3 THE INSPIRATION GAME

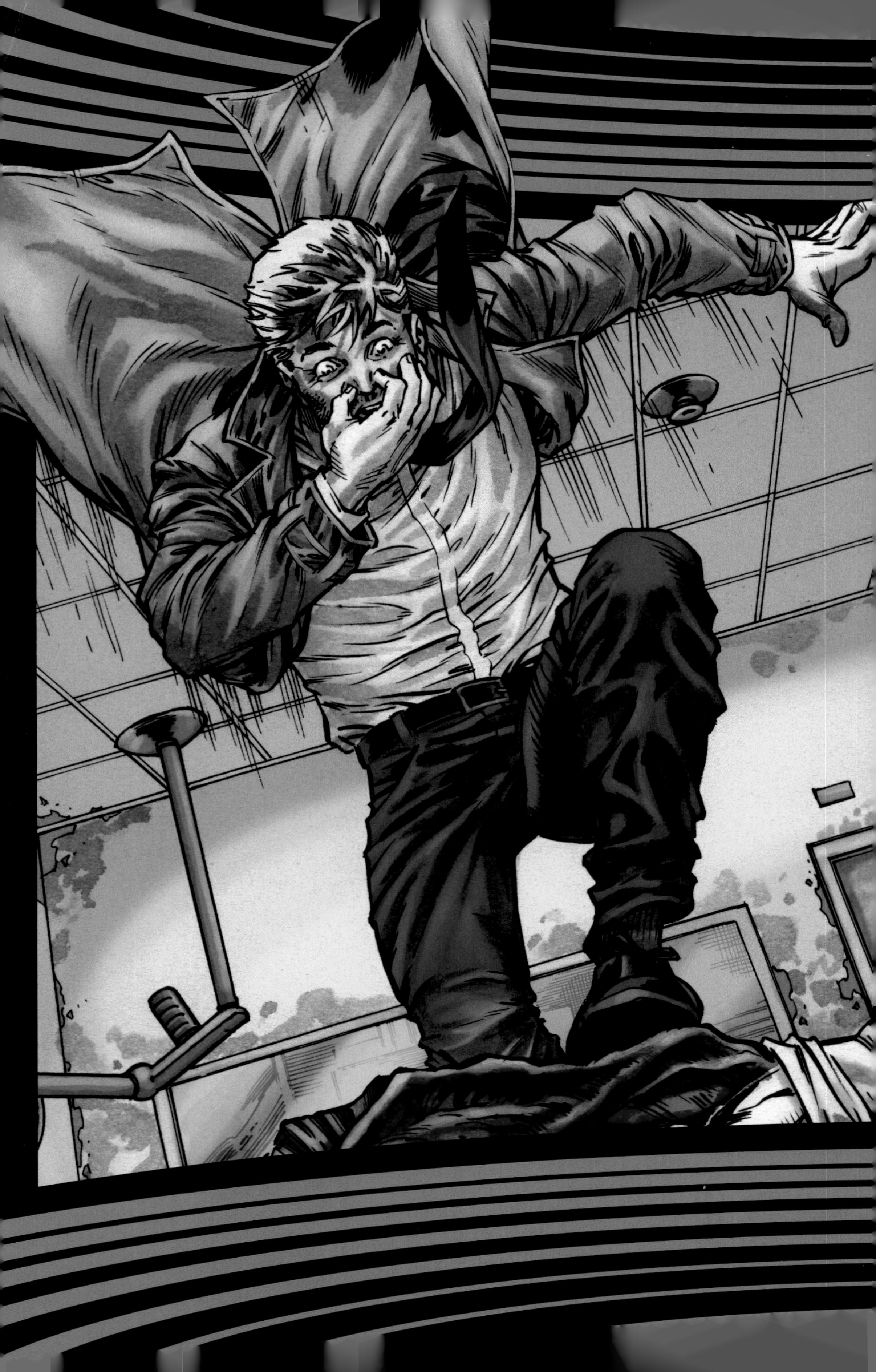

THE HELLBLAZER

VOL. 3 THE INSPIRATION GAME

TIM SEELEY * **RICHARD KADREY**
writers

JESÚS MERINO * **DAVIDE FABBRI** * **JOSÉ MARZÁN JR.**
artists

CARRIE STRACHAN
colorist

SAL CIPRIANO
letterer

TIM SEELEY with CHRIS SOTOMAYOR
collection cover art

TIM SEELEY with CHRIS SOTOMAYOR
JESÚS MERINO with CARRIE STRACHAN
original series covers

JOHN CONSTANTINE created by ALAN MOORE, STEVE BISSETTE,
JOHN TOTLEBEN and JAMIE DELANO & JOHN RIDGWAY

SUPERMAN created by JERRY SIEGEL and JOE SHUSTER
By special arrangement with THE JERRY SIEGEL FAMILY

KRISTY QUINN Editor - Original Series
JEB WOODARD Group Editor - Collected Editions * **SCOTT NYBAKKEN** Editor - Collected Edition
STEVE COOK Design Director - Books * **SHANNON STEWART** Publication Design

BOB HARRAS Senior VP - Editor-in-Chief, DC Comics
PAT McCALLUM Executive Editor, DC Comics

DIANE NELSON President * **DAN DiDIO** Publisher * **JIM LEE** Publisher * **GEOFF JOHNS** President & Chief Creative Officer
AMIT DESAI Executive VP - Business & Marketing Strategy, Direct to Consumer & Global Franchise Management
SAM ADES Senior VP & General Manager, Digital Services * **BOBBIE CHASE** VP & Executive Editor, Young Reader & Talent Development
MARK CHIARELLO Senior VP - Art, Design & Collected Editions * **JOHN CUNNINGHAM** Senior VP - Sales & Trade Marketing
ANNE DePIES Senior VP - Business Strategy, Finance & Administration * **DON FALLETTI** VP - Manufacturing Operations
LAWRENCE GANEM VP - Editorial Administration & Talent Relations * **ALISON GILL** Senior VP - Manufacturing & Operations
HANK KANALZ Senior VP - Editorial Strategy & Administration * **JAY KOGAN** VP - Legal Affairs
JACK MAHAN VP - Business Affairs * **NICK J. NAPOLITANO** VP - Manufacturing Administration * **EDDIE SCANNELL** VP - Consumer Marketing
COURTNEY SIMMONS Senior VP - Publicity & Communications * **JIM (SKI) SOKOLOWSKI** VP - Comic Book Specialty Sales & Trade Marketing
NANCY SPEARS VP - Mass, Book, Digital Sales & Trade Marketing * **MICHELE R. WELLS** VP - Content Strategy

THE HELLBLAZER VOL. 3: THE INSPIRATION GAME

DC Comics, 2900 West Alameda Ave., Burbank, CA 91505
Printed by LSC Communications, Kendallville, IN, USA. 2/2/18.
First Printing. ISBN: 978-1-4012-7801-4

Library of Congress Cataloging-in-Publication Data is available.

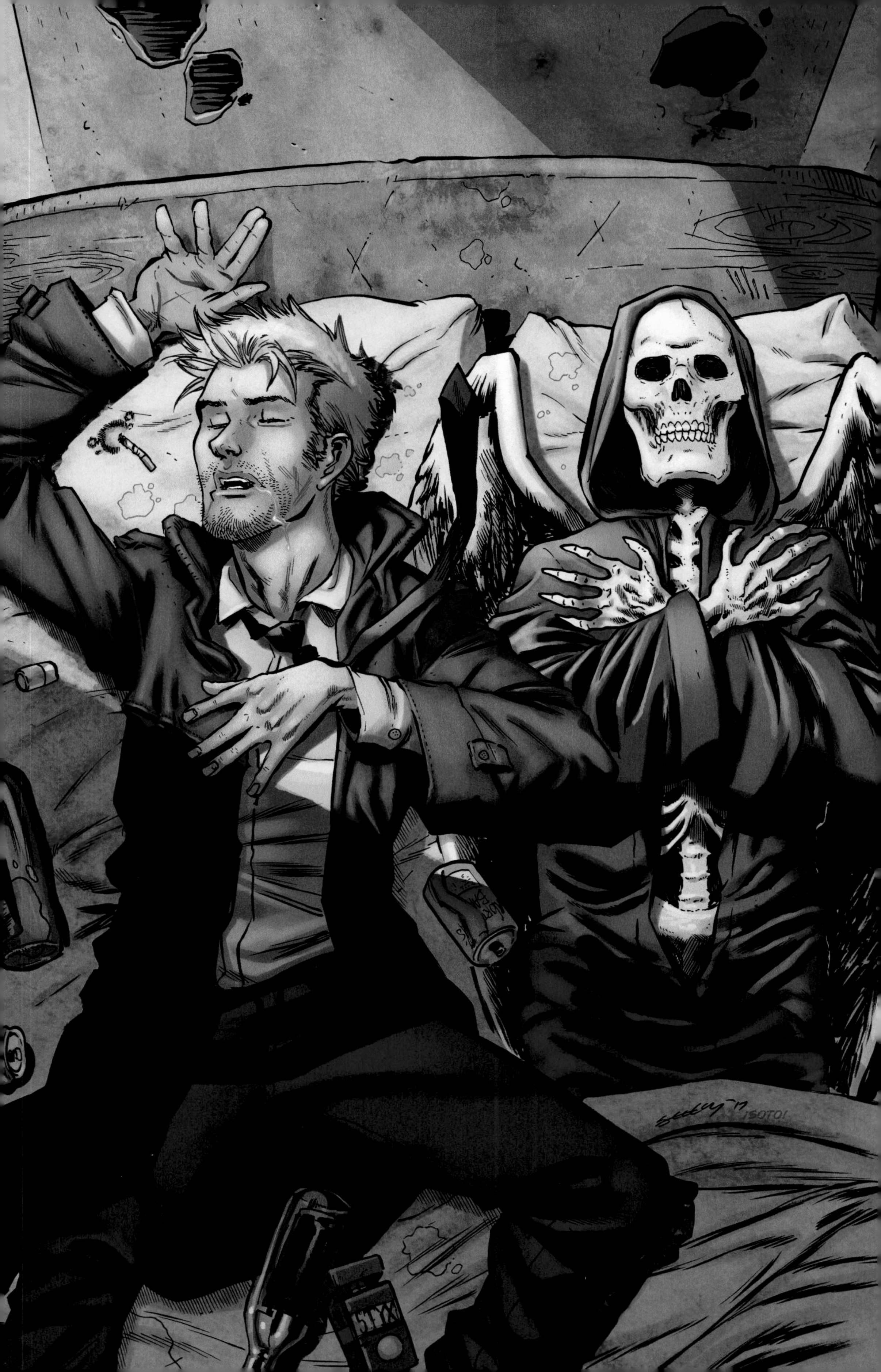
¡SOTO!
STYX

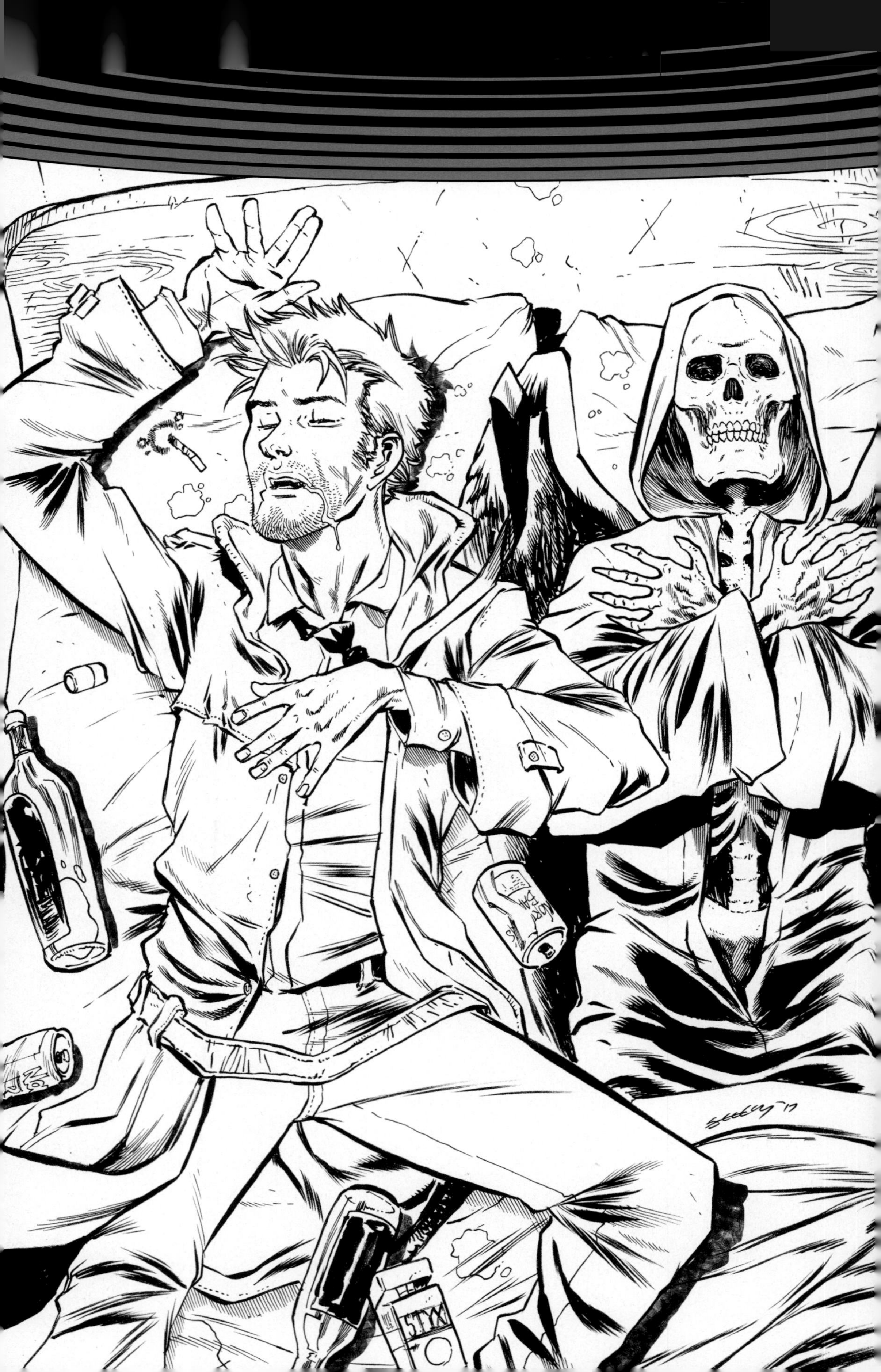
STYX

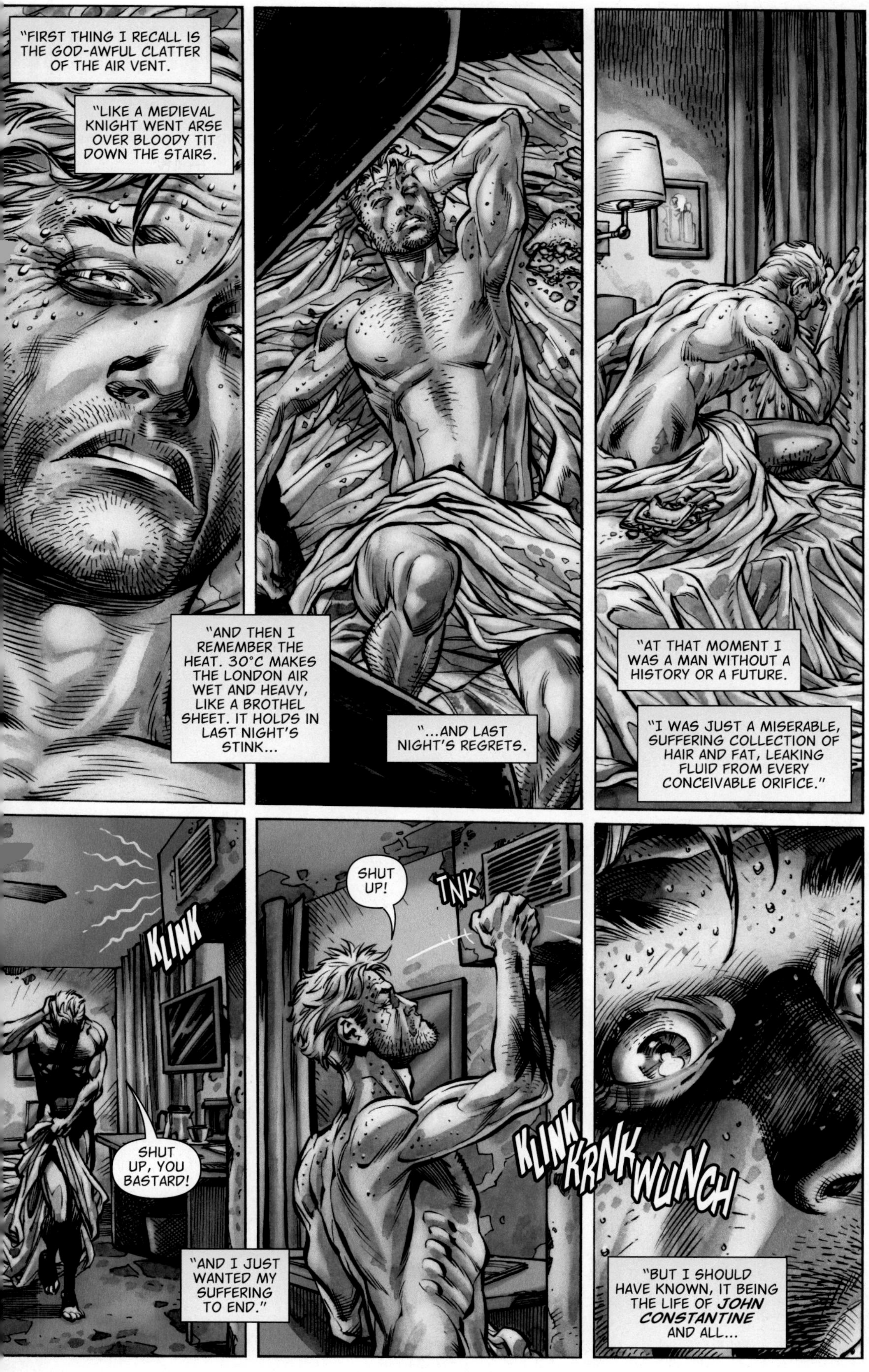
"FIRST THING I RECALL IS THE GOD-AWFUL CLATTER OF THE AIR VENT.
"LIKE A MEDIEVAL KNIGHT WENT ARSE OVER BLOODY TIT DOWN THE STAIRS.
"AND THEN I REMEMBER THE HEAT. 30°C MAKES THE LONDON AIR WET AND HEAVY, LIKE A BROTHEL SHEET. IT HOLDS IN LAST NIGHT'S STINK...
"...AND LAST NIGHT'S REGRETS.
"AT THAT MOMENT I WAS A MAN WITHOUT A HISTORY OR A FUTURE.
"I WAS JUST A MISERABLE, SUFFERING COLLECTION OF HAIR AND FAT, LEAKING FLUID FROM EVERY CONCEIVABLE ORIFICE."
KLINK
SHUT UP, YOU BASTARD!
"AND I JUST WANTED MY SUFFERING TO END."
SHUT UP!
TNK
KLINK KRNK WUNCH
"BUT I SHOULD HAVE KNOWN, IT BEING THE LIFE OF *JOHN CONSTANTINE* AND ALL...

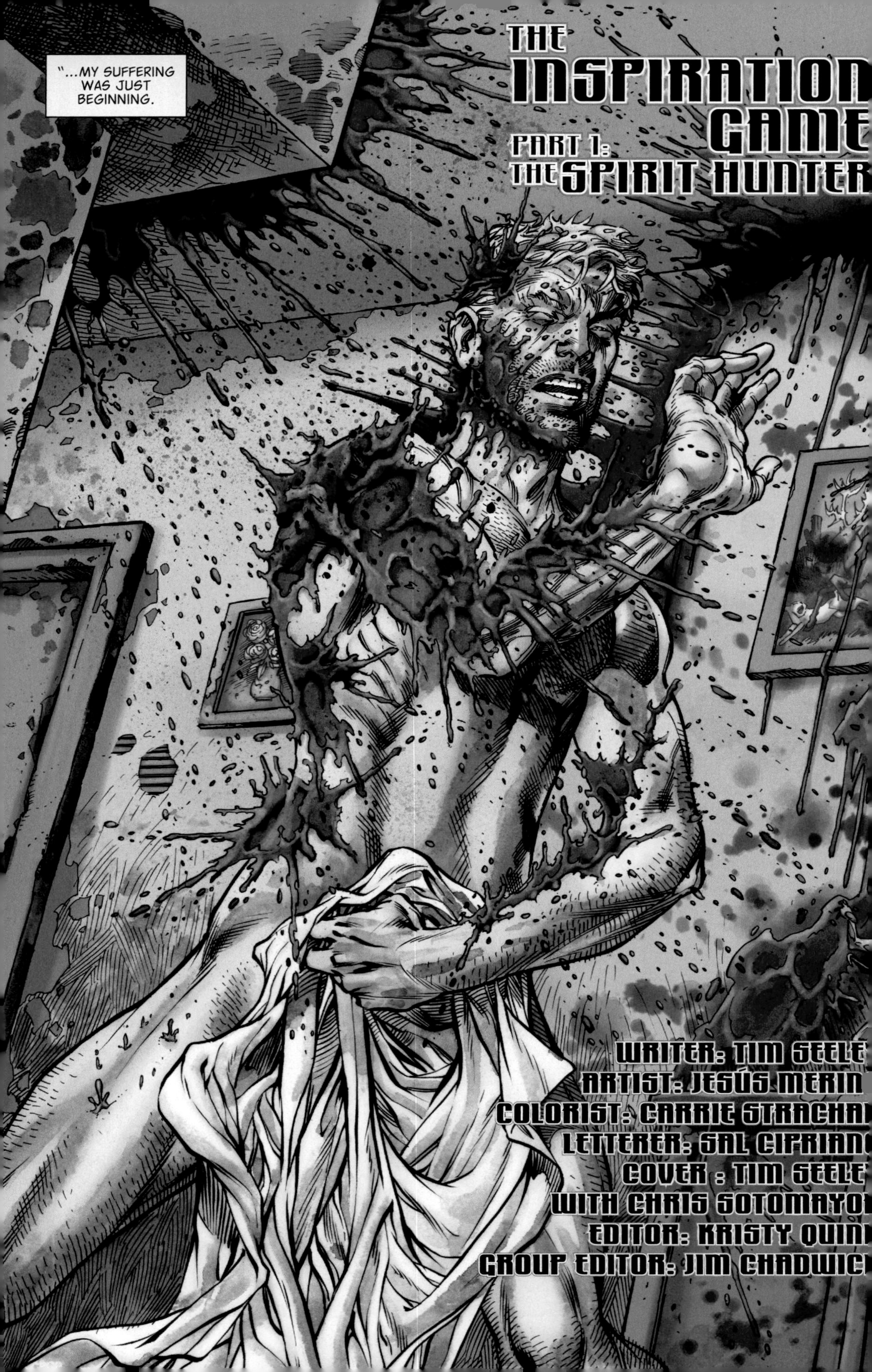
"...MY SUFFERING WAS JUST BEGINNING.
THE INSPIRATION GAME
PART 1: THE SPIRIT HUNTER
WRITER: TIM SEELE
ARTIST: JESÚS MERIN
COLORIST: CARRIE STRACHA
LETTERER: SAL CIPRIANO
COVER : TIM SEELE
WITH CHRIS SOTOMAYO
EDITOR: KRISTY QUIN
GROUP EDITOR: JIM CHADWIC

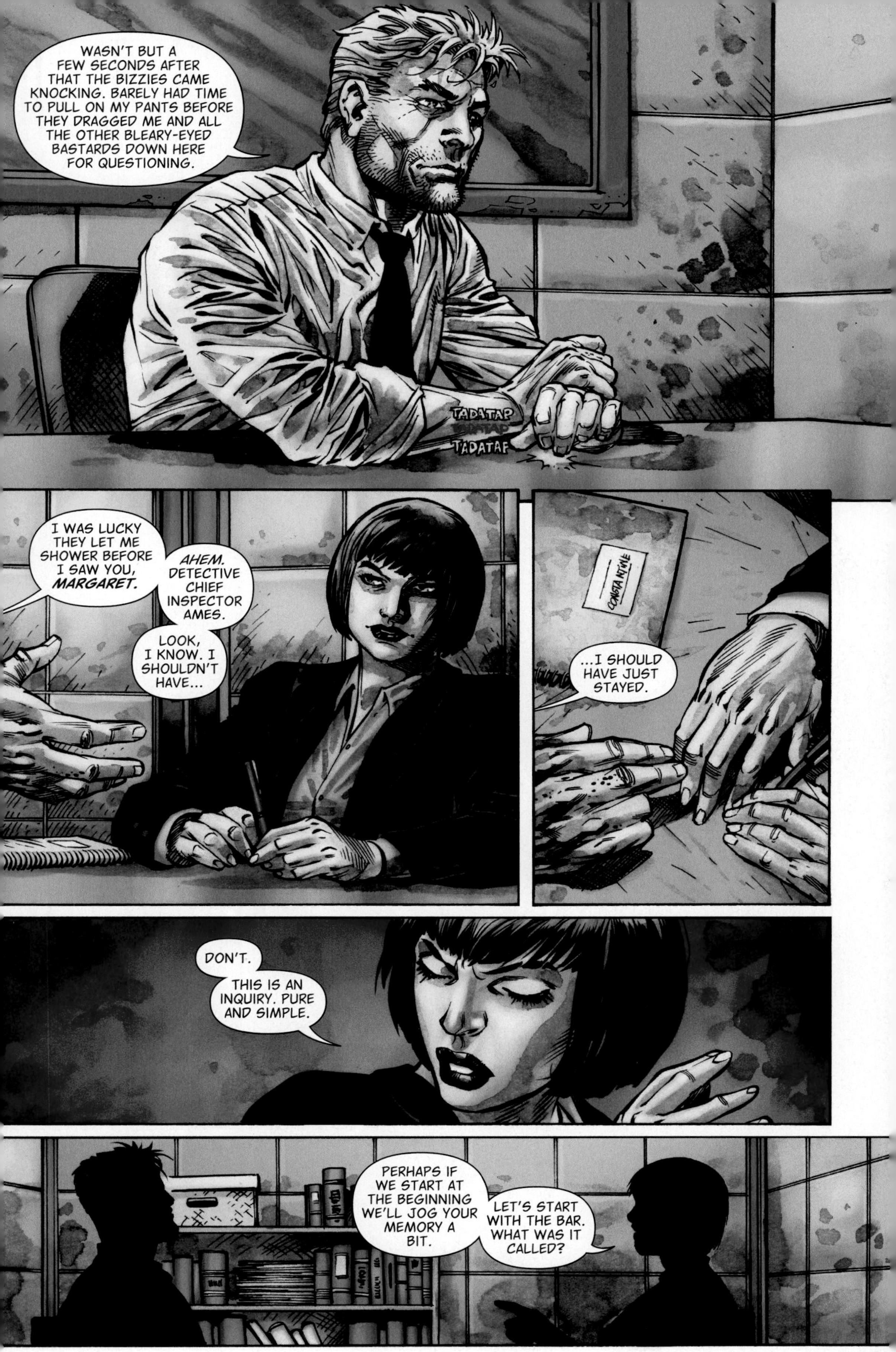
WASN'T BUT A FEW SECONDS AFTER THAT THE BIZZIES CAME KNOCKING. BARELY HAD TIME TO PULL ON MY PANTS BEFORE THEY DRAGGED ME AND ALL THE OTHER BLEARY-EYED BASTARDS DOWN HERE FOR QUESTIONING.
TADATAP
TADATAP
I WAS LUCKY THEY LET ME SHOWER BEFORE I SAW YOU, MARGARET.
AHEM. DETECTIVE CHIEF INSPECTOR AMES.
LOOK, I KNOW. I SHOULDN'T HAVE...
CONSTANTINE
...I SHOULD HAVE JUST STAYED.
DON'T.
THIS IS AN INQUIRY. PURE AND SIMPLE.
PERHAPS IF WE START AT THE BEGINNING WE'LL JOG YOUR MEMORY A BIT.
LET'S START WITH THE BAR. WHAT WAS IT CALLED?

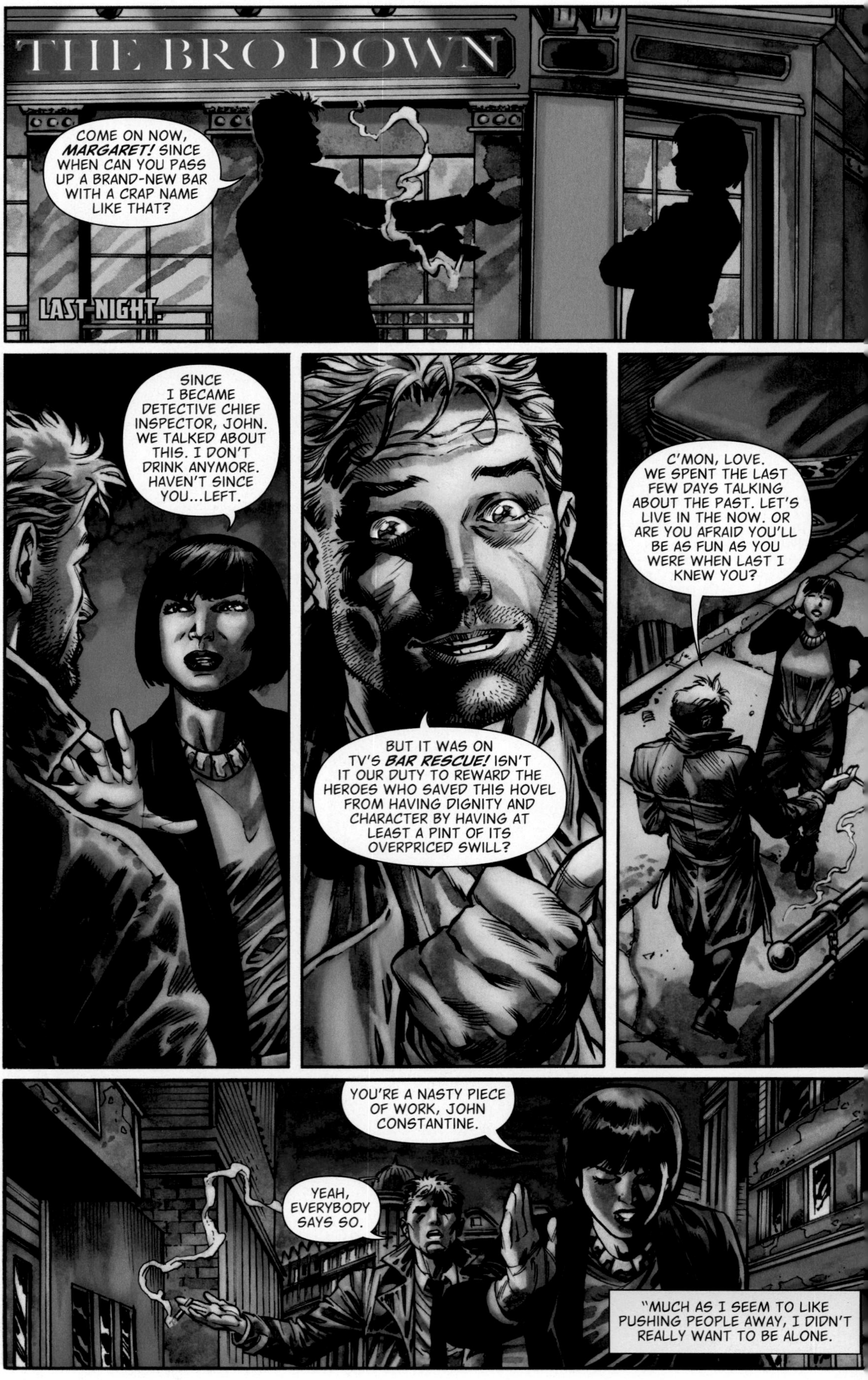
THE BRO DOWN
COME ON NOW, MARGARET! SINCE WHEN CAN YOU PASS UP A BRAND-NEW BAR WITH A CRAP NAME LIKE THAT?
LAST NIGHT.
SINCE I BECAME DETECTIVE CHIEF INSPECTOR, JOHN. WE TALKED ABOUT THIS. I DON'T DRINK ANYMORE. HAVEN'T SINCE YOU...LEFT.
BUT IT WAS ON TV'S BAR RESCUE! ISN'T IT OUR DUTY TO REWARD THE HEROES WHO SAVED THIS HOVEL FROM HAVING DIGNITY AND CHARACTER BY HAVING AT LEAST A PINT OF ITS OVERPRICED SWILL?
C'MON, LOVE. WE SPENT THE LAST FEW DAYS TALKING ABOUT THE PAST. LET'S LIVE IN THE NOW. OR ARE YOU AFRAID YOU'LL BE AS FUN AS YOU WERE WHEN LAST I KNEW YOU?
YOU'RE A NASTY PIECE OF WORK, JOHN CONSTANTINE.
YEAH, EVERYBODY SAYS SO.
"MUCH AS I SEEM TO LIKE PUSHING PEOPLE AWAY, I DIDN'T REALLY WANT TO BE ALONE.

"SITUATIONS LIKE THAT I TEND TO OVERCOMPENSATE. I USUALLY TRADE ONE FOR TWO."

WHAT ARE WE HAVING THEN, MATES?

"THEY WERE ONE OF THOSE YOUNG, ATTRACTIVE COUPLES RUINING LONDON. HIS NAME WAS *WENDALL*. HE ORDERED CHEAP BEER IRONICALLY AND THEN WINCED AT EVERY SIP."

"HER NAME WAS *ERAJ*. SHE SAID SHE WORKED AT A STRIP BAR. WHEN I ASKED HER ABOUT HER POLE WORK, SHE EXPLAINED SHE MANAGED A CLUB OF ALL MALE DANCERS. CALLED HERSELF *'THE SAUSAGE SERGEANT.'*"

"I THOUGHT SHE'D BE A BETTER THAN AVERAGE WAY TO GET BACK AT YOU AND STICK IT TO WINCING WENDALL AT THE SAME TIME."

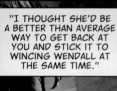

OH! MY FRIEND IS HERE.

MARTIN! COME OVER HERE!

"HER FRIEND'S NAME WAS *MARTIN GERMAN.* WIMPY SORT. WOULDN'T HAVE LOOKED HIS WAY NORMALLY. BUT THEN ERAJ TOLD ME WHAT OL' MARTY DID FOR A LIVING."

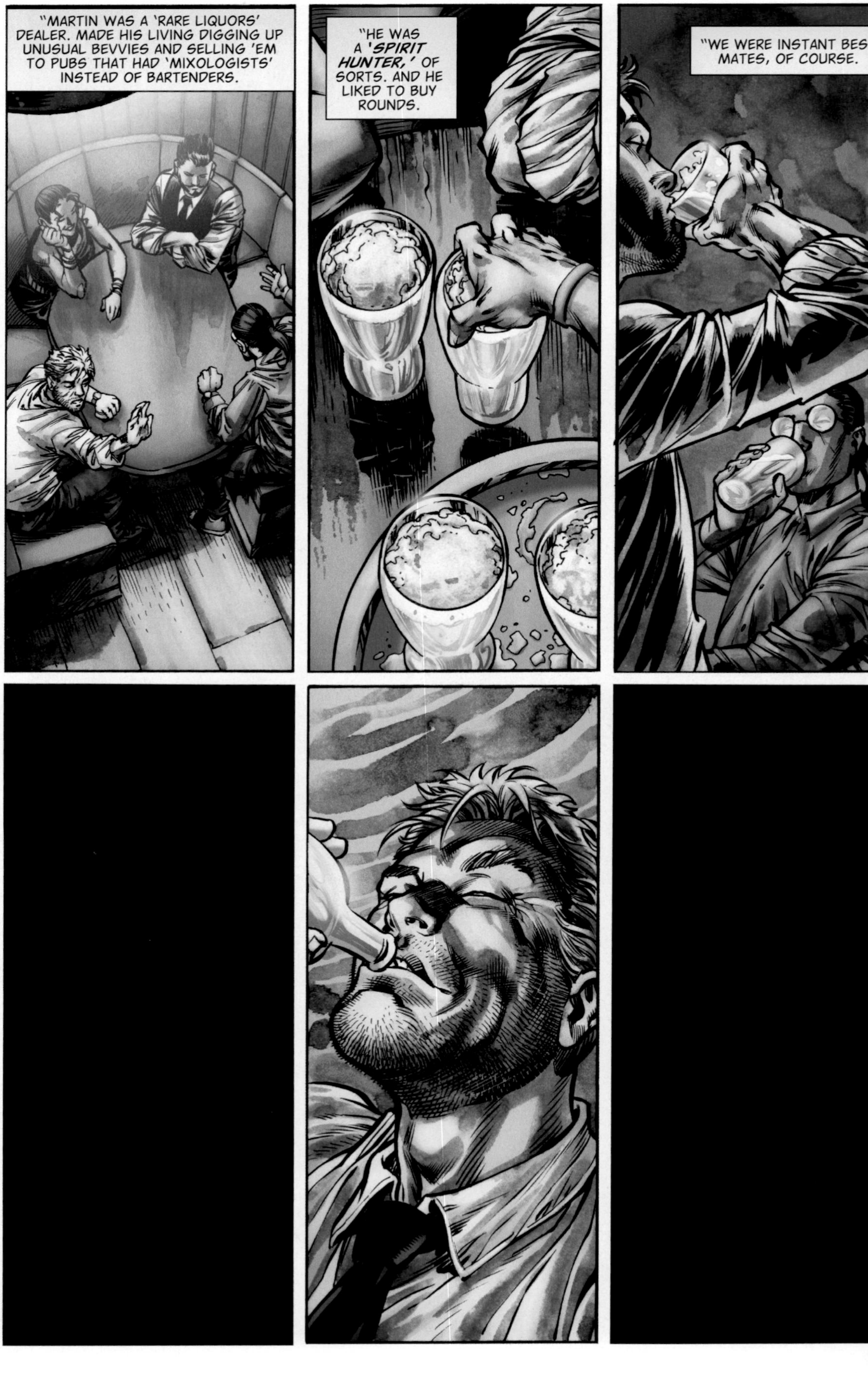
"MARTIN WAS A 'RARE LIQUORS' DEALER. MADE HIS LIVING DIGGING UP UNUSUAL BEVVIES AND SELLING 'EM TO PUBS THAT HAD 'MIXOLOGISTS' INSTEAD OF BARTENDERS.
"HE WAS A 'SPIRIT HUNTER,' OF SORTS. AND HE LIKED TO BUY ROUNDS.
"WE WERE INSTANT BES
MATES, OF COURSE.

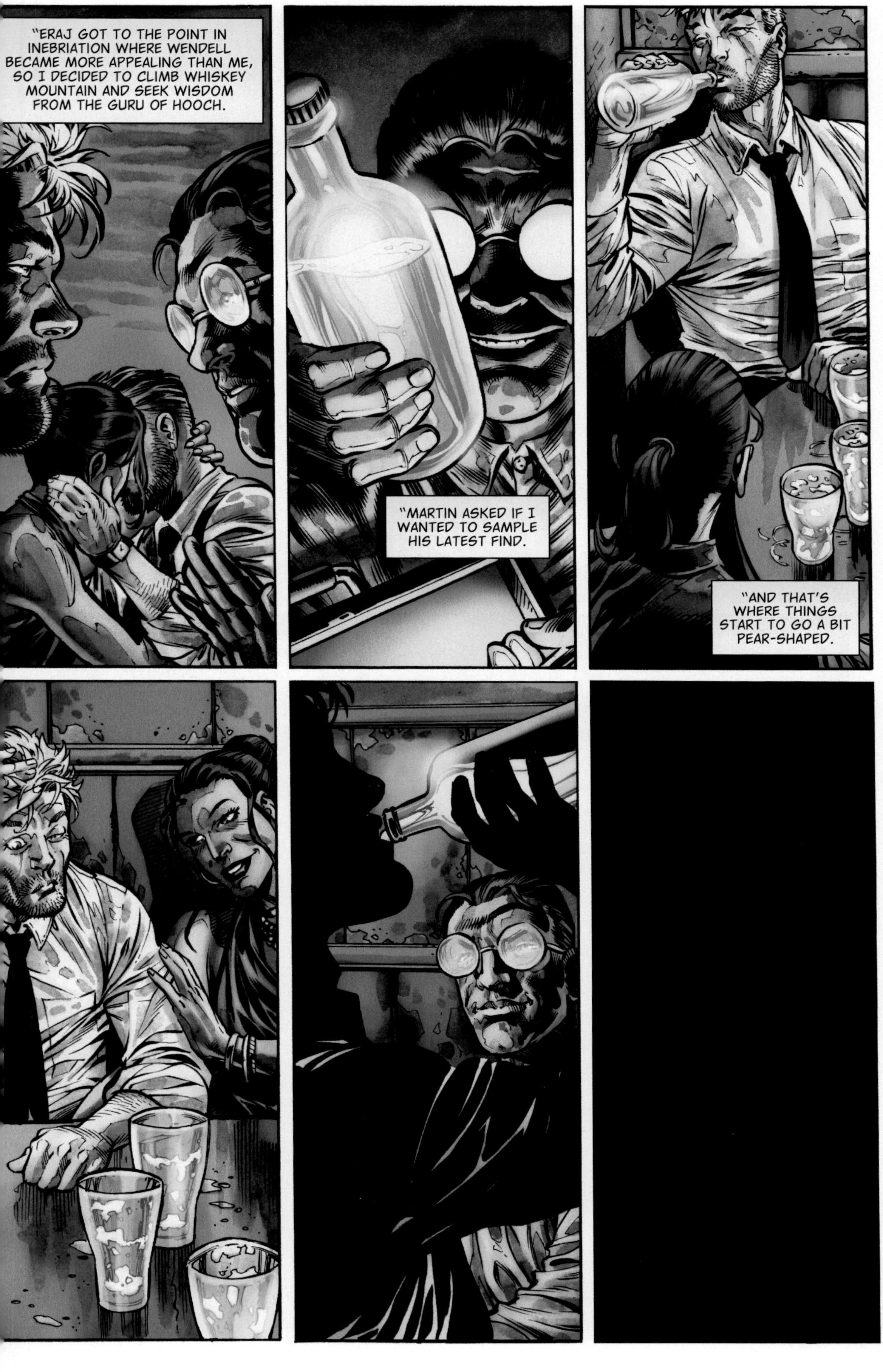
"ERAJ GOT TO THE POINT IN INEBRIATION WHERE WENDELL BECAME MORE APPEALING THAN ME, SO I DECIDED TO CLIMB WHISKEY MOUNTAIN AND SEEK WISDOM FROM THE GURU OF HOOCH.
"MARTIN ASKED IF I WANTED TO SAMPLE HIS LATEST FIND.
"AND THAT'S WHERE THINGS START TO GO A BIT PEAR-SHAPED.

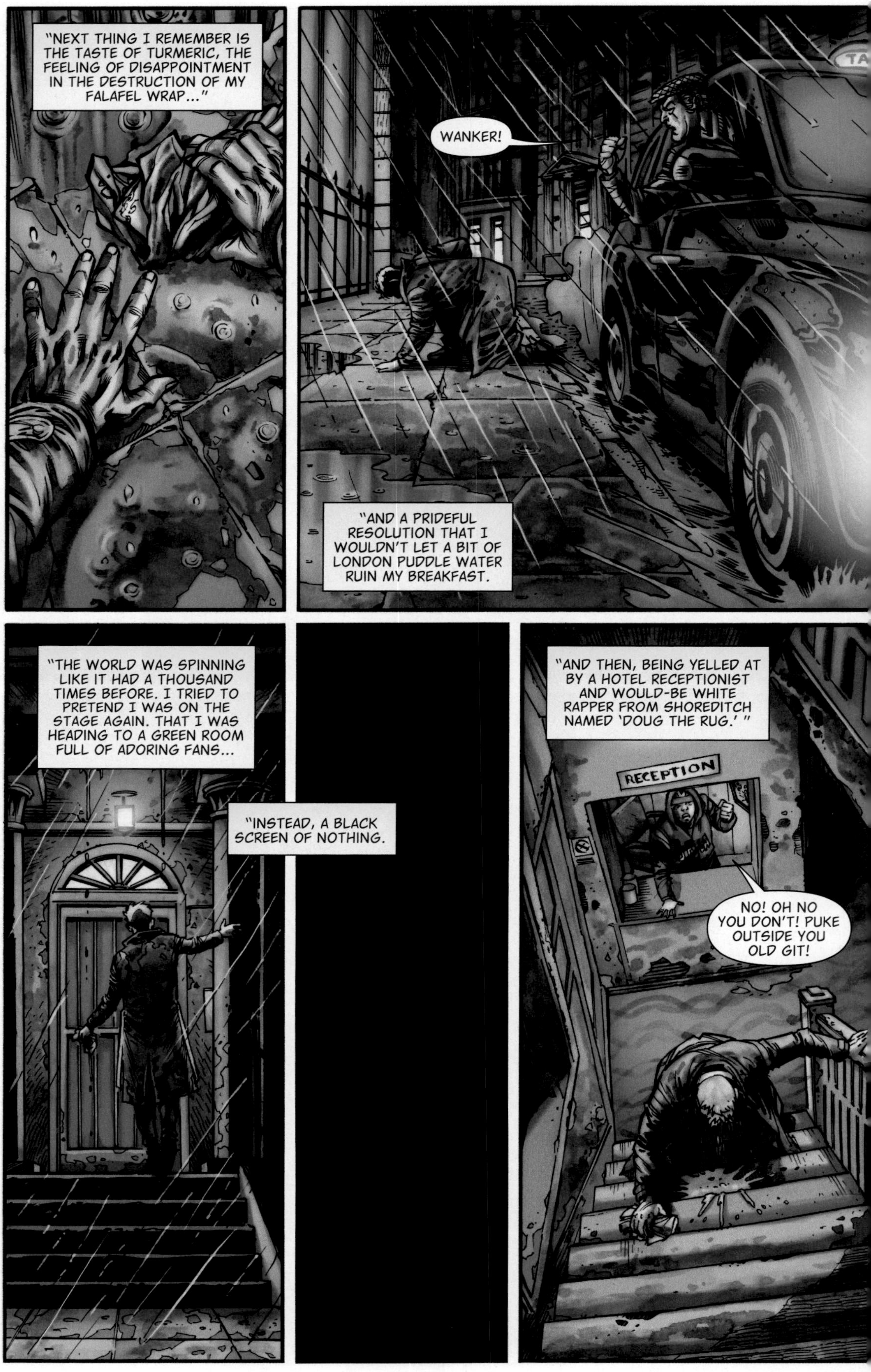
"NEXT THING I REMEMBER IS THE TASTE OF TURMERIC, THE FEELING OF DISAPPOINTMENT IN THE DESTRUCTION OF MY FALAFEL WRAP..."
WANKER!
"AND A PRIDEFUL RESOLUTION THAT I WOULDN'T LET A BIT OF LONDON PUDDLE WATER RUIN MY BREAKFAST.
"THE WORLD WAS SPINNING LIKE IT HAD A THOUSAND TIMES BEFORE. I TRIED TO PRETEND I WAS ON THE STAGE AGAIN. THAT I WAS HEADING TO A GREEN ROOM FULL OF ADORING FANS...
"INSTEAD, A BLACK SCREEN OF NOTHING.
"AND THEN, BEING YELLED AT BY A HOTEL RECEPTIONIST AND WOULD-BE WHITE RAPPER FROM SHOREDITCH NAMED 'DOUG THE RUG.' "
RECEPTION
NO! OH NO YOU DON'T! PUKE OUTSIDE YOU OLD GIT!

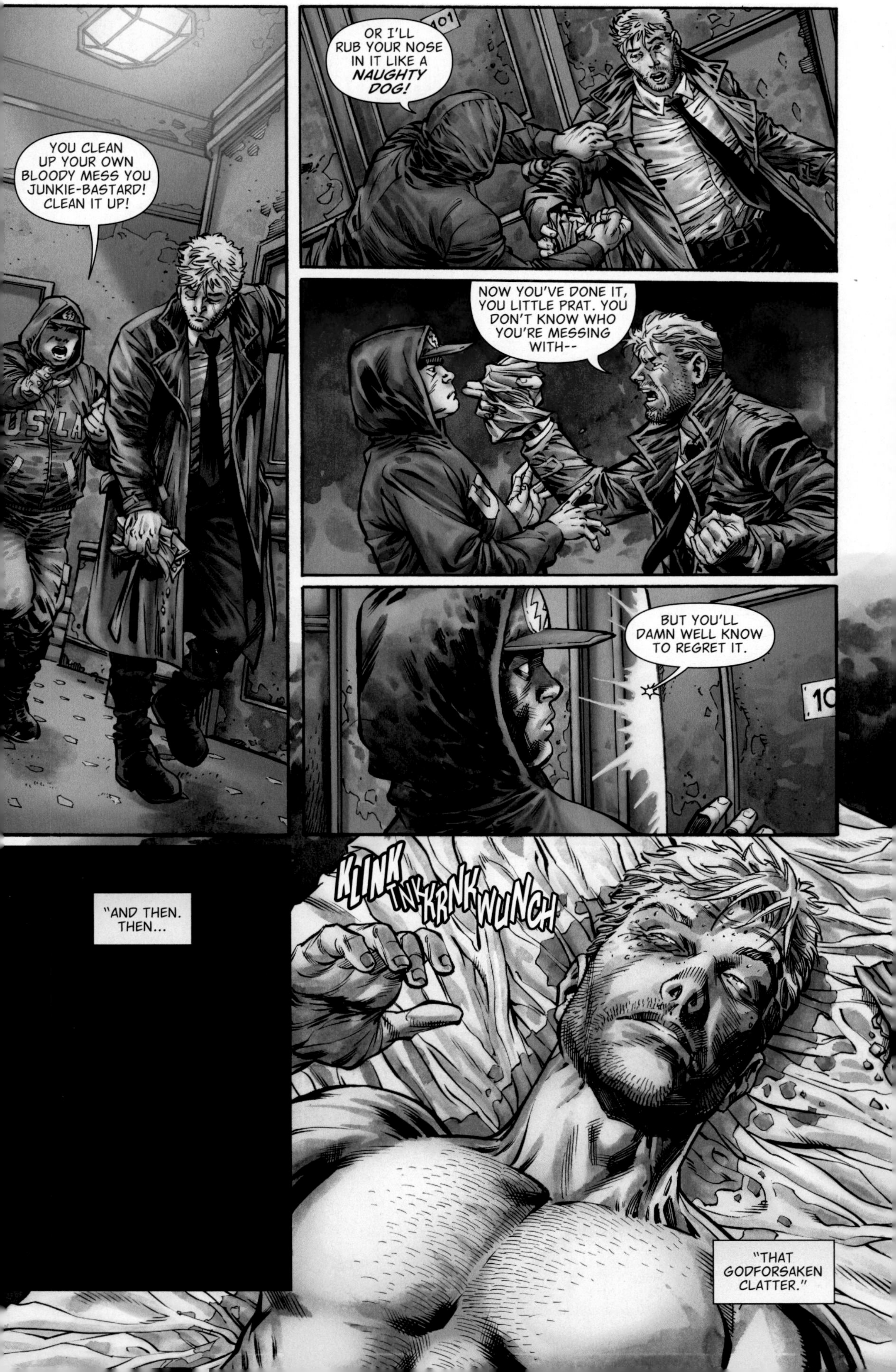
YOU CLEAN UP YOUR OWN BLOODY MESS YOU JUNKIE-BASTARD! CLEAN IT UP!
OR I'LL RUB YOUR NOSE IN IT LIKE A NAUGHTY DOG!
101
USLA
NOW YOU'VE DONE IT, YOU LITTLE PRAT. YOU DON'T KNOW WHO YOU'RE MESSING WITH--
BUT YOU'LL DAMN WELL KNOW TO REGRET IT.
10
"AND THEN. THEN...
KLINK TNK KRNK WUNCH
"THAT GODFORSAKEN CLATTER."

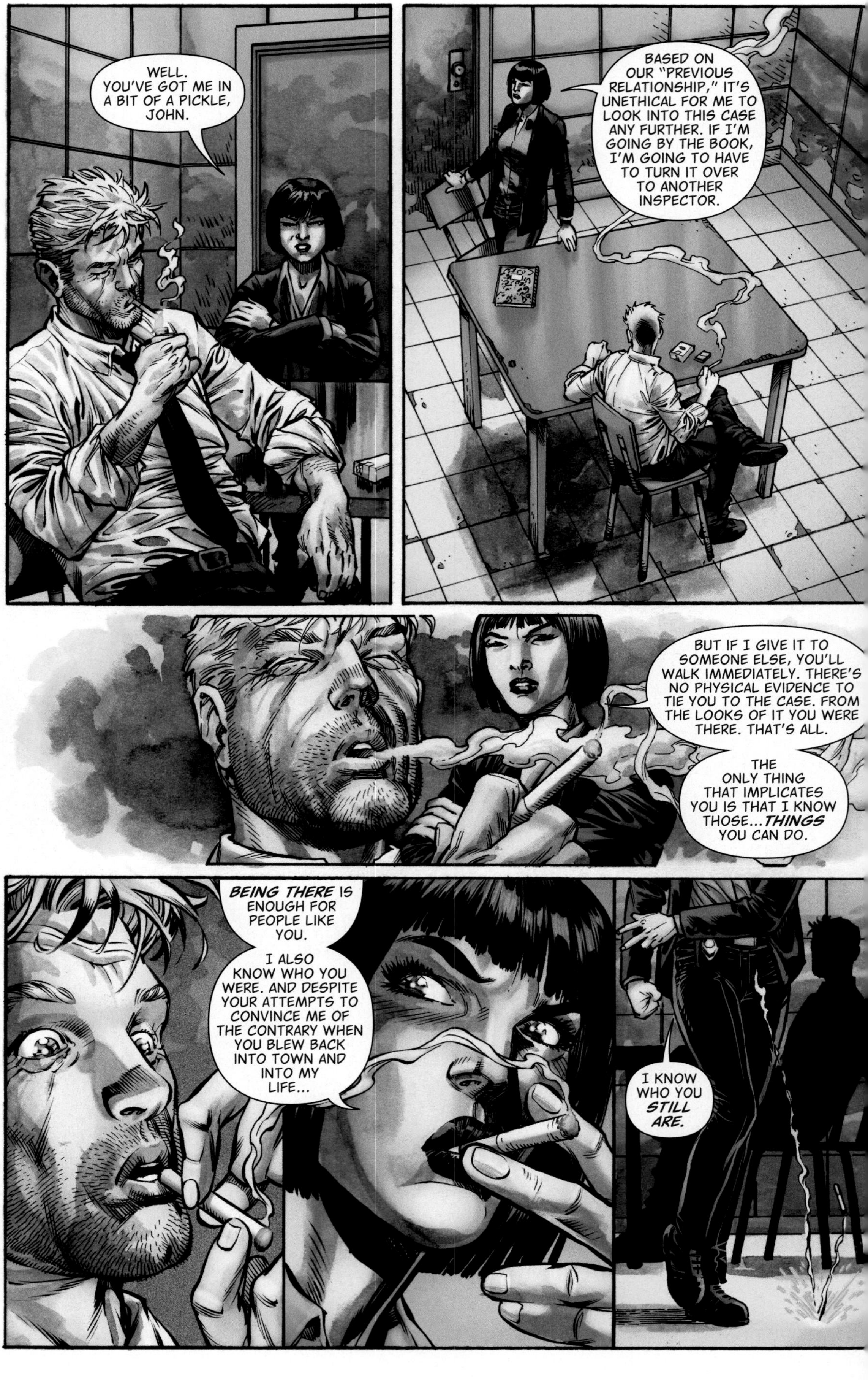
WELL. YOU'VE GOT ME IN A BIT OF A PICKLE, JOHN.
BASED ON OUR "PREVIOUS RELATIONSHIP," IT'S UNETHICAL FOR ME TO LOOK INTO THIS CASE ANY FURTHER. IF I'M GOING BY THE BOOK, I'M GOING TO HAVE TO TURN IT OVER TO ANOTHER INSPECTOR.
BUT IF I GIVE IT TO SOMEONE ELSE, YOU'LL WALK IMMEDIATELY. THERE'S NO PHYSICAL EVIDENCE TO TIE YOU TO THE CASE. FROM THE LOOKS OF IT YOU WERE THERE. THAT'S ALL.
THE ONLY THING THAT IMPLICATES YOU IS THAT I KNOW THOSE...*THINGS* YOU CAN DO.
BEING THERE IS ENOUGH FOR PEOPLE LIKE YOU.
I ALSO KNOW WHO YOU WERE. AND DESPITE YOUR ATTEMPTS TO CONVINCE ME OF THE CONTRARY WHEN YOU BLEW BACK INTO TOWN AND INTO MY LIFE...
I KNOW WHO YOU ***STILL ARE.***

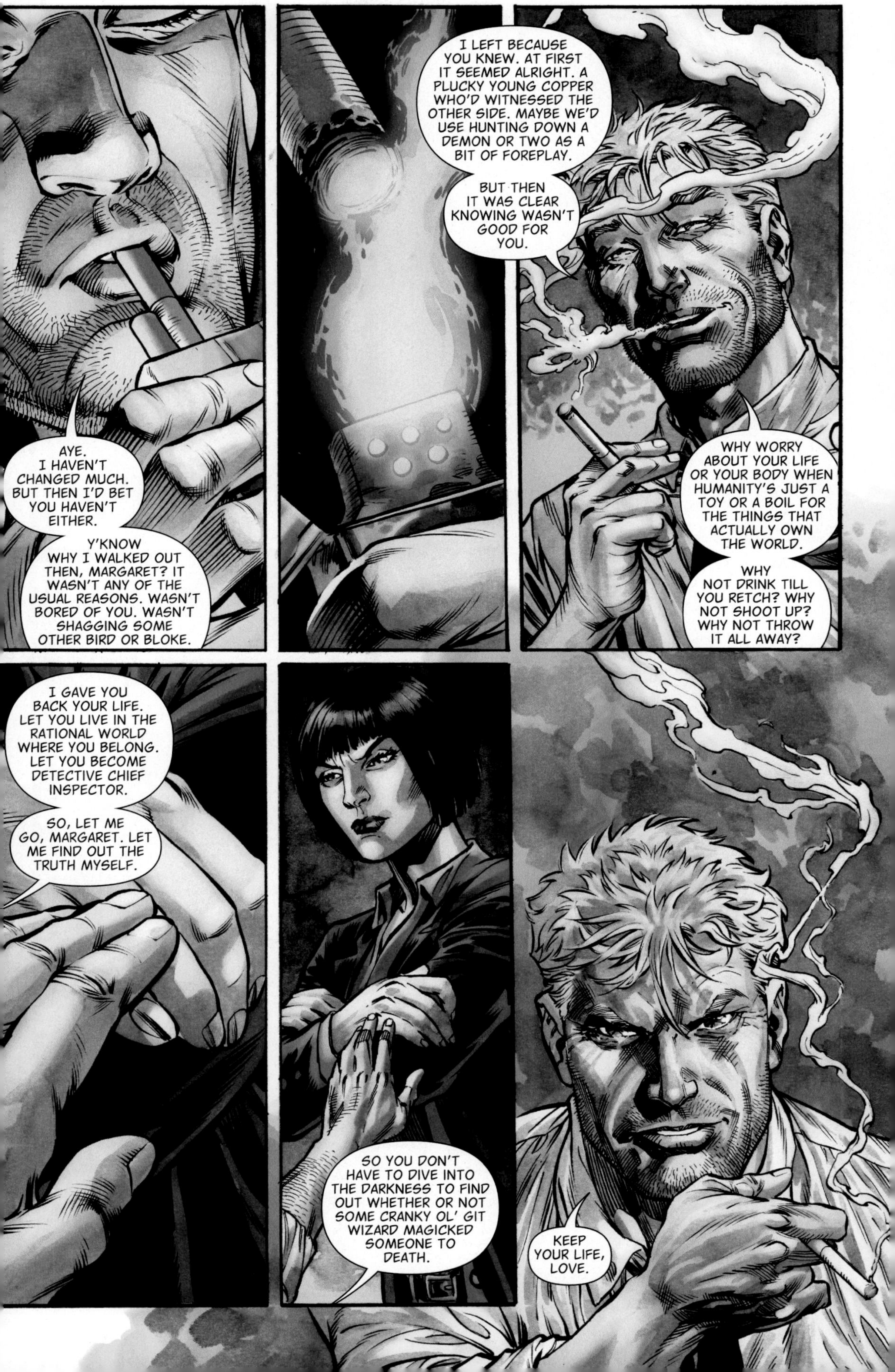
AYE. I HAVEN'T CHANGED MUCH. BUT THEN I'D BET YOU HAVEN'T EITHER.
Y'KNOW WHY I WALKED OUT THEN, MARGARET? IT WASN'T ANY OF THE USUAL REASONS. WASN'T BORED OF YOU. WASN'T SHAGGING SOME OTHER BIRD OR BLOKE.
I LEFT BECAUSE YOU KNEW. AT FIRST IT SEEMED ALRIGHT. A PLUCKY YOUNG COPPER WHO'D WITNESSED THE OTHER SIDE. MAYBE WE'D USE HUNTING DOWN A DEMON OR TWO AS A BIT OF FOREPLAY.
BUT THEN IT WAS CLEAR KNOWING WASN'T GOOD FOR YOU.
WHY WORRY ABOUT YOUR LIFE OR YOUR BODY WHEN HUMANITY'S JUST A TOY OR A BOIL FOR THE THINGS THAT ACTUALLY OWN THE WORLD.
WHY NOT DRINK TILL YOU RETCH? WHY NOT SHOOT UP? WHY NOT THROW IT ALL AWAY?
I GAVE YOU BACK YOUR LIFE. LET YOU LIVE IN THE RATIONAL WORLD WHERE YOU BELONG. LET YOU BECOME DETECTIVE CHIEF INSPECTOR.
SO, LET ME GO, MARGARET. LET ME FIND OUT THE TRUTH MYSELF.
SO YOU DON'T HAVE TO DIVE INTO THE DARKNESS TO FIND OUT WHETHER OR NOT SOME CRANKY OL' GIT WIZARD MAGICKED SOMEONE TO DEATH.
KEEP YOUR LIFE, LOVE.

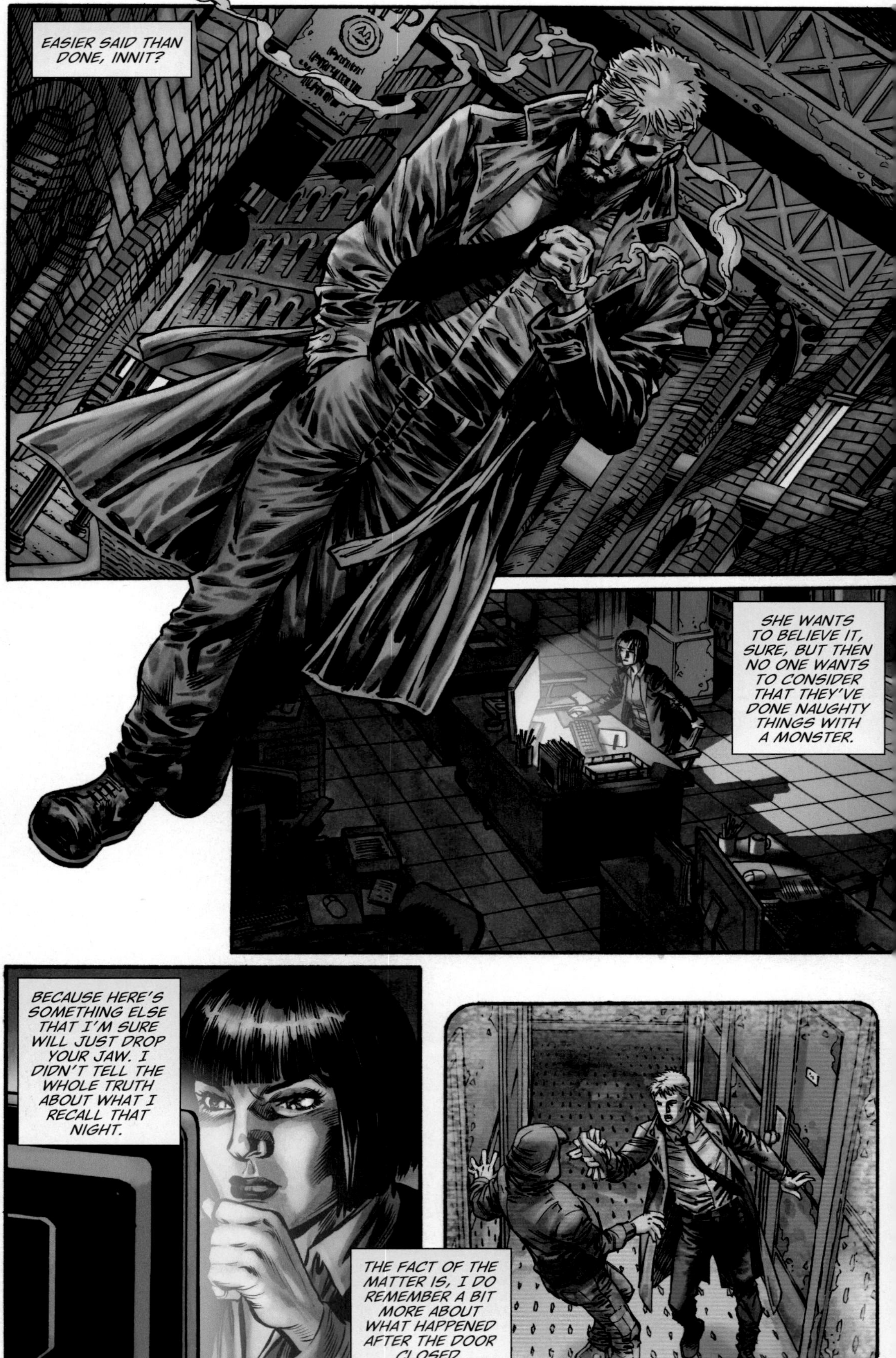
EASIER SAID THAN DONE, INNIT?
SHE WANTS TO BELIEVE IT, SURE, BUT THEN NO ONE WANTS TO CONSIDER THAT THEY'VE DONE NAUGHTY THINGS WITH A MONSTER.
BECAUSE HERE'S SOMETHING ELSE THAT I'M SURE WILL JUST DROP YOUR JAW. I DIDN'T TELL THE WHOLE TRUTH ABOUT WHAT I RECALL THAT NIGHT.
THE FACT OF THE MATTER IS, I DO REMEMBER A BIT MORE ABOUT WHAT HAPPENED AFTER THE DOOR CLOSED.

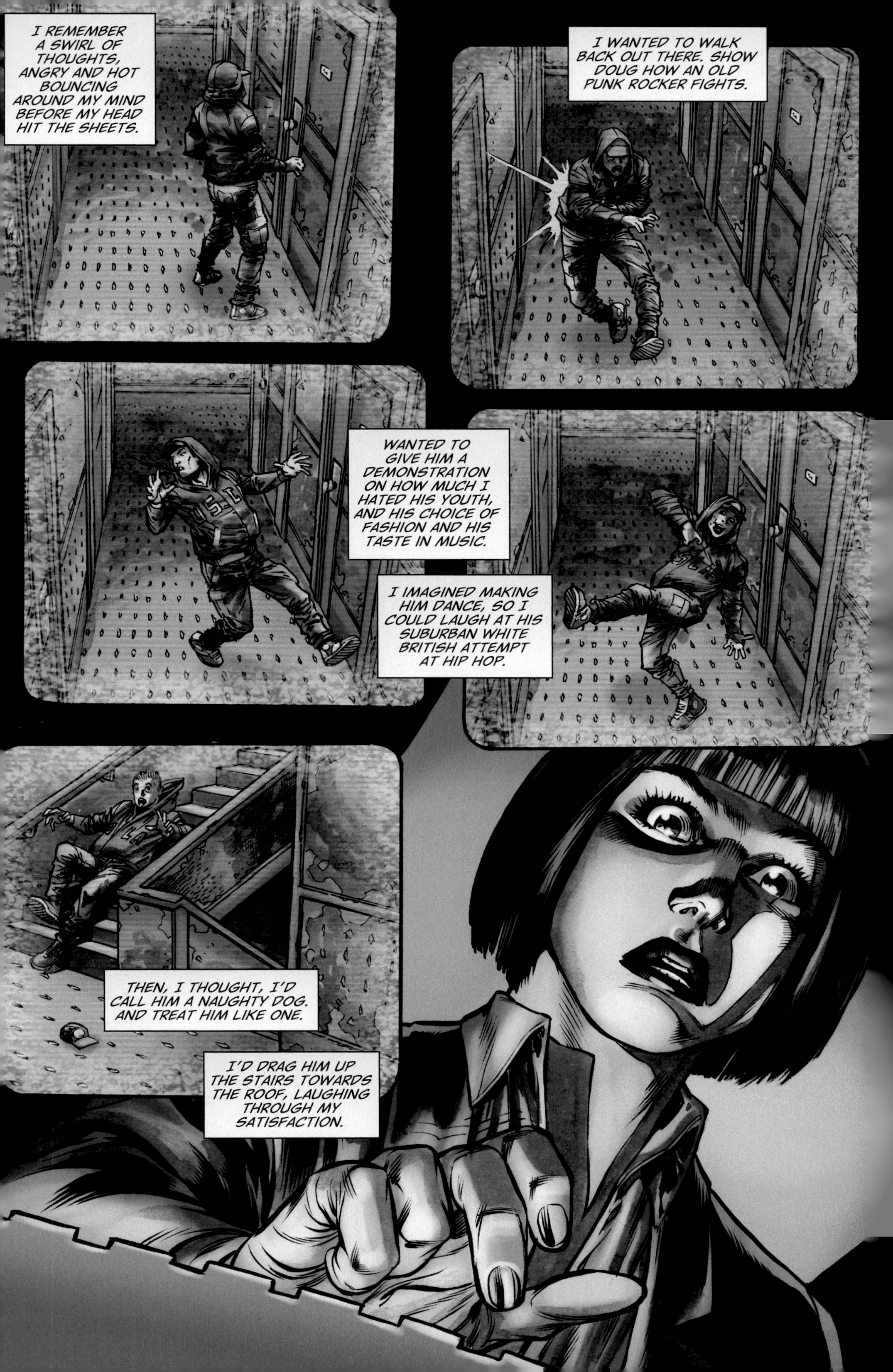
I REMEMBER A SWIRL OF THOUGHTS, ANGRY AND HOT BOUNCING AROUND MY MIND BEFORE MY HEAD HIT THE SHEETS.
I WANTED TO WALK BACK OUT THERE. SHOW DOUG HOW AN OLD PUNK ROCKER FIGHTS.
WANTED TO GIVE HIM A DEMONSTRATION ON HOW MUCH I HATED HIS YOUTH, AND HIS CHOICE OF FASHION AND HIS TASTE IN MUSIC.
I IMAGINED MAKING HIM DANCE, SO I COULD LAUGH AT HIS SUBURBAN WHITE BRITISH ATTEMPT AT HIP HOP.
THEN, I THOUGHT, I'D CALL HIM A NAUGHTY DOG. AND TREAT HIM LIKE ONE.
I'D DRAG HIM UP THE STAIRS TOWARDS THE ROOF, LAUGHING THROUGH MY SATISFACTION.

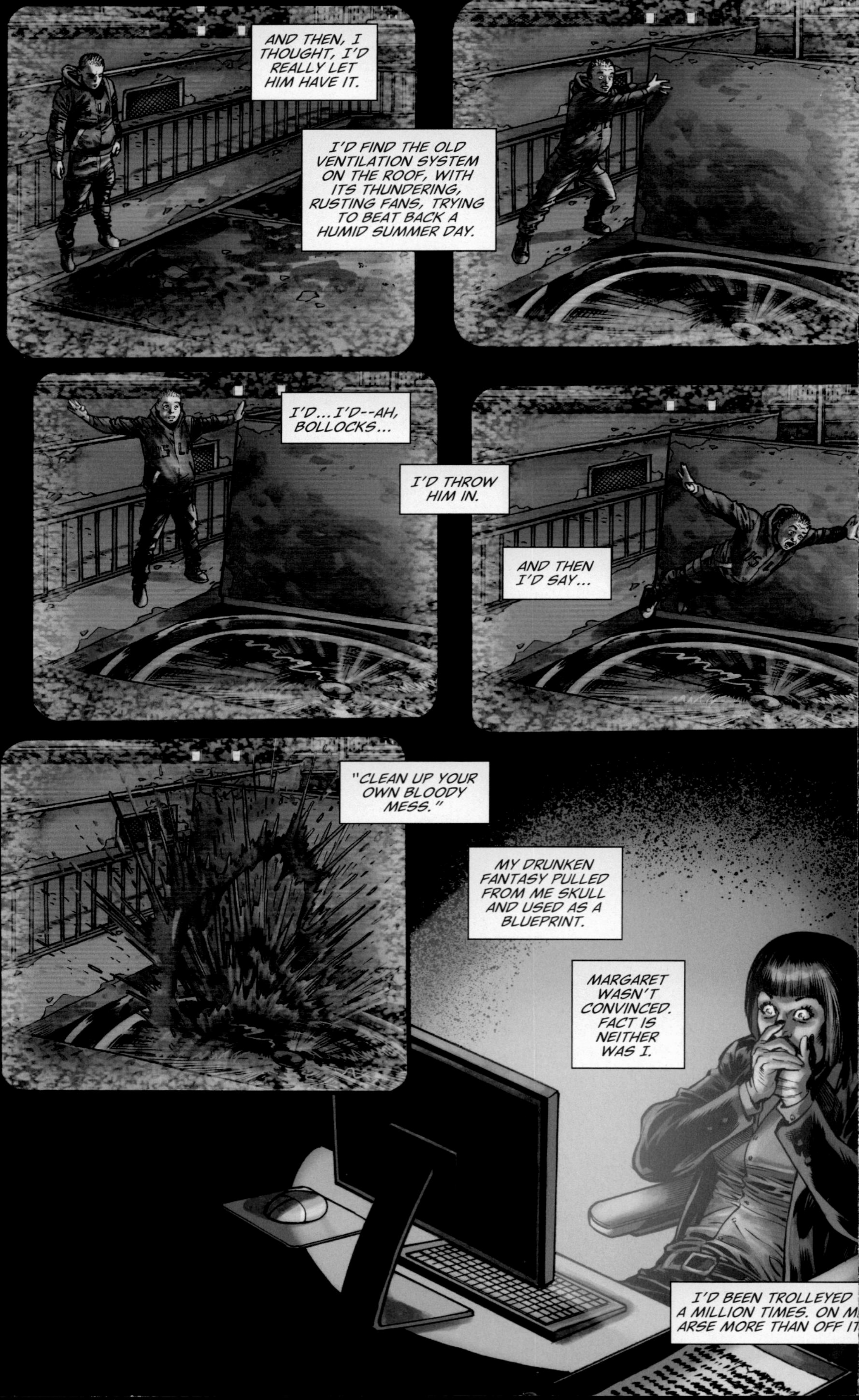
AND THEN, I THOUGHT, I'D REALLY LET HIM HAVE IT.
I'D FIND THE OLD VENTILATION SYSTEM ON THE ROOF, WITH ITS THUNDERING, RUSTING FANS, TRYING TO BEAT BACK A HUMID SUMMER DAY.
I'D... I'D--AH, BOLLOCKS...
I'D THROW HIM IN.
AND THEN I'D SAY...
"CLEAN UP YOUR OWN BLOODY MESS."
MY DRUNKEN FANTASY PULLED FROM ME SKULL AND USED AS A BLUEPRINT.
MARGARET WASN'T CONVINCED. FACT IS NEITHER WAS I.
I'D BEEN TROLLEYED A MILLION TIMES. ON M ARSE MORE THAN OFF IT

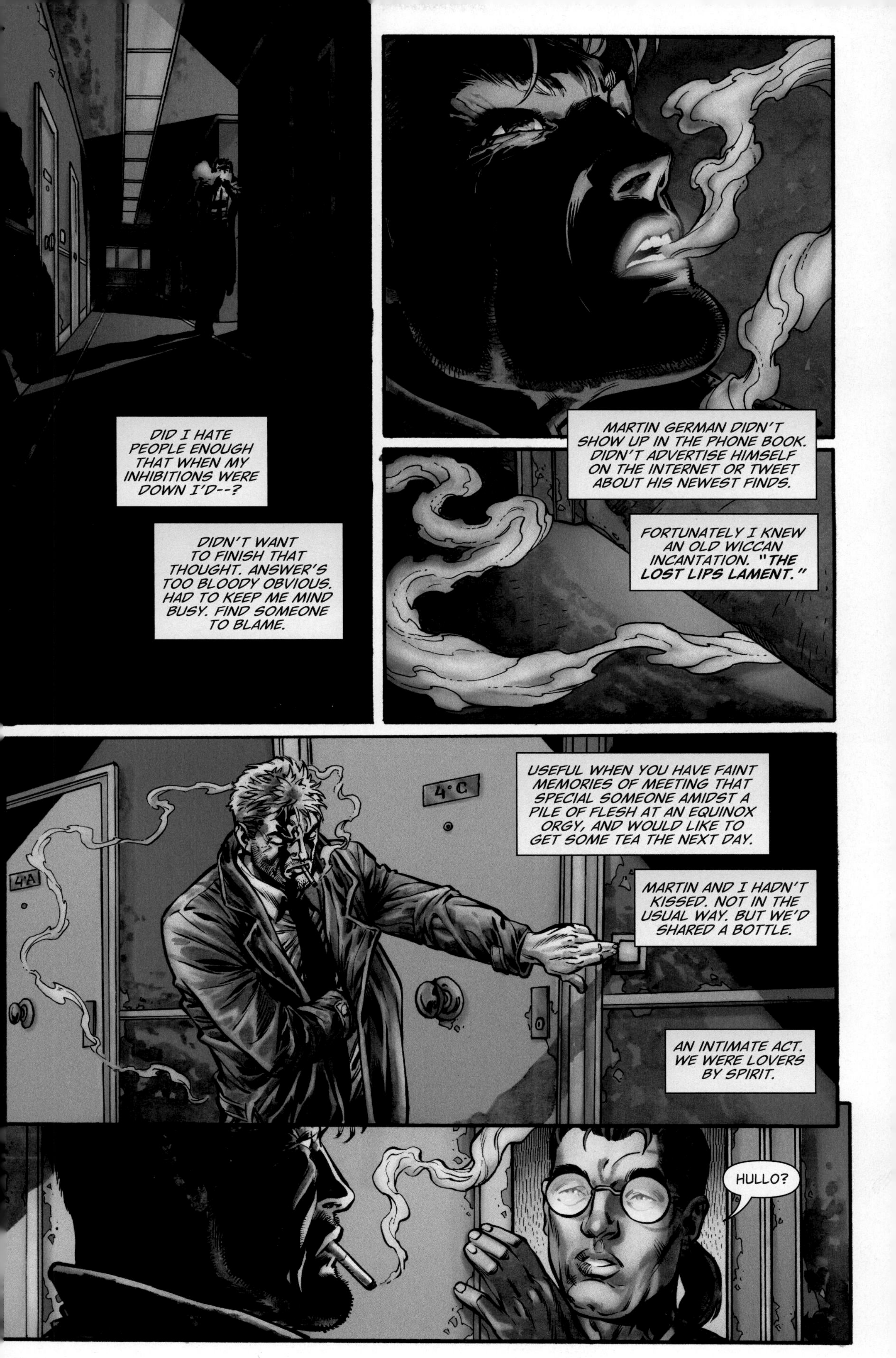
MARTIN GERMAN DIDN'T SHOW UP IN THE PHONE BOOK. DIDN'T ADVERTISE HIMSELF ON THE INTERNET OR TWEET ABOUT HIS NEWEST FINDS.
DID I HATE PEOPLE ENOUGH THAT WHEN MY INHIBITIONS WERE DOWN I'D--?
DIDN'T WANT TO FINISH THAT THOUGHT. ANSWER'S TOO BLOODY OBVIOUS. HAD TO KEEP ME MIND BUSY. FIND SOMEONE TO BLAME.
FORTUNATELY I KNEW AN OLD WICCAN INCANTATION. "THE LOST LIPS LAMENT."
4A
4C
USEFUL WHEN YOU HAVE FAINT MEMORIES OF MEETING THAT SPECIAL SOMEONE AMIDST A PILE OF FLESH AT AN EQUINOX ORGY, AND WOULD LIKE TO GET SOME TEA THE NEXT DAY.
MARTIN AND I HADN'T KISSED. NOT IN THE USUAL WAY. BUT WE'D SHARED A BOTTLE.
AN INTIMATE ACT. WE WERE LOVERS BY SPIRIT.
HULLO?

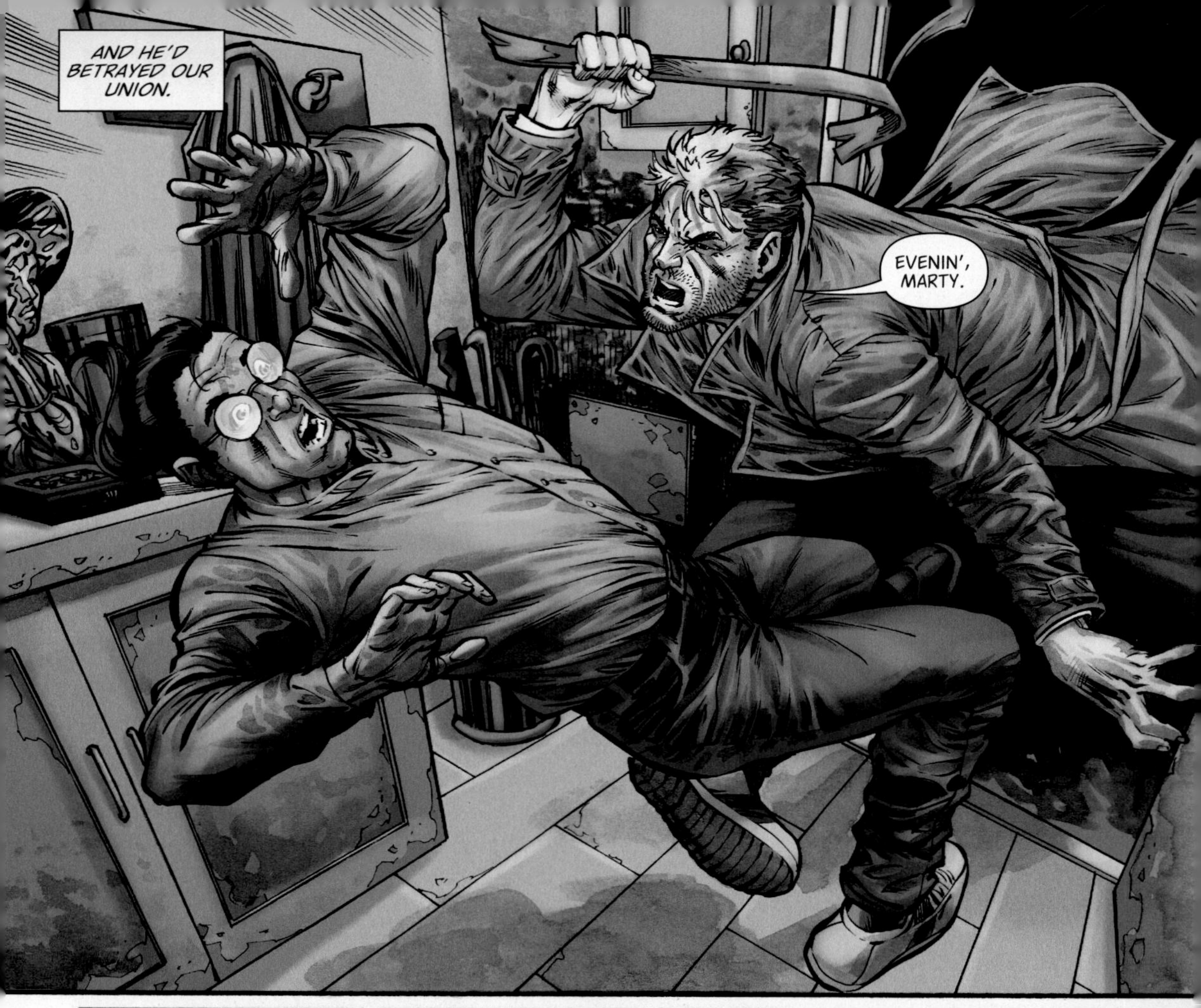
AND HE'D BETRAYED OUR UNION.
EVENIN', MARTY.
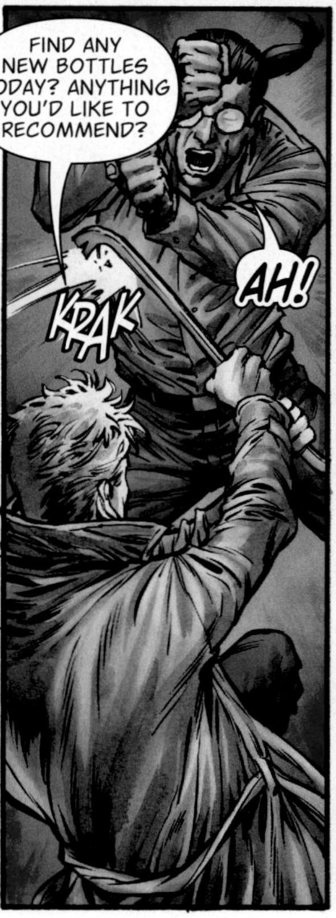
FIND ANY NEW BOTTLES TODAY? ANYTHING YOU'D LIKE TO RECOMMEND?
KRAK
AH!
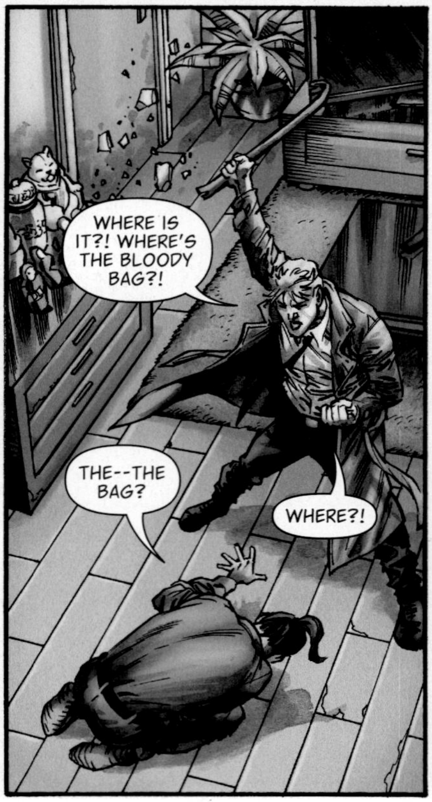
WHERE IS IT?! WHERE'S THE BLOODY BAG?!
THE--THE BAG?
WHERE?!
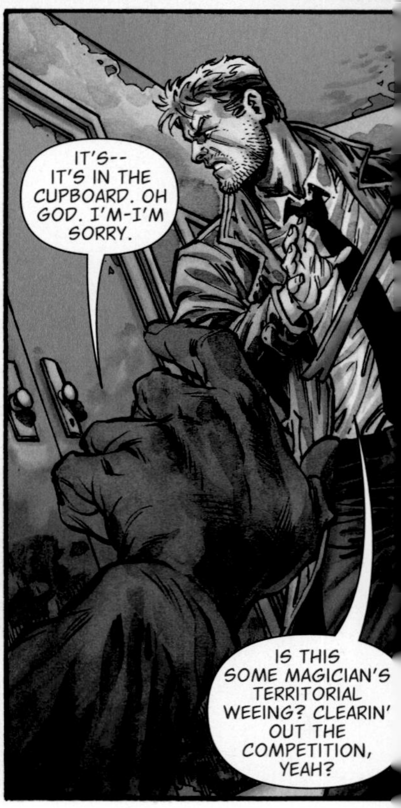
IT'S-- IT'S IN THE CUPBOARD. OH GOD. I'M-I'M SORRY.
IS THIS SOME MAGICIAN'S TERRITORIAL WEEING? CLEARIN' OUT THE COMPETITION, YEAH?

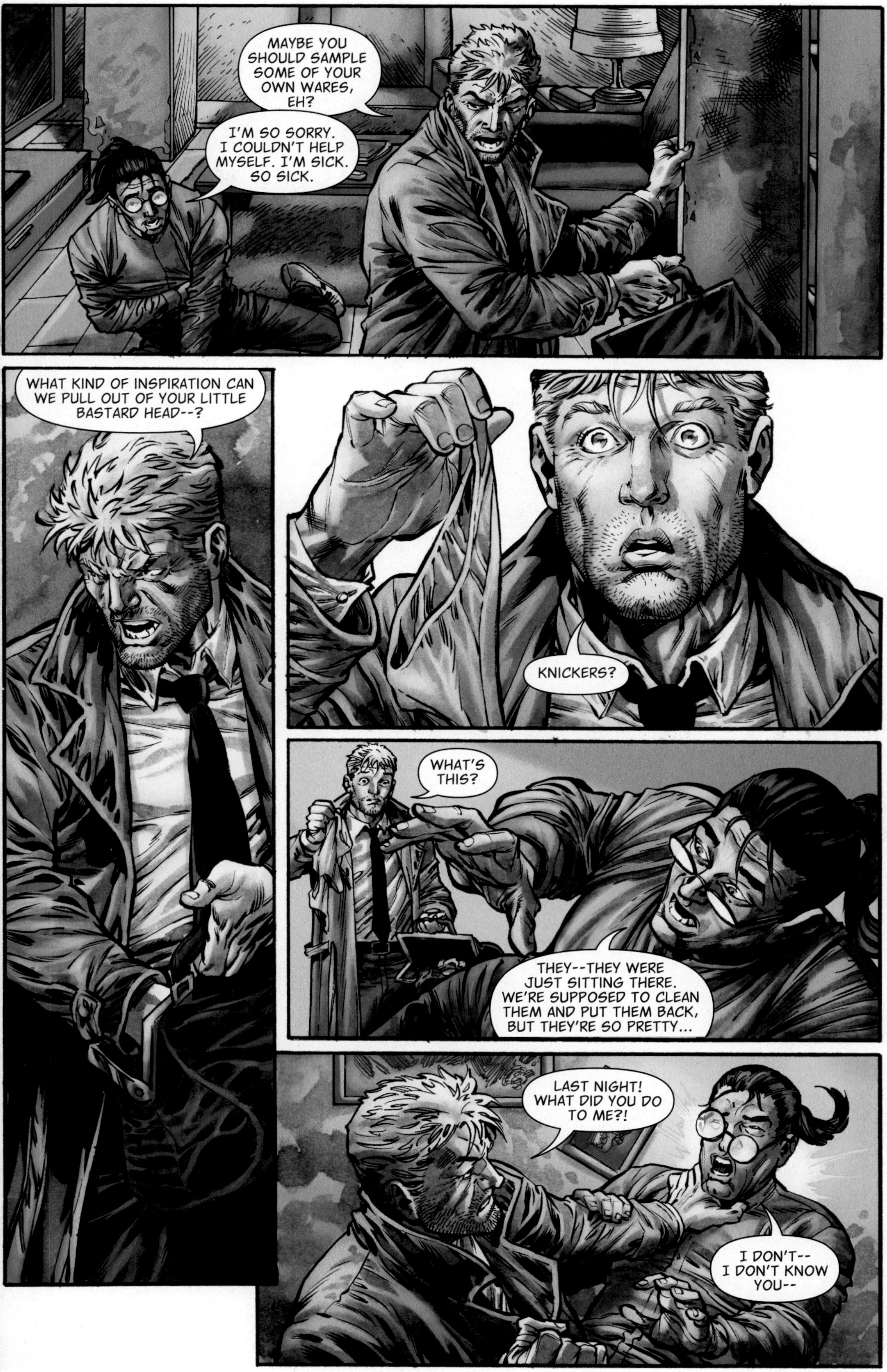
MAYBE YOU SHOULD SAMPLE SOME OF YOUR OWN WARES, EH?
I'M SO SORRY. I COULDN'T HELP MYSELF. I'M SICK. SO SICK.
WHAT KIND OF INSPIRATION CAN WE PULL OUT OF YOUR LITTLE BASTARD HEAD--?
KNICKERS?
WHAT'S THIS?
THEY--THEY WERE JUST SITTING THERE. WE'RE SUPPOSED TO CLEAN THEM AND PUT THEM BACK, BUT THEY'RE SO PRETTY...
LAST NIGHT! WHAT DID YOU DO TO ME?!
I DON'T-- I DON'T KNOW YOU--

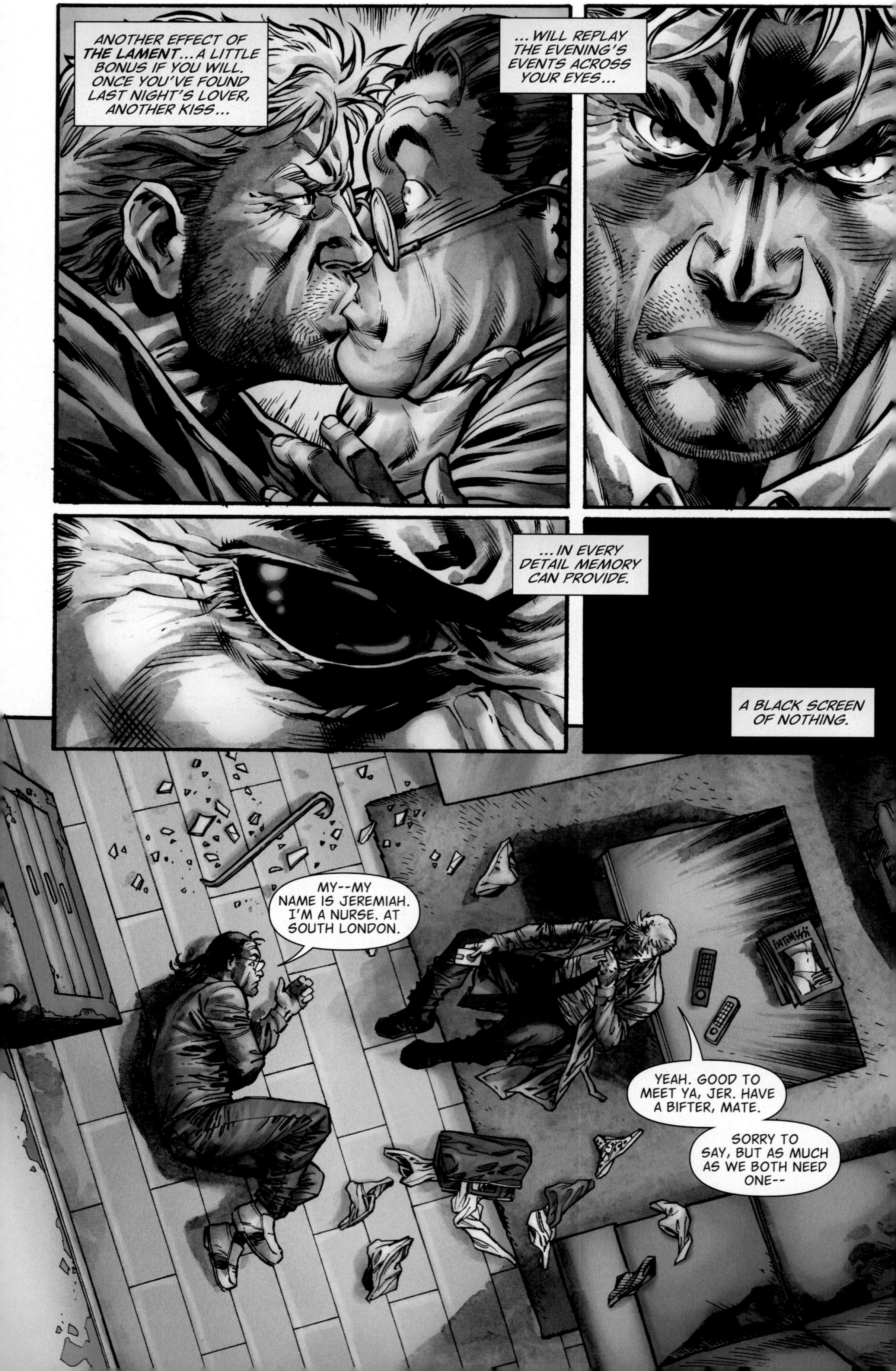
ANOTHER EFFECT OF THE LAMENT... A LITTLE BONUS IF YOU WILL. ONCE YOU'VE FOUND LAST NIGHT'S LOVER, ANOTHER KISS...
...WILL REPLAY THE EVENING'S EVENTS ACROSS YOUR EYES...
...IN EVERY DETAIL MEMORY CAN PROVIDE.
A BLACK SCREEN OF NOTHING.
MY--MY NAME IS JEREMIAH. I'M A NURSE. AT SOUTH LONDON.
YEAH. GOOD TO MEET YA, JER. HAVE A BIFTER, MATE.
SORRY TO SAY, BUT AS MUCH AS WE BOTH NEED ONE--

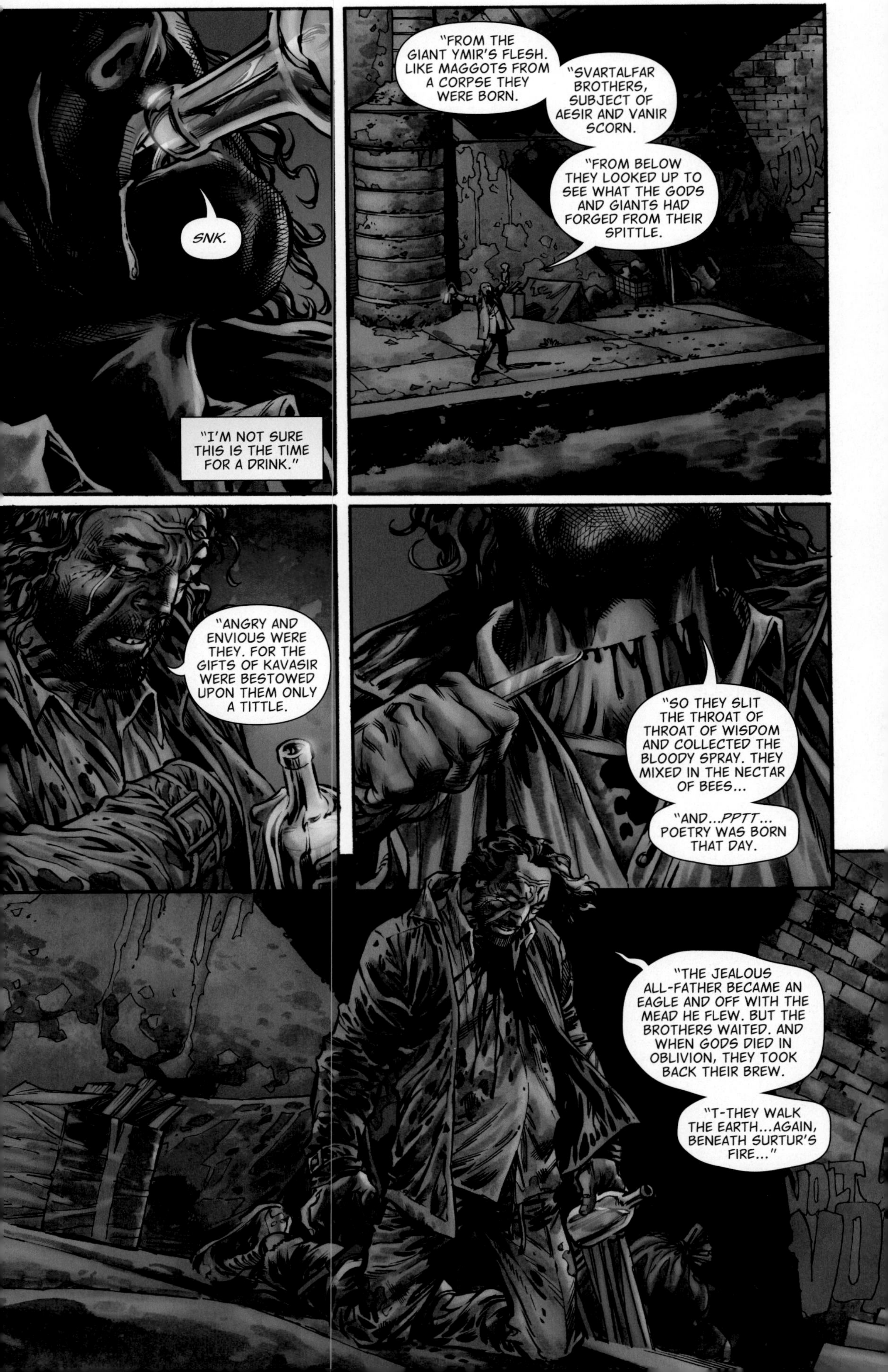
SNK.
"I'M NOT SURE THIS IS THE TIME FOR A DRINK."
"FROM THE GIANT YMIR'S FLESH. LIKE MAGGOTS FROM A CORPSE THEY WERE BORN.
"SVARTALFAR BROTHERS, SUBJECT OF AESIR AND VANIR SCORN.
"FROM BELOW THEY LOOKED UP TO SEE WHAT THE GODS AND GIANTS HAD FORGED FROM THEIR SPITTLE.
"ANGRY AND ENVIOUS WERE THEY. FOR THE GIFTS OF KAVASIR WERE BESTOWED UPON THEM ONLY A TITTLE.
"SO THEY SLIT THE THROAT OF THROAT OF WISDOM AND COLLECTED THE BLOODY SPRAY. THEY MIXED IN THE NECTAR OF BEES...
"AND...*PPTT*... POETRY WAS BORN THAT DAY.
"THE JEALOUS ALL-FATHER BECAME AN EAGLE AND OFF WITH THE MEAD HE FLEW. BUT THE BROTHERS WAITED. AND WHEN GODS DIED IN OBLIVION, THEY TOOK BACK THEIR BREW.
"T-THEY WALK THE EARTH...AGAIN, BENEATH SURTUR'S FIRE..."

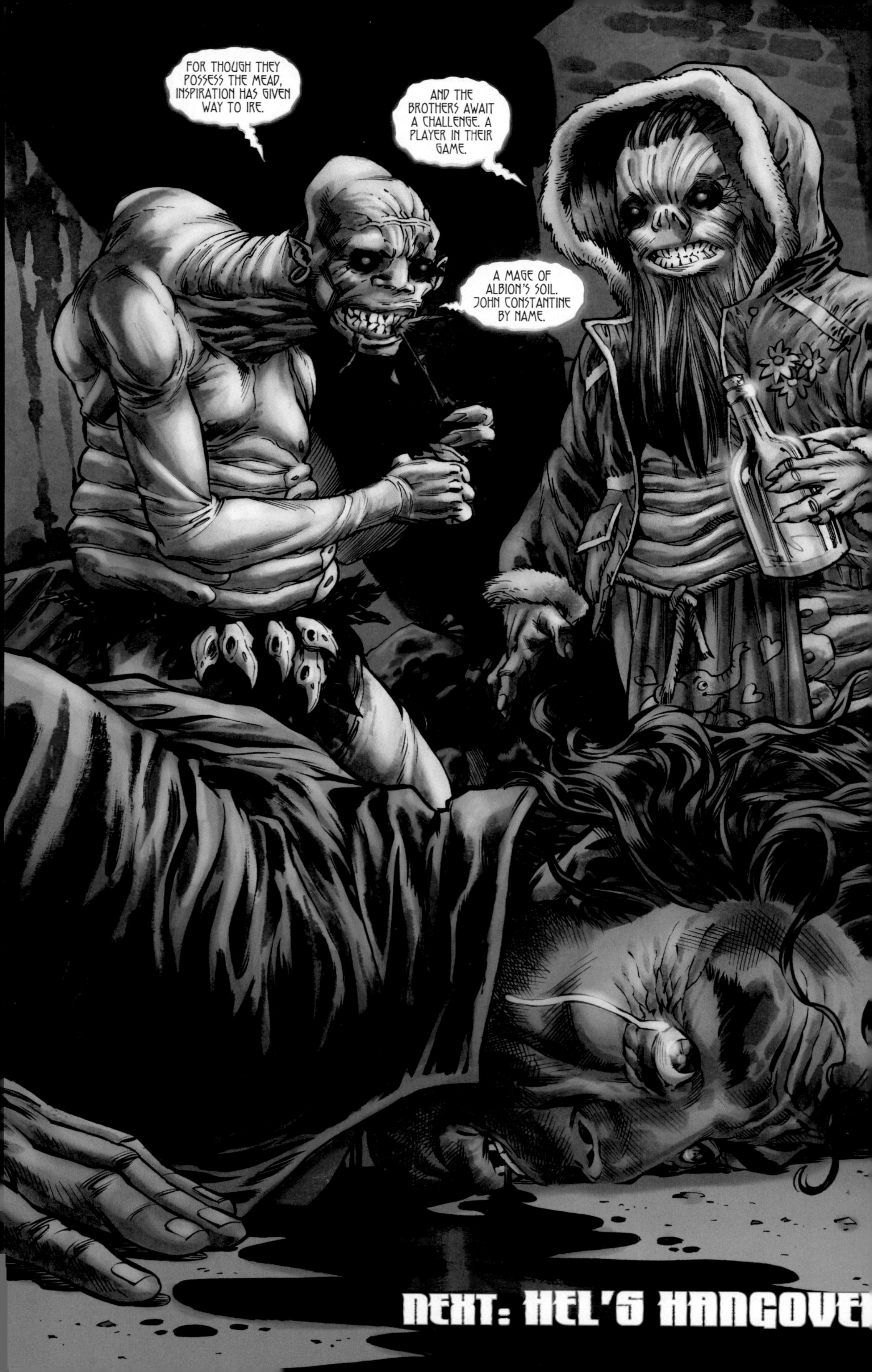
FOR THOUGH THEY POSSESS THE MEAD, INSPIRATION HAS GIVEN WAY TO IRE.
AND THE BROTHERS AWAIT A CHALLENGE. A PLAYER IN THEIR GAME.
A MAGE OF ALBION'S SOIL. JOHN CONSTANTINE BY NAME.
NEXT: HEL'S HANGOVER

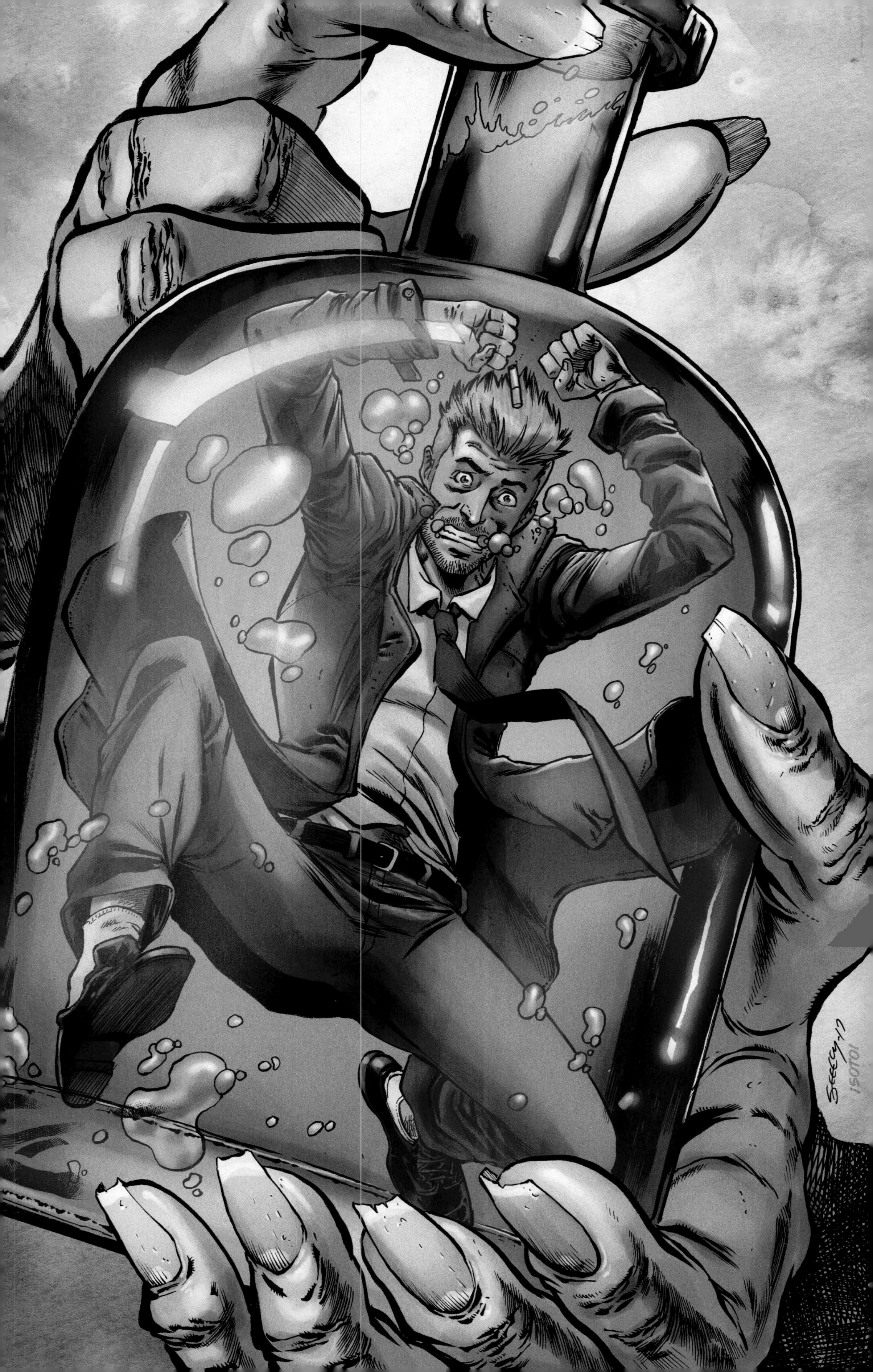

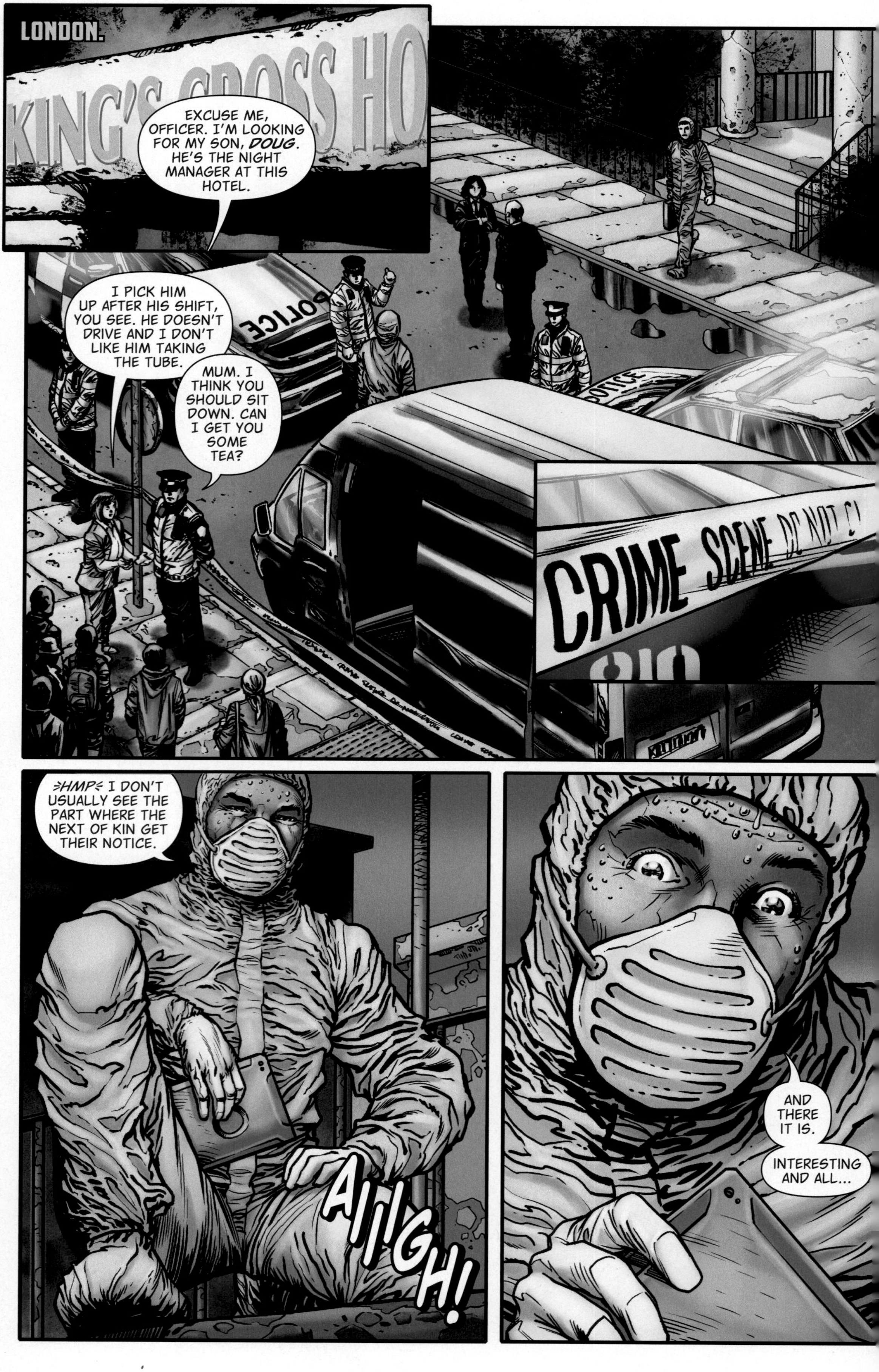

LONDON.
KING'S CROSS HO
EXCUSE ME, OFFICER. I'M LOOKING FOR MY SON, *DOUG*. HE'S THE NIGHT MANAGER AT THIS HOTEL.
I PICK HIM UP AFTER HIS SHIFT, YOU SEE. HE DOESN'T DRIVE AND I DON'T LIKE HIM TAKING THE TUBE.
POLICE
MUM. I THINK YOU SHOULD SIT DOWN. CAN I GET YOU SOME TEA?
CRIME SCENE DO NOT C
HMP I DON'T USUALLY SEE THE PART WHERE THE NEXT OF KIN GET THEIR NOTICE.
AIIIGH!
AND THERE IT IS.
INTERESTING AND ALL...

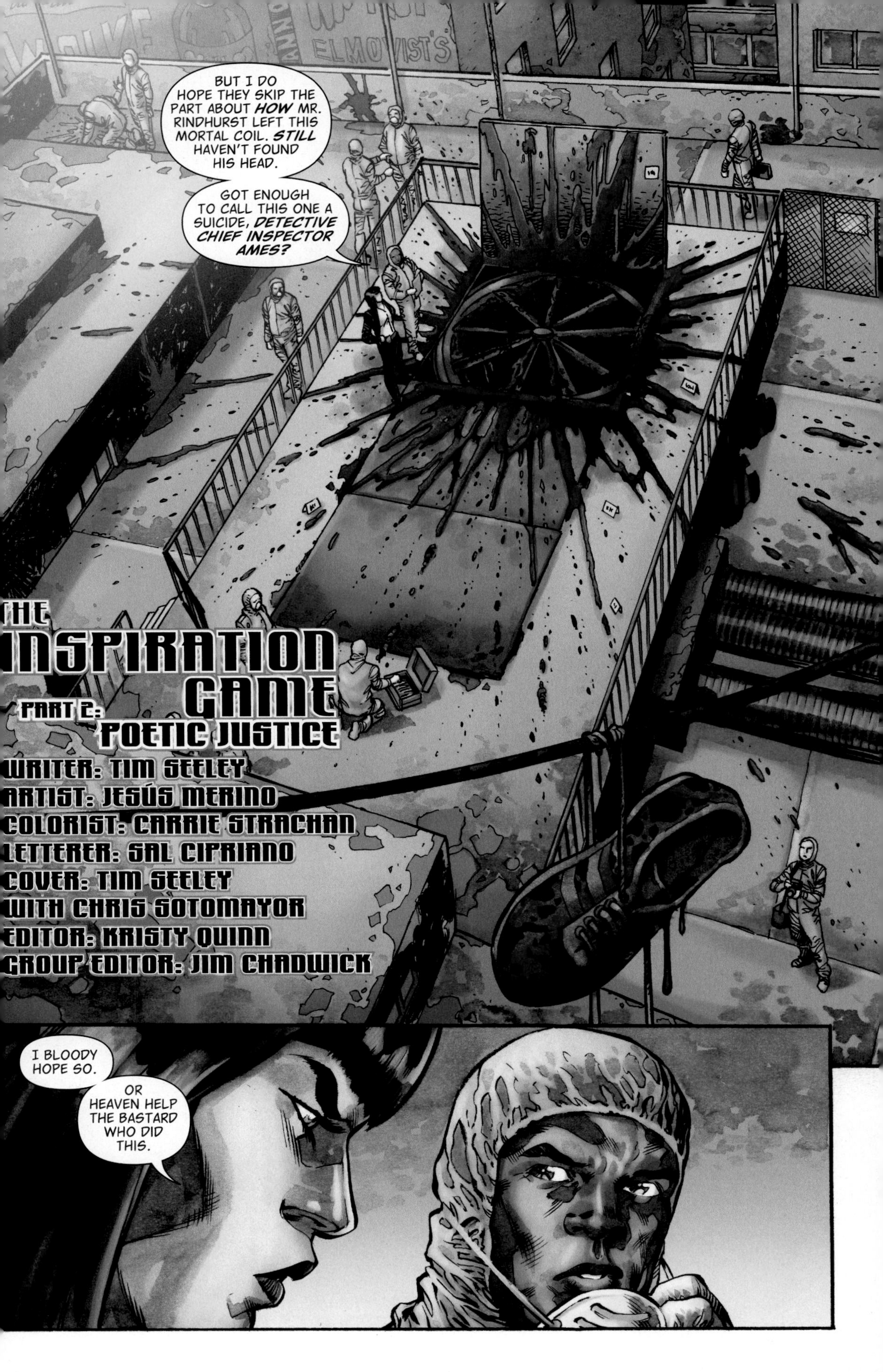
BUT I DO HOPE THEY SKIP THE PART ABOUT *HOW* MR. RINDHURST LEFT THIS MORTAL COIL. *STILL* HAVEN'T FOUND HIS HEAD.
GOT ENOUGH TO CALL THIS ONE A SUICIDE, *DETECTIVE CHIEF INSPECTOR AMES?*
THE INSPIRATION GAME
PART 2: POETIC JUSTICE
WRITER: TIM SEELEY
ARTIST: JESÚS MERINO
COLORIST: CARRIE STRACHAN
LETTERER: SAL CIPRIANO
COVER: TIM SEELEY WITH CHRIS SOTOMAYOR
EDITOR: KRISTY QUINN
GROUP EDITOR: JIM CHADWICK
I BLOODY HOPE SO.
OR HEAVEN HELP THE BASTARD WHO DID THIS.

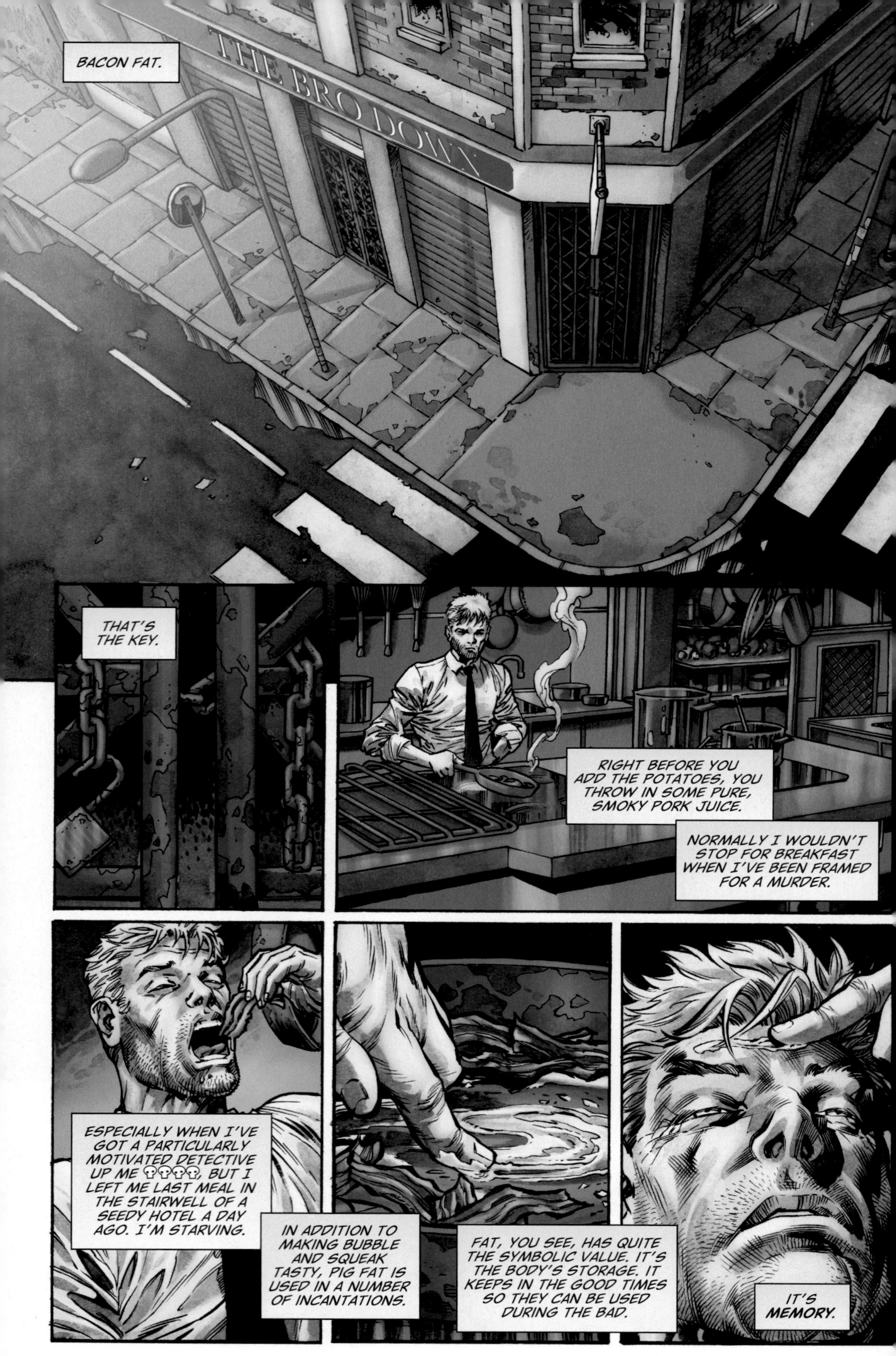
BACON FAT.
THE BRO DOWN
THAT'S THE KEY.
RIGHT BEFORE YOU ADD THE POTATOES, YOU THROW IN SOME PURE, SMOKY PORK JUICE.
NORMALLY I WOULDN'T STOP FOR BREAKFAST WHEN I'VE BEEN FRAMED FOR A MURDER.
ESPECIALLY WHEN I'VE GOT A PARTICULARLY MOTIVATED DETECTIVE UP ME, BUT I LEFT ME LAST MEAL IN THE STAIRWELL OF A SEEDY HOTEL A DAY AGO. I'M STARVING.
IN ADDITION TO MAKING BUBBLE AND SQUEAK TASTY, PIG FAT IS USED IN A NUMBER OF INCANTATIONS.
FAT, YOU SEE, HAS QUITE THE SYMBOLIC VALUE. IT'S THE BODY'S STORAGE. IT KEEPS IN THE GOOD TIMES SO THEY CAN BE USED DURING THE BAD.
IT'S MEMORY.

AND SINCE MY OWN IS A BIT SHABBY, I'M GOING TO NEED SOME HELP RECREATING THE EVENTS THAT LED TO THE UNTIMELY DEATH OF DOUG RINDHURST...

FROM *THE BRO DOWN BAR.*

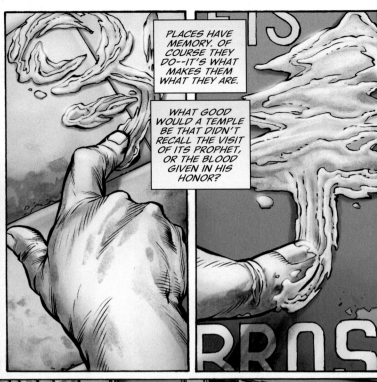

PLACES HAVE MEMORY. OF COURSE THEY DO--IT'S WHAT MAKES THEM WHAT THEY ARE.

WHAT GOOD WOULD A TEMPLE BE THAT DIDN'T RECALL THE VISIT OF ITS PROPHET, OR THE BLOOD GIVEN IN HIS HONOR?

BROS

THE THING IS, MOST PLACES DON'T WANT TO TELL YOU THEIR SECRETS RIGHT OFF THE BAT.

YOU NEED TO BUILD TRUST. A REPARTEE.

AND THEN WARM THEM UP WITH A LITTLE FLASHBACK FOREPLAY.

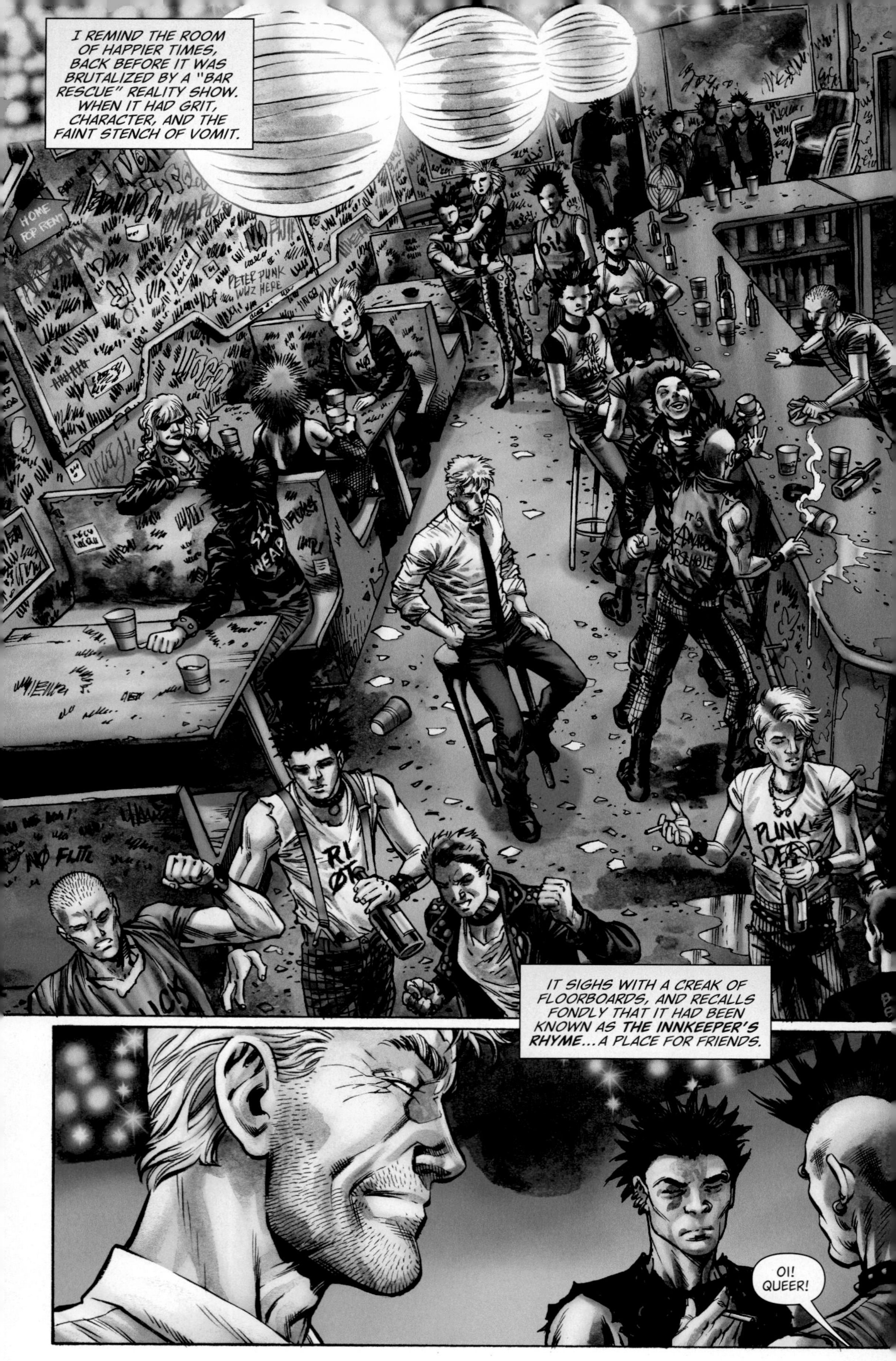

I REMIND THE ROOM OF HAPPIER TIMES, BACK BEFORE IT WAS BRUTALIZED BY A "BAR RESCUE" REALITY SHOW. WHEN IT HAD GRIT, CHARACTER, AND THE FAINT STENCH OF VOMIT.
IT SIGHS WITH A CREAK OF FLOORBOARDS, AND RECALLS FONDLY THAT IT HAD BEEN KNOWN AS **THE INNKEEPER'S RHYME**... A PLACE FOR FRIENDS.
OI! QUEER!

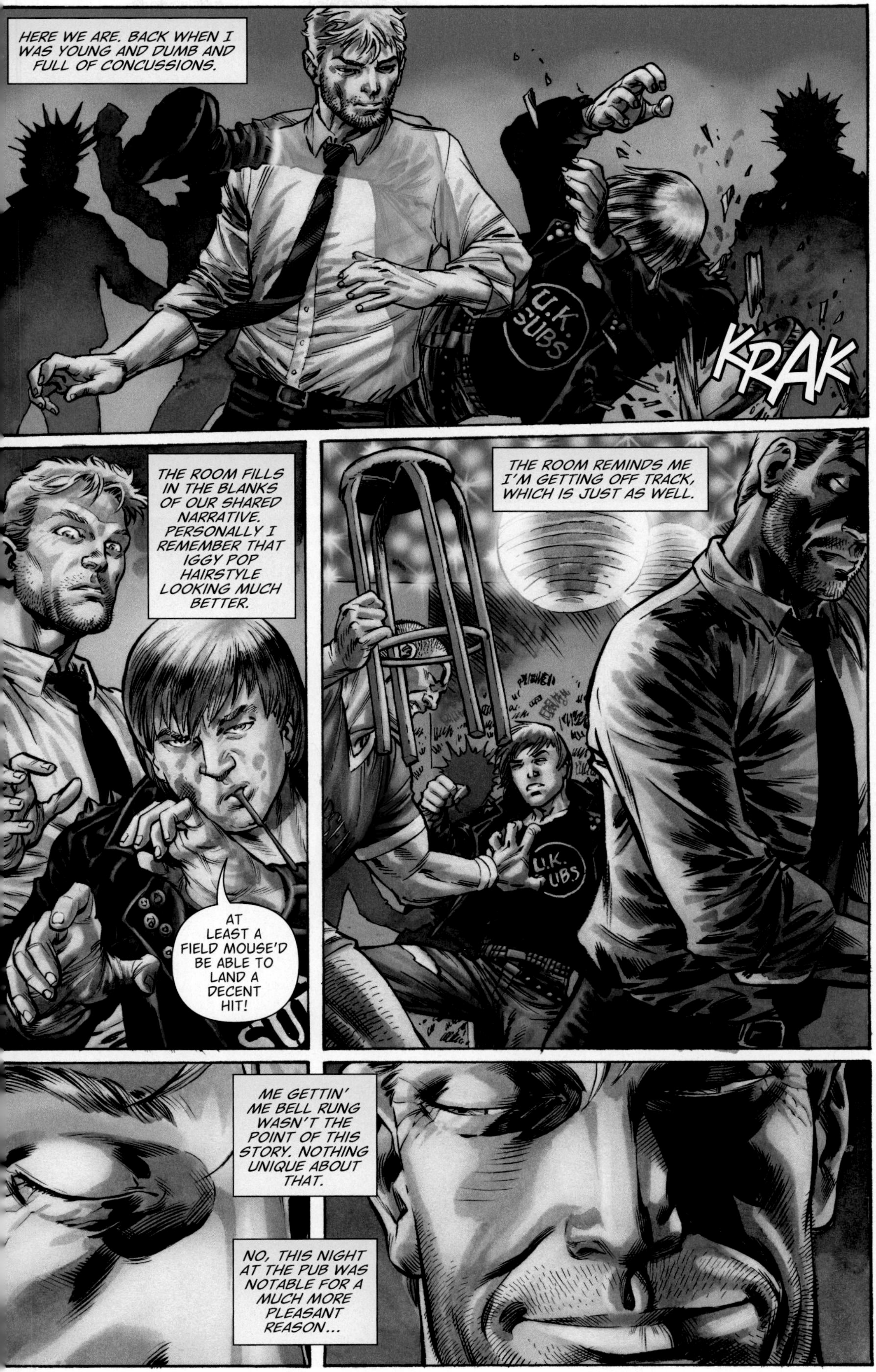
HERE WE ARE. BACK WHEN I WAS YOUNG AND DUMB AND FULL OF CONCUSSIONS.
U.K. SUBS
KRAK
THE ROOM FILLS IN THE BLANKS OF OUR SHARED NARRATIVE. PERSONALLY I REMEMBER THAT IGGY POP HAIRSTYLE LOOKING MUCH BETTER.
AT LEAST A FIELD MOUSE'D BE ABLE TO LAND A DECENT HIT!
THE ROOM REMINDS ME I'M GETTING OFF TRACK, WHICH IS JUST AS WELL.
ME GETTIN' ME BELL RUNG WASN'T THE POINT OF THIS STORY. NOTHING UNIQUE ABOUT THAT.
NO, THIS NIGHT AT THE PUB WAS NOTABLE FOR A MUCH MORE PLEASANT REASON...

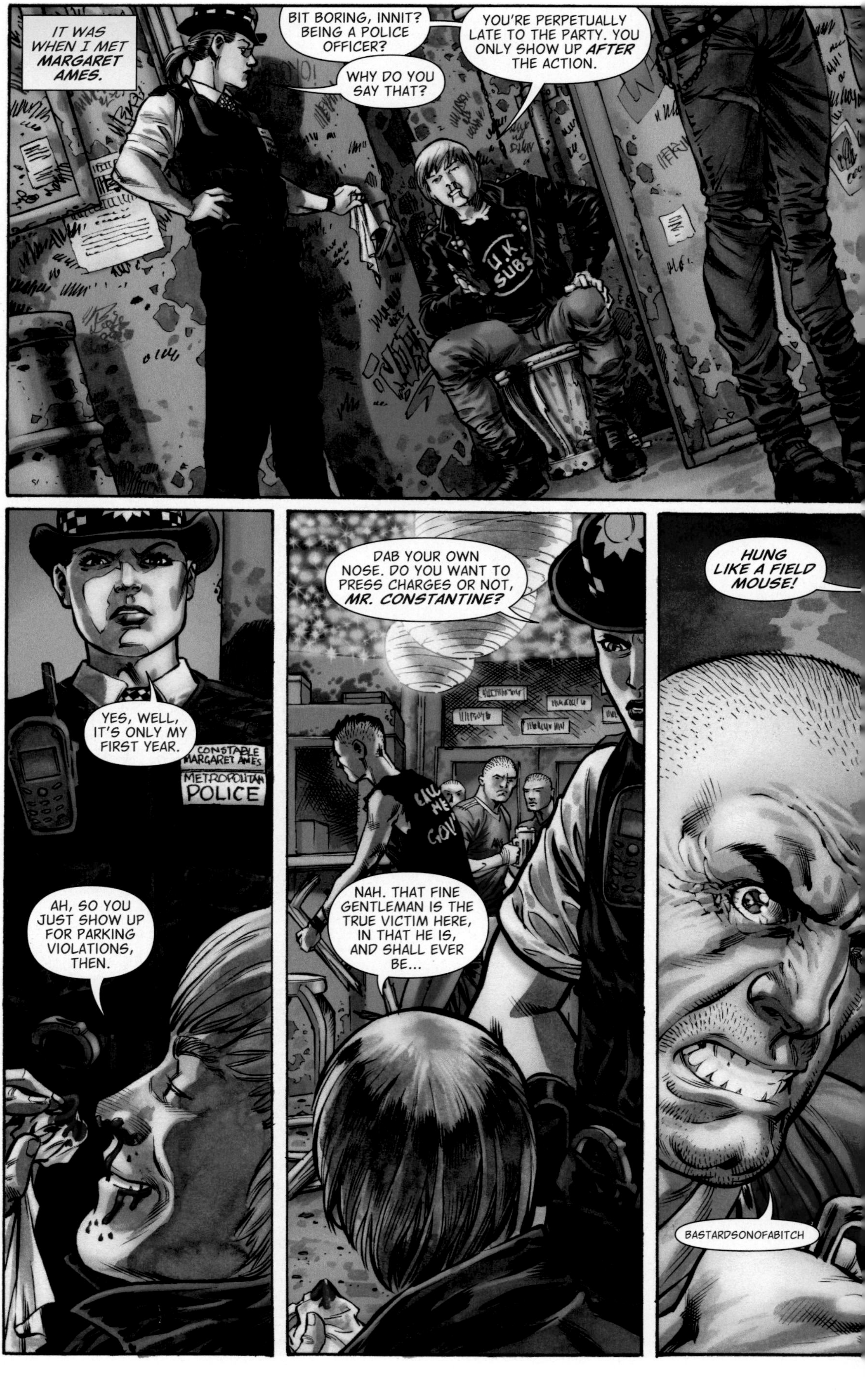
IT WAS WHEN I MET MARGARET AMES.
BIT BORING, INNIT? BEING A POLICE OFFICER?
WHY DO YOU SAY THAT?
YOU'RE PERPETUALLY LATE TO THE PARTY. YOU ONLY SHOW UP AFTER THE ACTION.
U.K. SUBS
YES, WELL, IT'S ONLY MY FIRST YEAR.
CONSTABLE MARGARET AMES
METROPOLITAN POLICE
AH, SO YOU JUST SHOW UP FOR PARKING VIOLATIONS, THEN.
DAB YOUR OWN NOSE. DO YOU WANT TO PRESS CHARGES OR NOT, MR. CONSTANTINE?
NAH. THAT FINE GENTLEMAN IS THE TRUE VICTIM HERE, IN THAT HE IS, AND SHALL EVER BE...
HUNG LIKE A FIELD MOUSE!
BASTARDSONOFABITCH

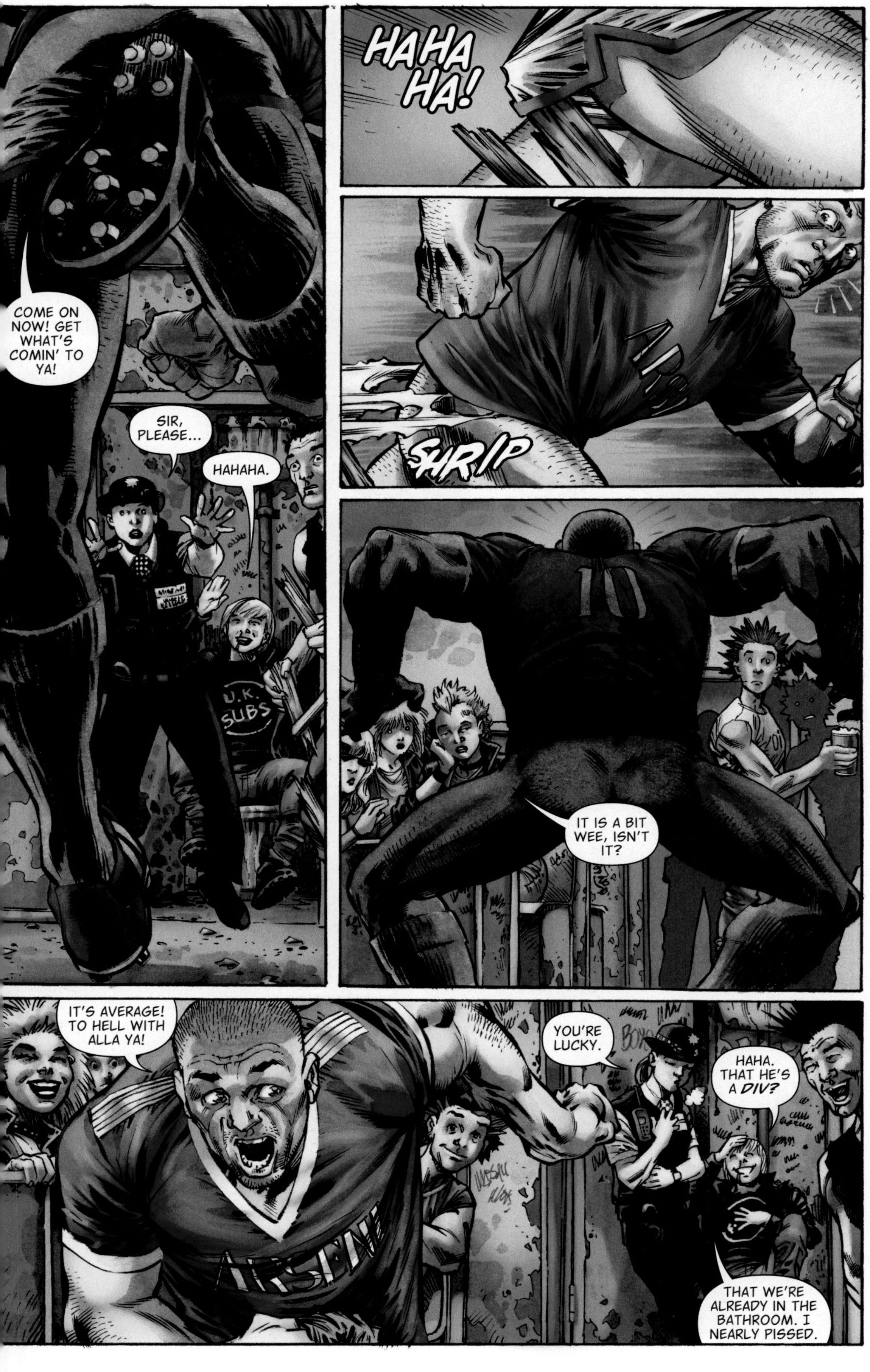
HAHA HA!
COME ON NOW! GET WHAT'S COMIN' TO YA!
SIR, PLEASE...
HAHAHA.
U.K. SUBS
SHRIP
IT IS A BIT WEE, ISN'T IT?
IT'S AVERAGE! TO HELL WITH ALLA YA!
YOU'RE LUCKY.
HAHA. THAT HE'S A *DIV?*
THAT WE'RE ALREADY IN THE BATHROOM. I NEARLY PISSED.

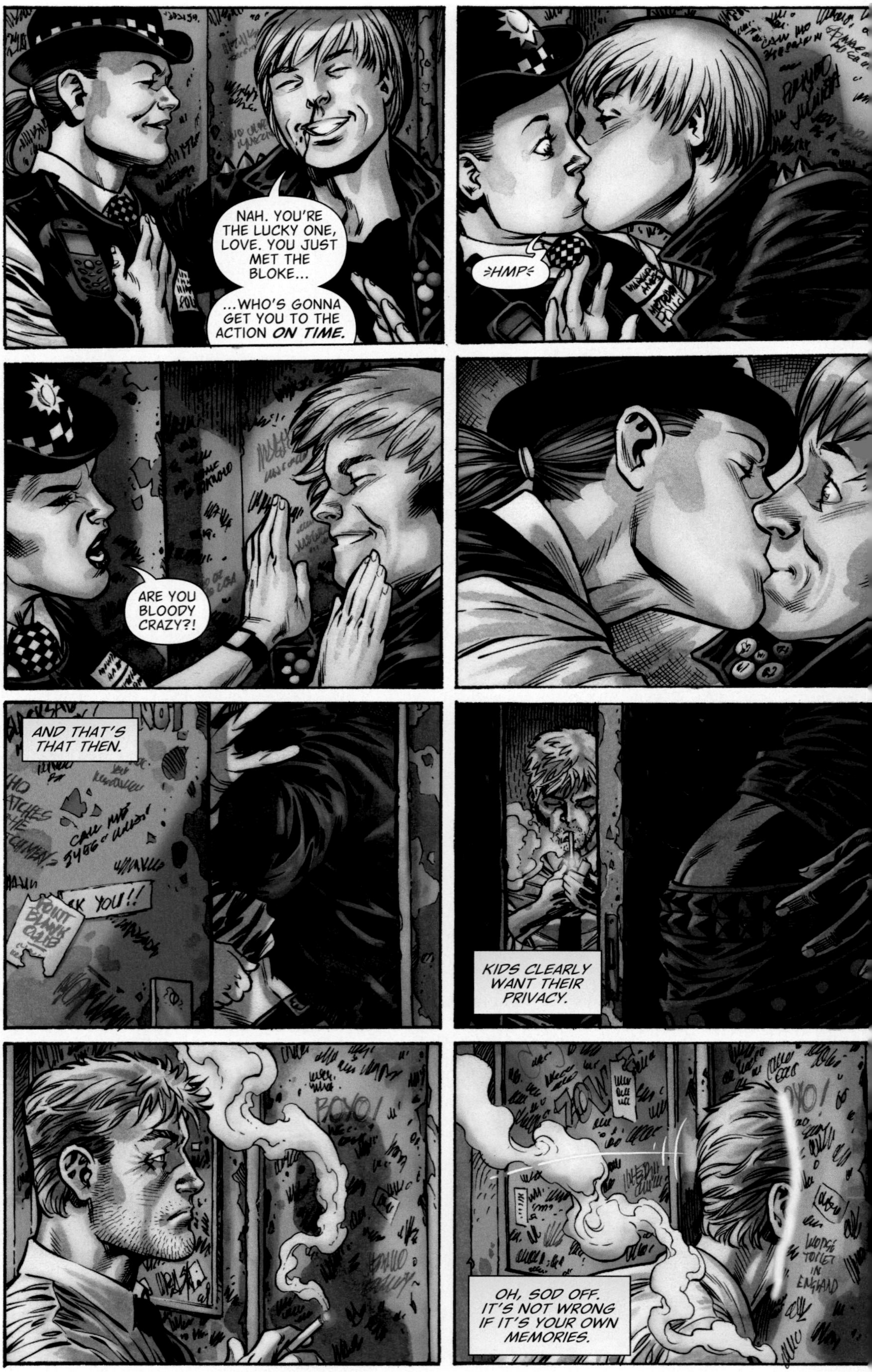
NAH. YOU'RE THE LUCKY ONE, LOVE. YOU JUST MET THE BLOKE...
...WHO'S GONNA GET YOU TO THE ACTION ON TIME.
HMP
ARE YOU BLOODY CRAZY?!
AND THAT'S THAT THEN.
KIDS CLEARLY WANT THEIR PRIVACY.
OH, SOD OFF. IT'S NOT WRONG IF IT'S YOUR OWN MEMORIES.

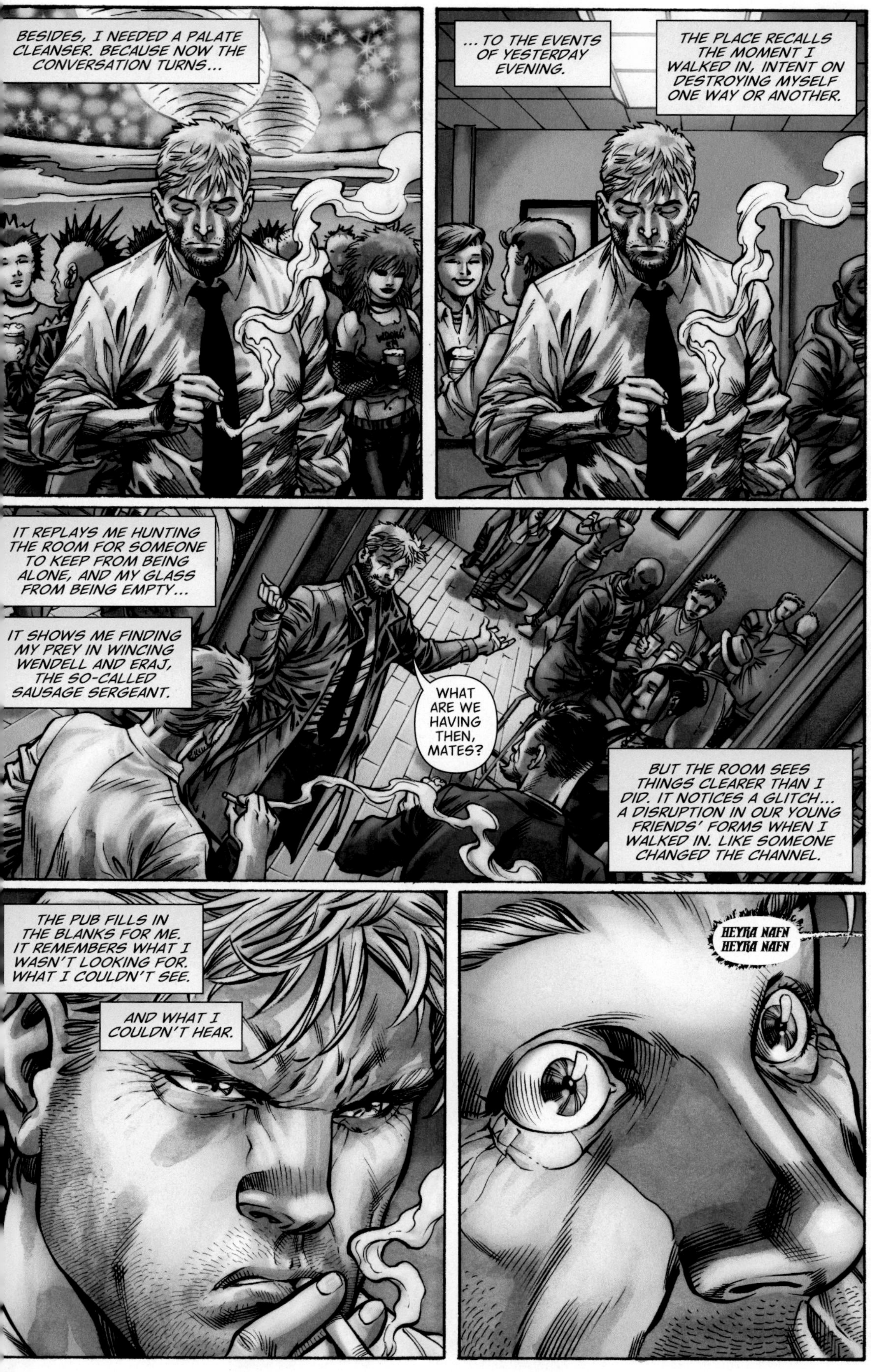
BESIDES, I NEEDED A PALATE CLEANSER. BECAUSE NOW THE CONVERSATION TURNS...
...TO THE EVENTS OF YESTERDAY EVENING.
THE PLACE RECALLS THE MOMENT I WALKED IN, INTENT ON DESTROYING MYSELF ONE WAY OR ANOTHER.
IT REPLAYS ME HUNTING THE ROOM FOR SOMEONE TO KEEP FROM BEING ALONE, AND MY GLASS FROM BEING EMPTY...
IT SHOWS ME FINDING MY PREY IN WINCING WENDELL AND ERAJ, THE SO-CALLED SAUSAGE SERGEANT.
WHAT ARE WE HAVING THEN, MATES?
BUT THE ROOM SEES THINGS CLEARER THAN I DID. IT NOTICES A GLITCH... A DISRUPTION IN OUR YOUNG FRIENDS' FORMS WHEN I WALKED IN. LIKE SOMEONE CHANGED THE CHANNEL.
THE PUB FILLS IN THE BLANKS FOR ME. IT REMEMBERS WHAT I WASN'T LOOKING FOR. WHAT I COULDN'T SEE.
AND WHAT I COULDN'T HEAR.
HEYRA NAFN
HEYRA NAFN

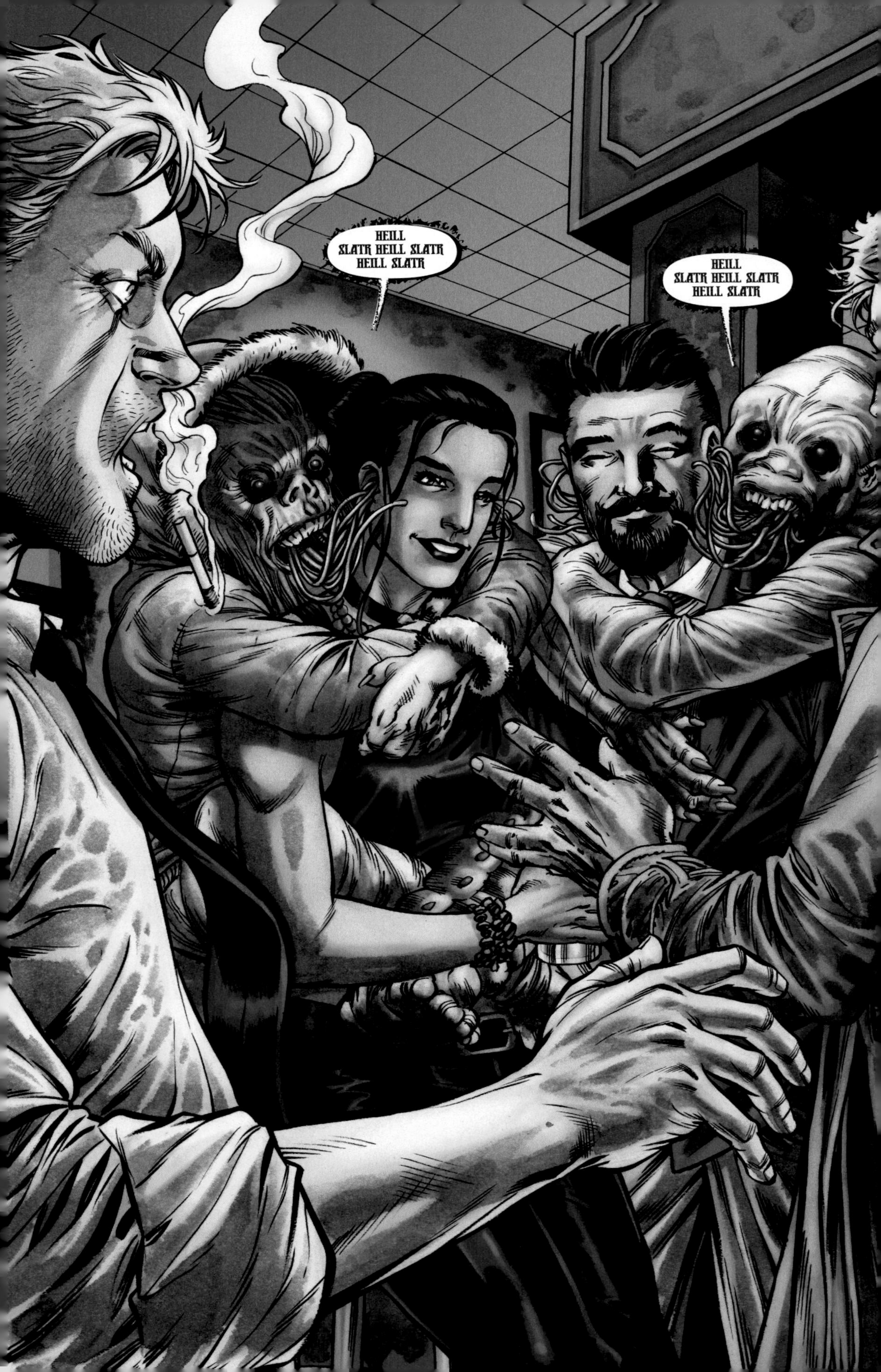
HEILL SLATR HEILL SLATR HEILL SLATR
HEILL SLATR HEILL SLATR HEILL SLATR

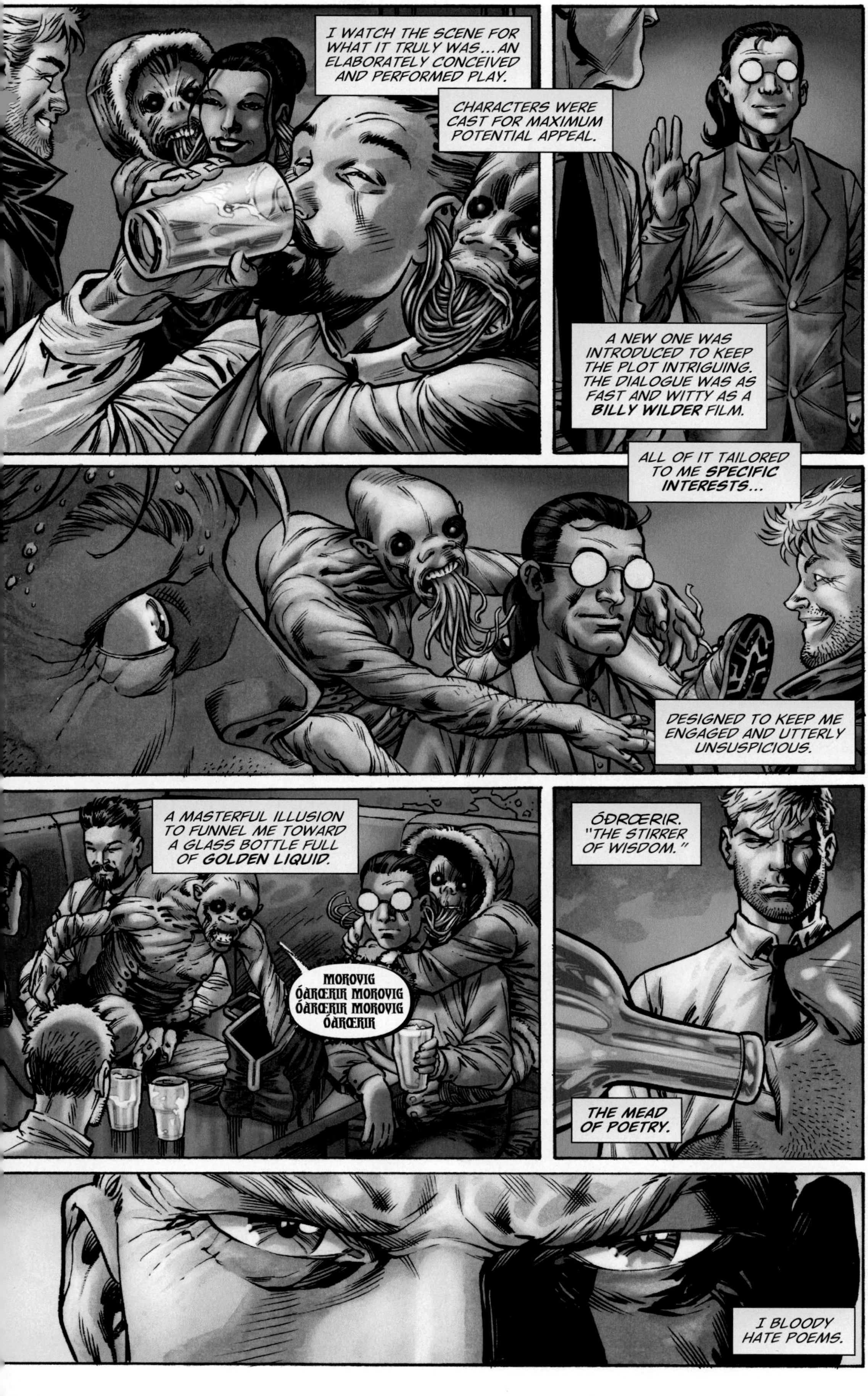
I WATCH THE SCENE FOR WHAT IT TRULY WAS... AN ELABORATELY CONCEIVED AND PERFORMED PLAY.
CHARACTERS WERE CAST FOR MAXIMUM POTENTIAL APPEAL.
A NEW ONE WAS INTRODUCED TO KEEP THE PLOT INTRIGUING. THE DIALOGUE WAS AS FAST AND WITTY AS A **BILLY WILDER** FILM.
ALL OF IT TAILORED TO ME **SPECIFIC INTERESTS...**
DESIGNED TO KEEP ME ENGAGED AND UTTERLY UNSUSPICIOUS.
A MASTERFUL ILLUSION TO FUNNEL ME TOWARD A GLASS BOTTLE FULL OF **GOLDEN LIQUID.**
MOROVIG ÓÐRŒRIR MOROVIG ÓÐRŒRIR MOROVIG ÓÐRŒRIR
ÓÐRŒRIR. "THE STIRRER OF WISDOM."
THE MEAD OF POETRY.
I BLOODY HATE POEMS.

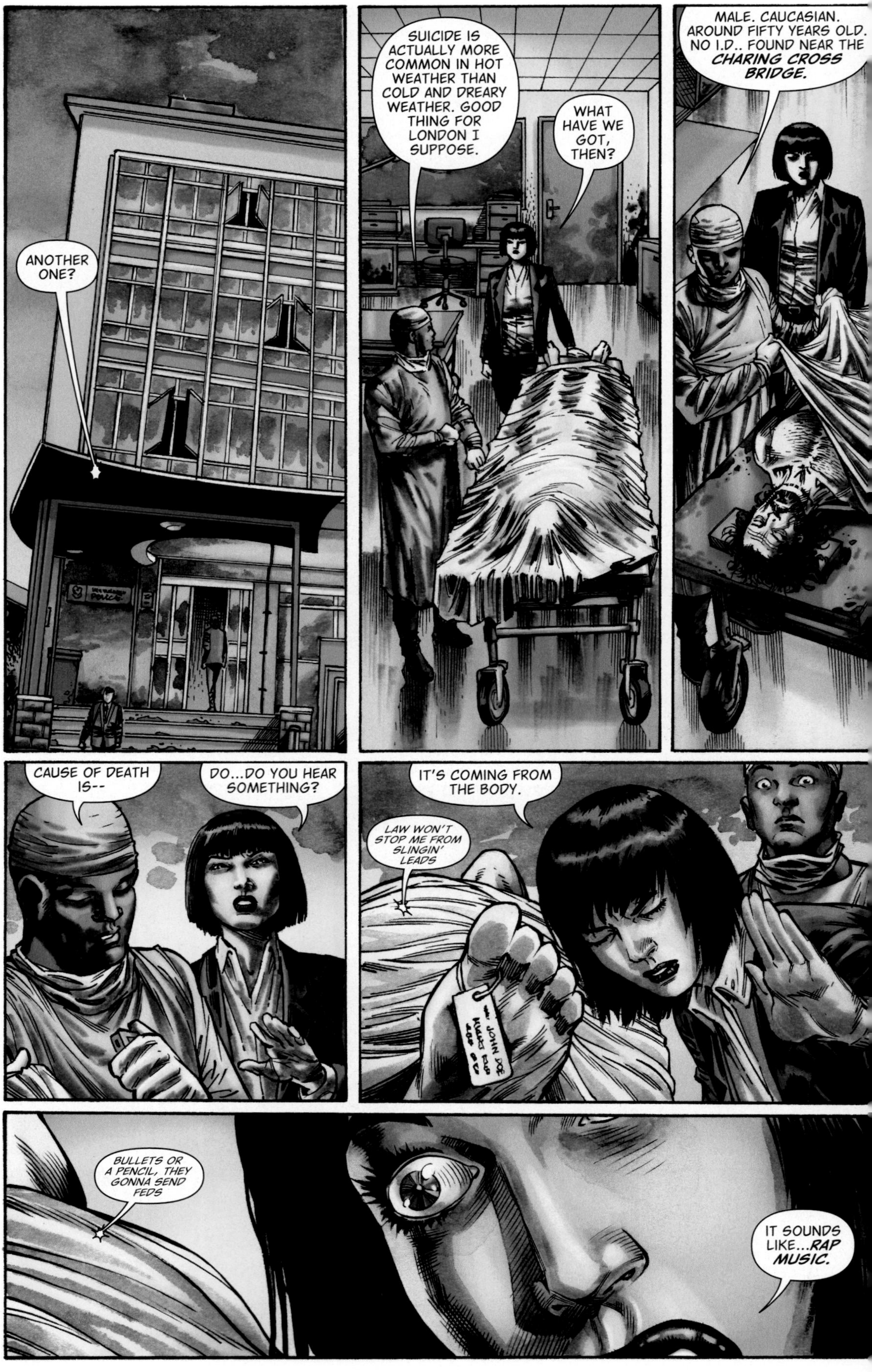
ANOTHER ONE?
SUICIDE IS ACTUALLY MORE COMMON IN HOT WEATHER THAN COLD AND DREARY WEATHER. GOOD THING FOR LONDON I SUPPOSE.
WHAT HAVE WE GOT, THEN?
MALE. CAUCASIAN. AROUND FIFTY YEARS OLD. NO I.D.. FOUND NEAR THE CHARING CROSS BRIDGE.
CAUSE OF DEATH IS--
DO...DO YOU HEAR SOMETHING?
IT'S COMING FROM THE BODY.
LAW WON'T STOP ME FROM SLINGIN' LEADS
JOHN DOE
BULLETS OR A PENCIL, THEY GONNA SEND FEDS
IT SOUNDS LIKE...RAP MUSIC.

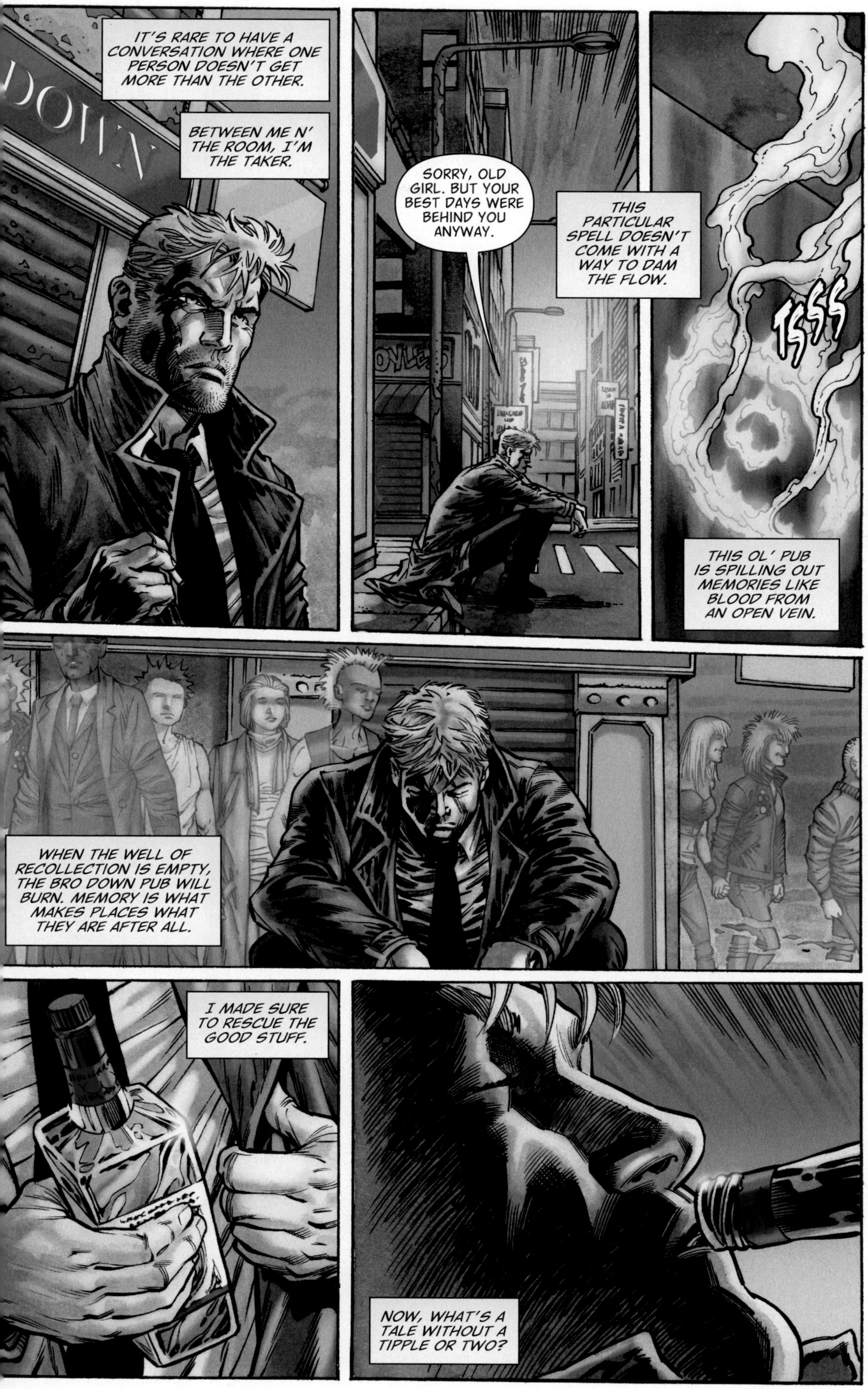
IT'S RARE TO HAVE A CONVERSATION WHERE ONE PERSON DOESN'T GET MORE THAN THE OTHER.
BETWEEN ME N' THE ROOM, I'M THE TAKER.
DOWN
SORRY, OLD GIRL. BUT YOUR BEST DAYS WERE BEHIND YOU ANYWAY.
THIS PARTICULAR SPELL DOESN'T COME WITH A WAY TO DAM THE FLOW.
TSSS
THIS OL' PUB IS SPILLING OUT MEMORIES LIKE BLOOD FROM AN OPEN VEIN.
WHEN THE WELL OF RECOLLECTION IS EMPTY, THE BRO DOWN PUB WILL BURN. MEMORY IS WHAT MAKES PLACES WHAT THEY ARE AFTER ALL.
I MADE SURE TO RESCUE THE GOOD STUFF.
NOW, WHAT'S A TALE WITHOUT A TIPPLE OR TWO?

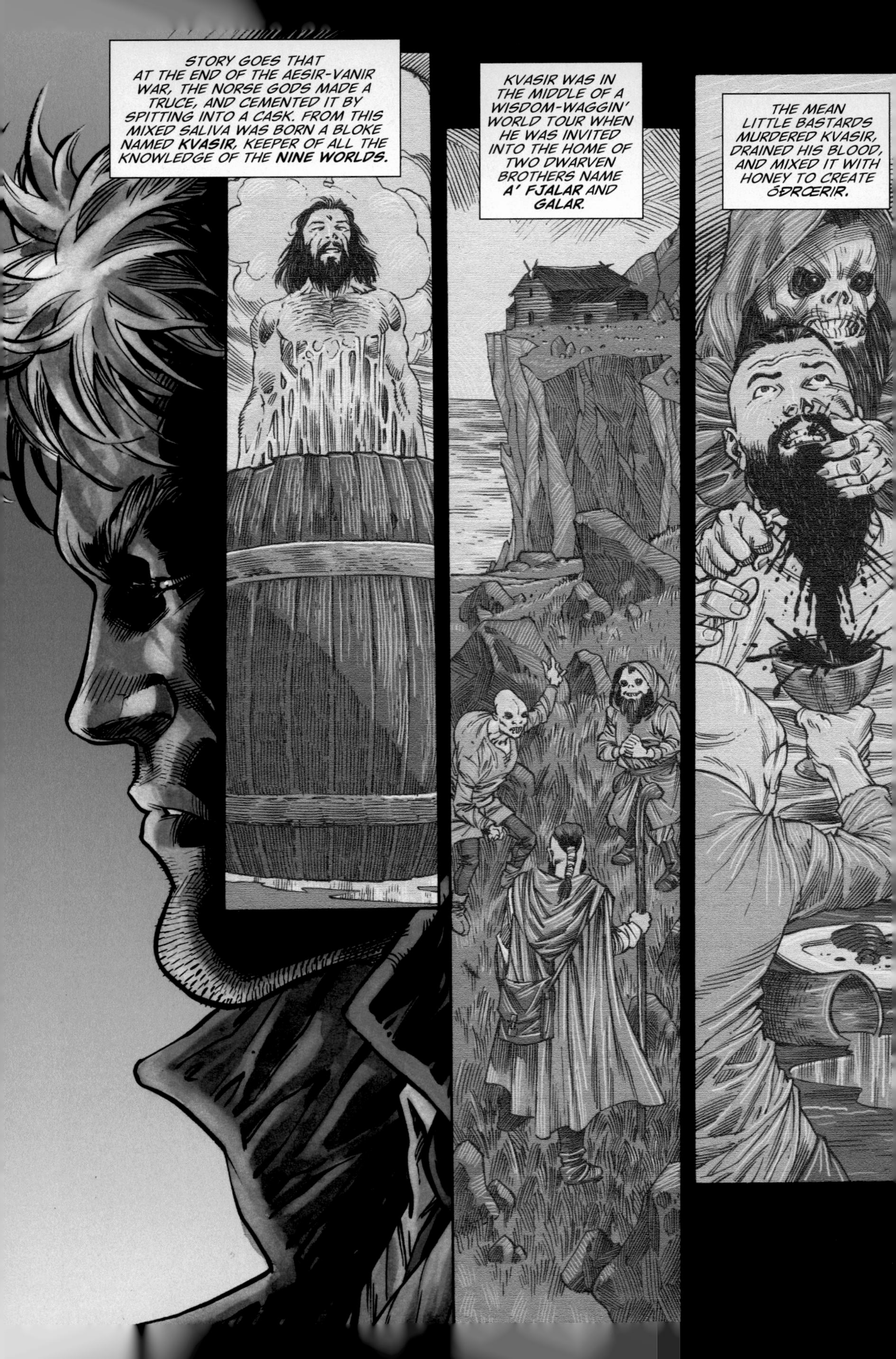
STORY GOES THAT AT THE END OF THE AESIR-VANIR WAR, THE NORSE GODS MADE A TRUCE, AND CEMENTED IT BY SPITTING INTO A CASK. FROM THIS MIXED SALIVA WAS BORN A BLOKE NAMED KVASIR, KEEPER OF ALL THE KNOWLEDGE OF THE NINE WORLDS.
KVASIR WAS IN THE MIDDLE OF A WISDOM-WAGGIN' WORLD TOUR WHEN HE WAS INVITED INTO THE HOME OF TWO DWARVEN BROTHERS NAME A' FJALAR AND GALAR.
THE MEAN LITTLE BASTARDS MURDERED KVASIR, DRAINED HIS BLOOD, AND MIXED IT WITH HONEY TO CREATE ÓÐRŒRIR.

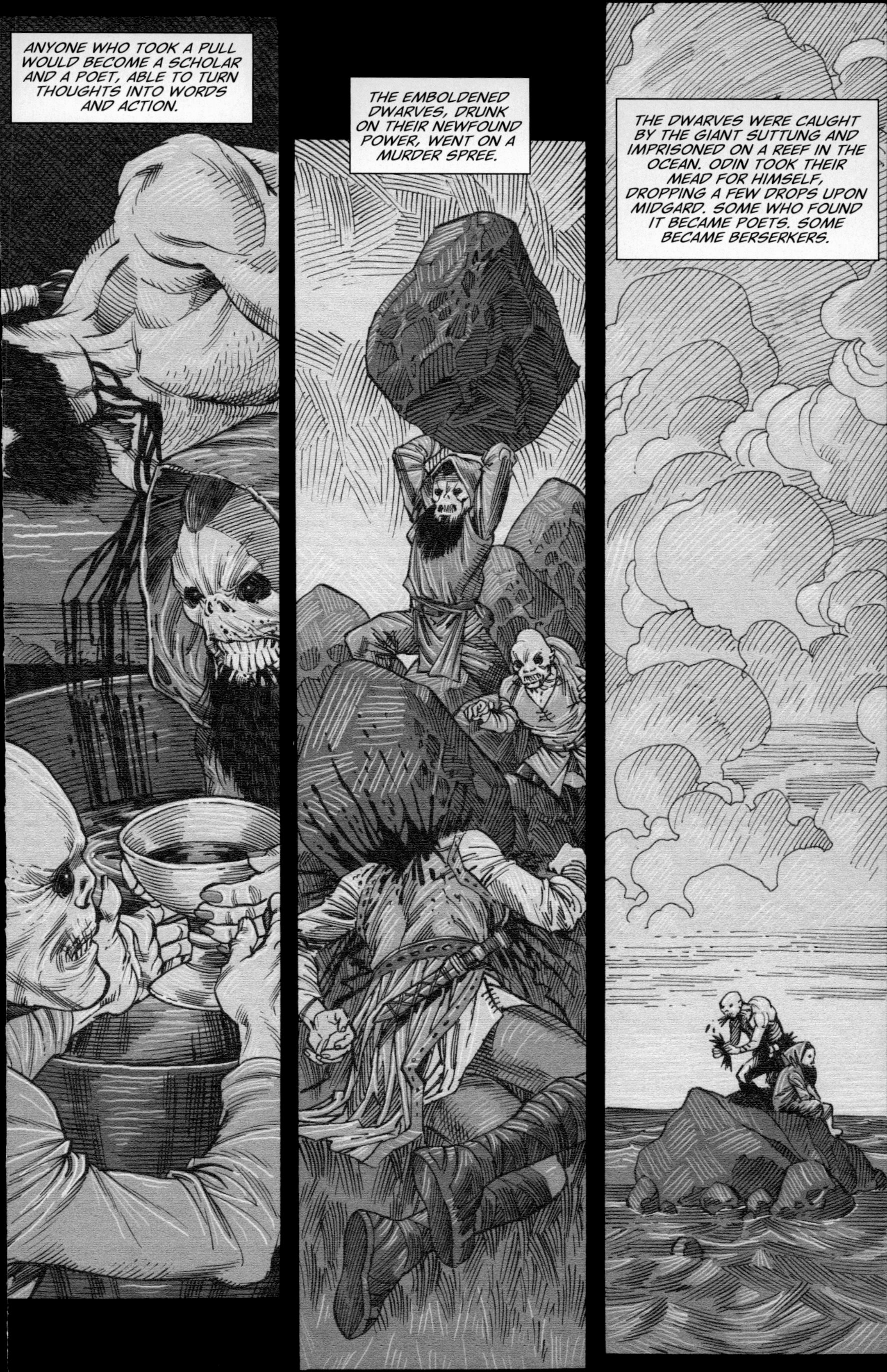
ANYONE WHO TOOK A PULL WOULD BECOME A SCHOLAR AND A POET, ABLE TO TURN THOUGHTS INTO WORDS AND ACTION.
THE EMBOLDENED DWARVES, DRUNK ON THEIR NEWFOUND POWER, WENT ON A MURDER SPREE.
THE DWARVES WERE CAUGHT BY THE GIANT SUTTUNG AND IMPRISONED ON A REEF IN THE OCEAN. ODIN TOOK THEIR MEAD FOR HIMSELF, DROPPING A FEW DROPS UPON MIDGARD. SOME WHO FOUND IT BECAME POETS. SOME BECAME BERSERKERS.

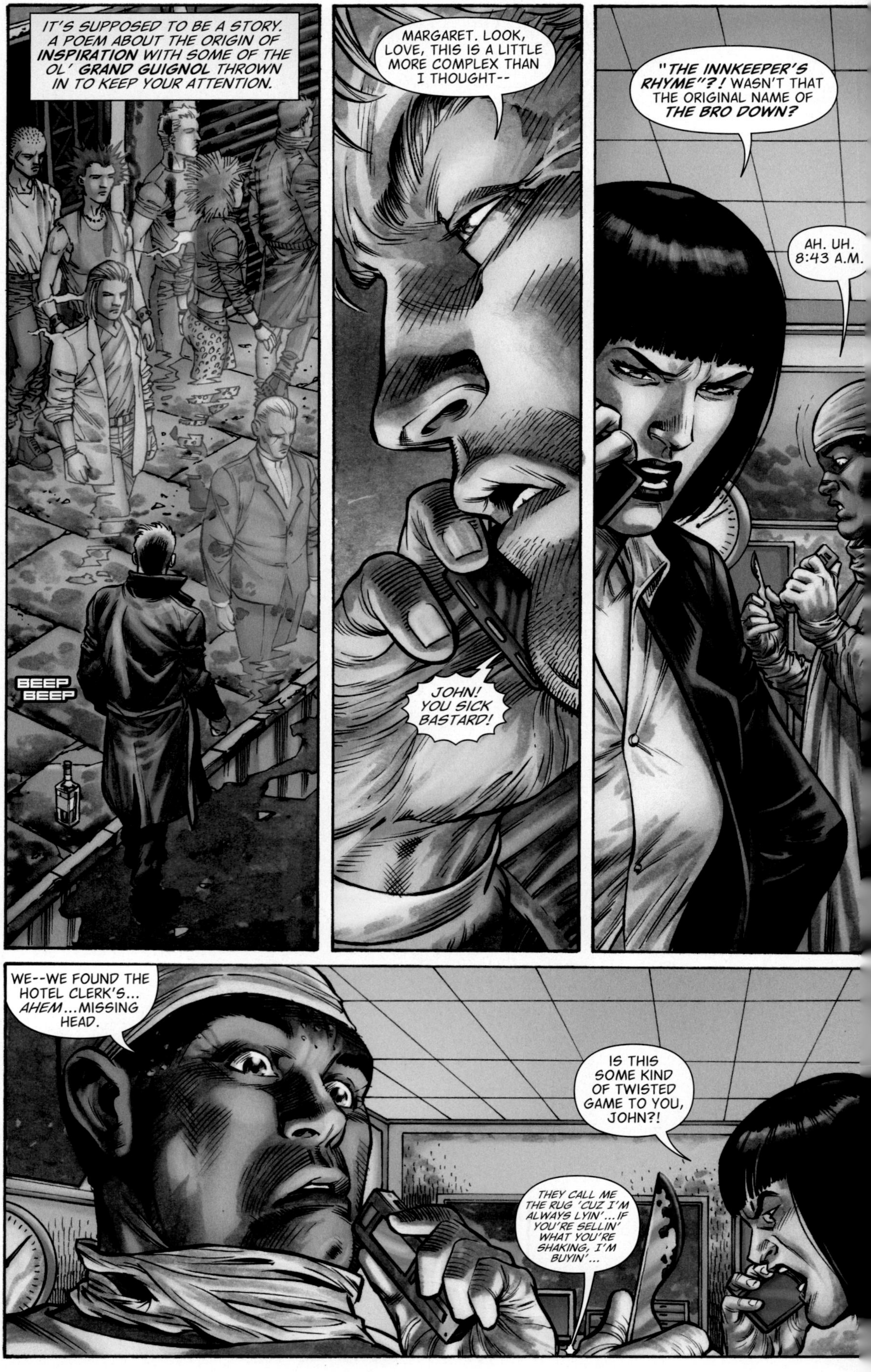
IT'S SUPPOSED TO BE A STORY. A POEM ABOUT THE ORIGIN OF INSPIRATION WITH SOME OF THE OL' GRAND GUIGNOL THROWN IN TO KEEP YOUR ATTENTION.
BEEP BEEP
MARGARET. LOOK, LOVE, THIS IS A LITTLE MORE COMPLEX THAN I THOUGHT--
JOHN! YOU SICK BASTARD!
"THE INNKEEPER'S RHYME"?! WASN'T THAT THE ORIGINAL NAME OF THE BRO DOWN?
AH. UH. 8:43 A.M.
WE--WE FOUND THE HOTEL CLERK'S... AHEM...MISSING HEAD.
IS THIS SOME KIND OF TWISTED GAME TO YOU, JOHN?!
THEY CALL ME THE RUG 'CUZ I'M ALWAYS LYIN'...IF YOU'RE SELLIN' WHAT YOU'RE SHAKING, I'M BUYIN'...

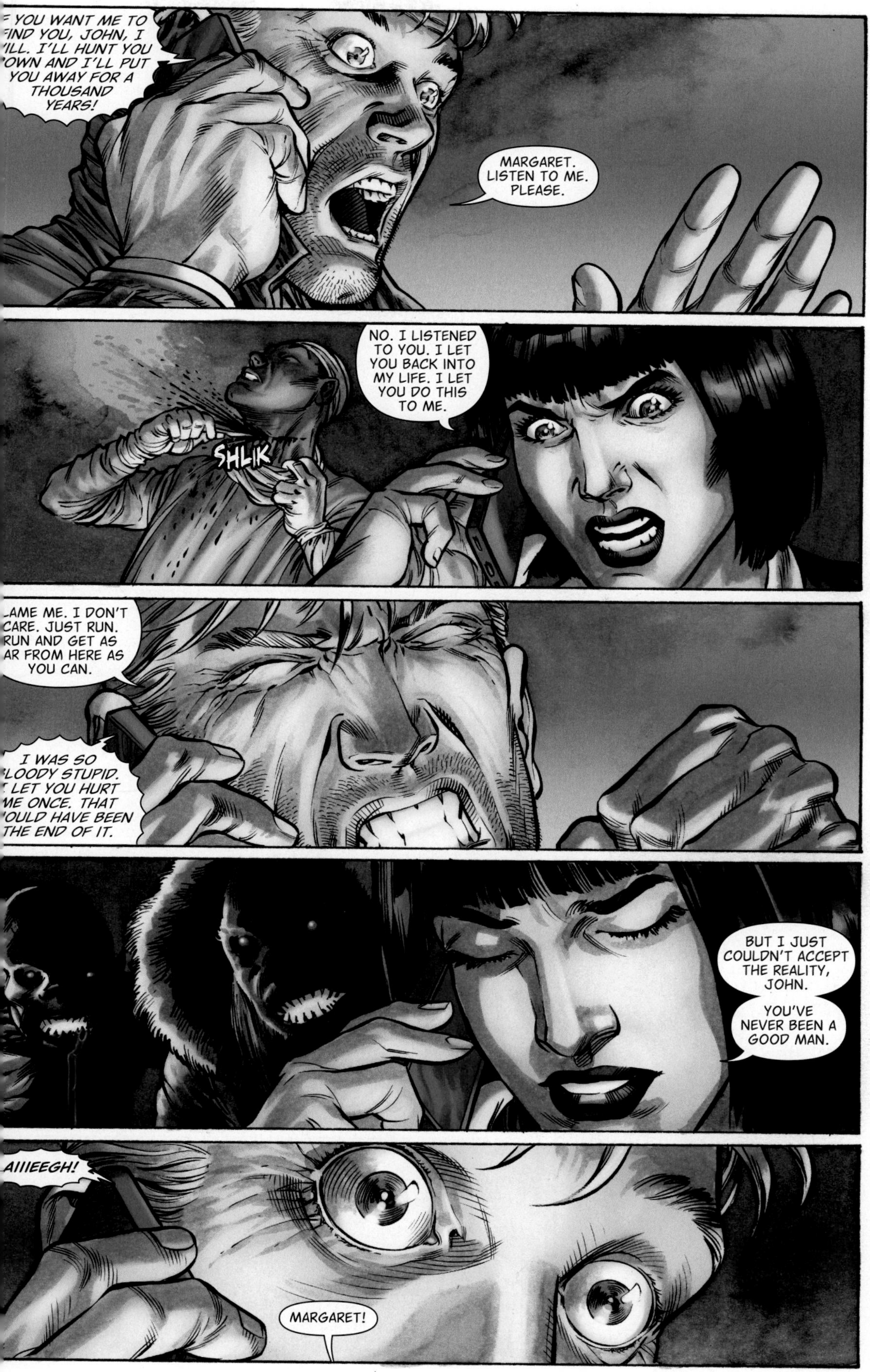
F YOU WANT ME TO FIND YOU, JOHN, I WILL. I'LL HUNT YOU DOWN AND I'LL PUT YOU AWAY FOR A THOUSAND YEARS!
MARGARET. LISTEN TO ME. PLEASE.
NO. I LISTENED TO YOU. I LET YOU BACK INTO MY LIFE. I LET YOU DO THIS TO ME.
SHLIK
LAME ME. I DON'T CARE. JUST RUN. RUN AND GET AS AR FROM HERE AS YOU CAN.
I WAS SO LOODY STUPID. I LET YOU HURT ME ONCE. THAT OULD HAVE BEEN THE END OF IT.
BUT I JUST COULDN'T ACCEPT THE REALITY, JOHN.
YOU'VE NEVER BEEN A GOOD MAN.
AIIIEEGH!
MARGARET!

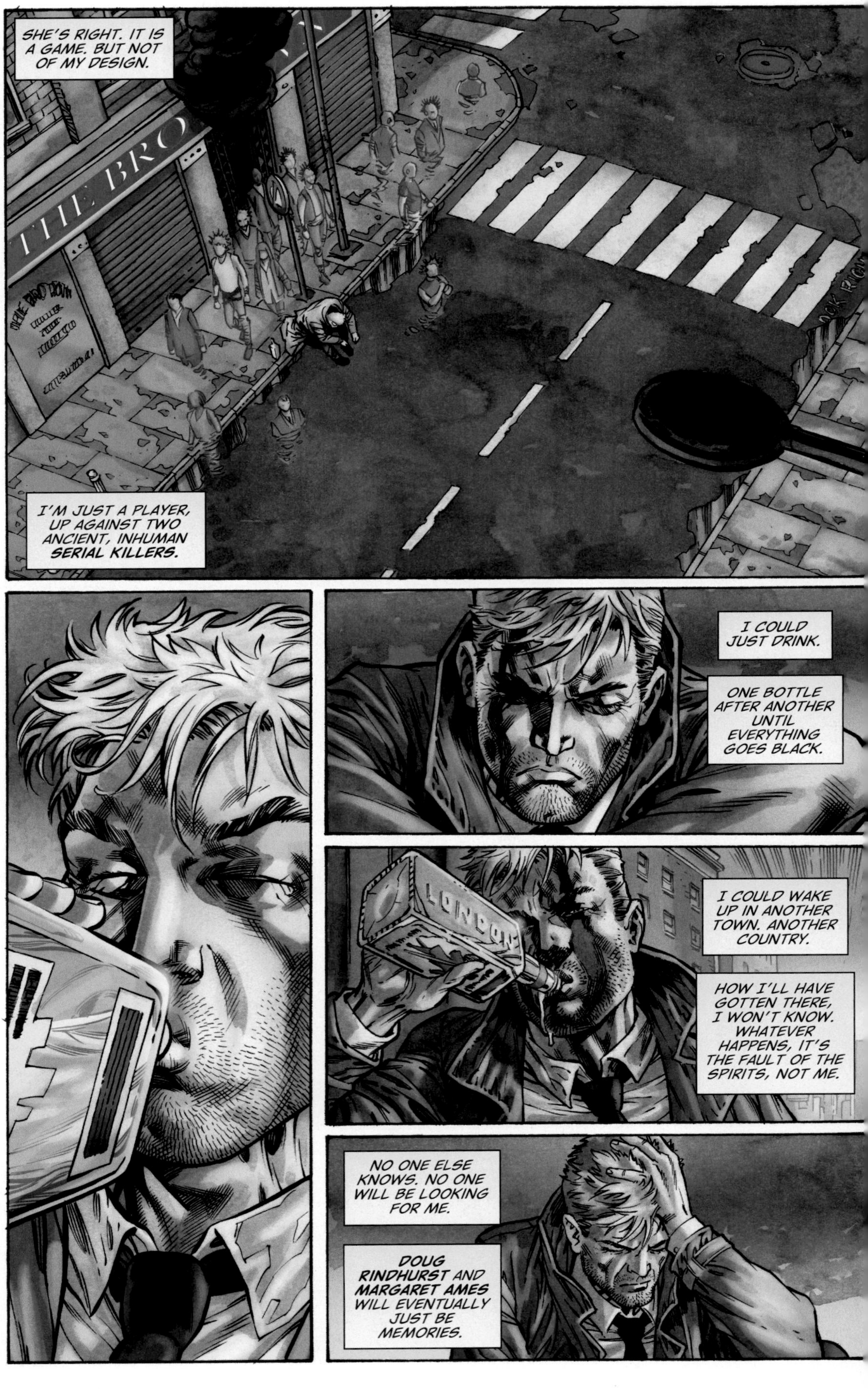
SHE'S RIGHT. IT IS A GAME. BUT NOT OF MY DESIGN.
THE BRO
I'M JUST A PLAYER, UP AGAINST TWO ANCIENT, INHUMAN SERIAL KILLERS.
I COULD JUST DRINK.
ONE BOTTLE AFTER ANOTHER UNTIL EVERYTHING GOES BLACK.
LONDON
I COULD WAKE UP IN ANOTHER TOWN. ANOTHER COUNTRY.
HOW I'LL HAVE GOTTEN THERE, I WON'T KNOW. WHATEVER HAPPENS, IT'S THE FAULT OF THE SPIRITS, NOT ME.
NO ONE ELSE KNOWS. NO ONE WILL BE LOOKING FOR ME.
DOUG RINDHURST AND MARGARET AMES WILL EVENTUALLY JUST BE MEMORIES.

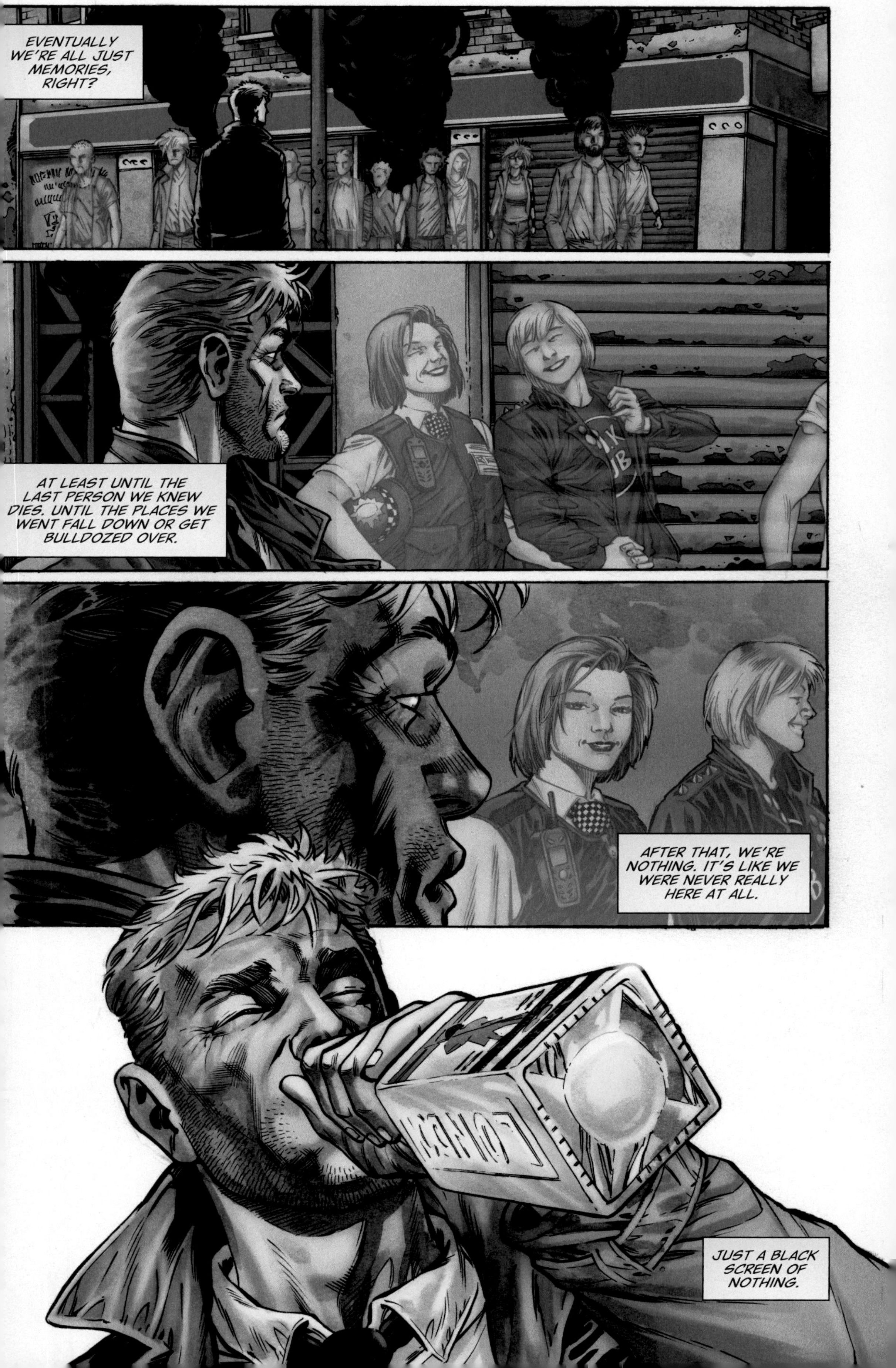

EVENTUALLY WE'RE ALL JUST MEMORIES, RIGHT?
AT LEAST UNTIL THE LAST PERSON WE KNEW DIES. UNTIL THE PLACES WE WENT FALL DOWN OR GET BULLDOZED OVER.
AFTER THAT, WE'RE NOTHING. IT'S LIKE WE WERE NEVER REALLY HERE AT ALL.
JUST A BLACK SCREEN OF NOTHING.

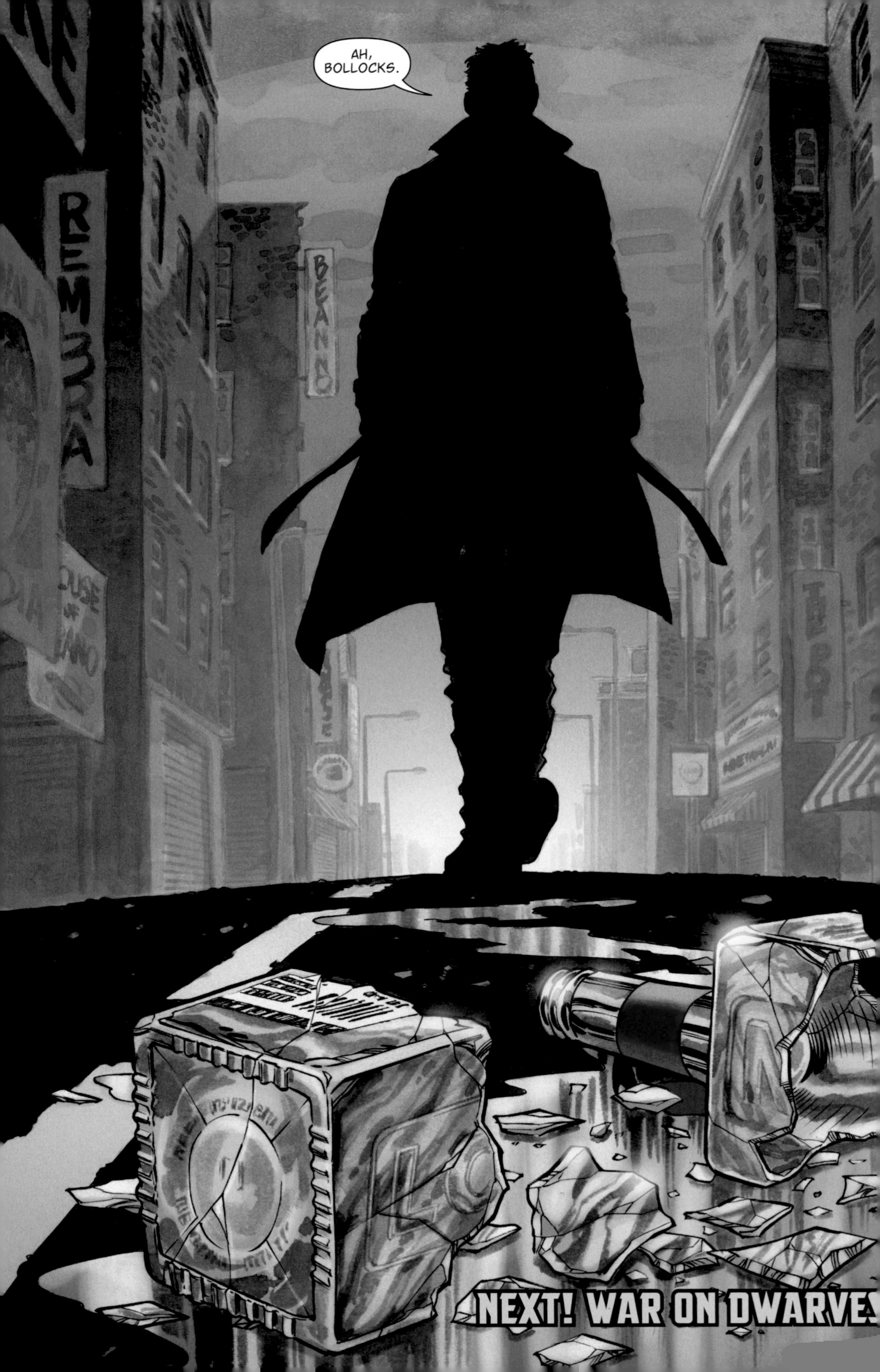
AH, BOLLOCKS.
NEXT! WAR ON DWARVES

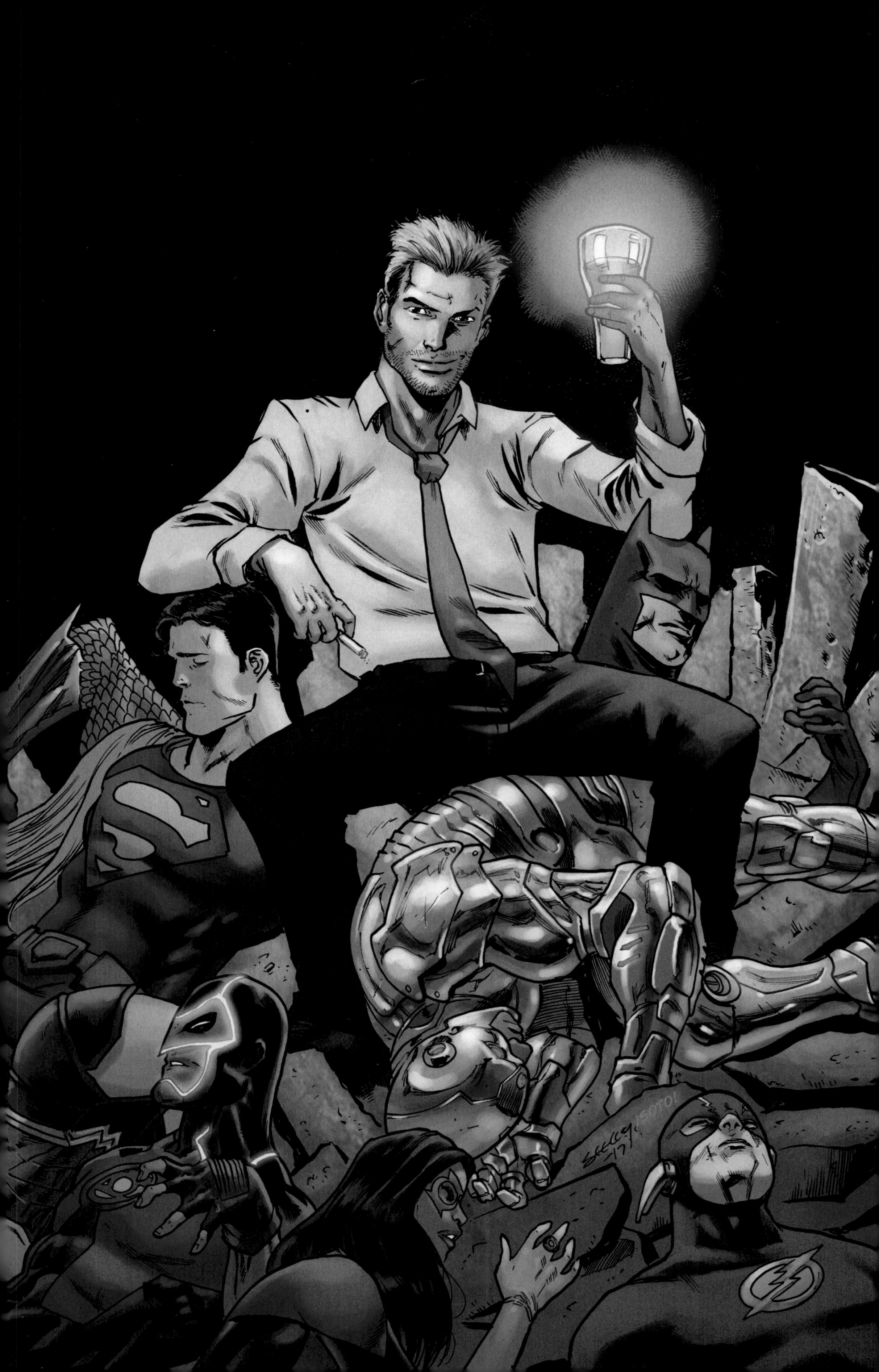

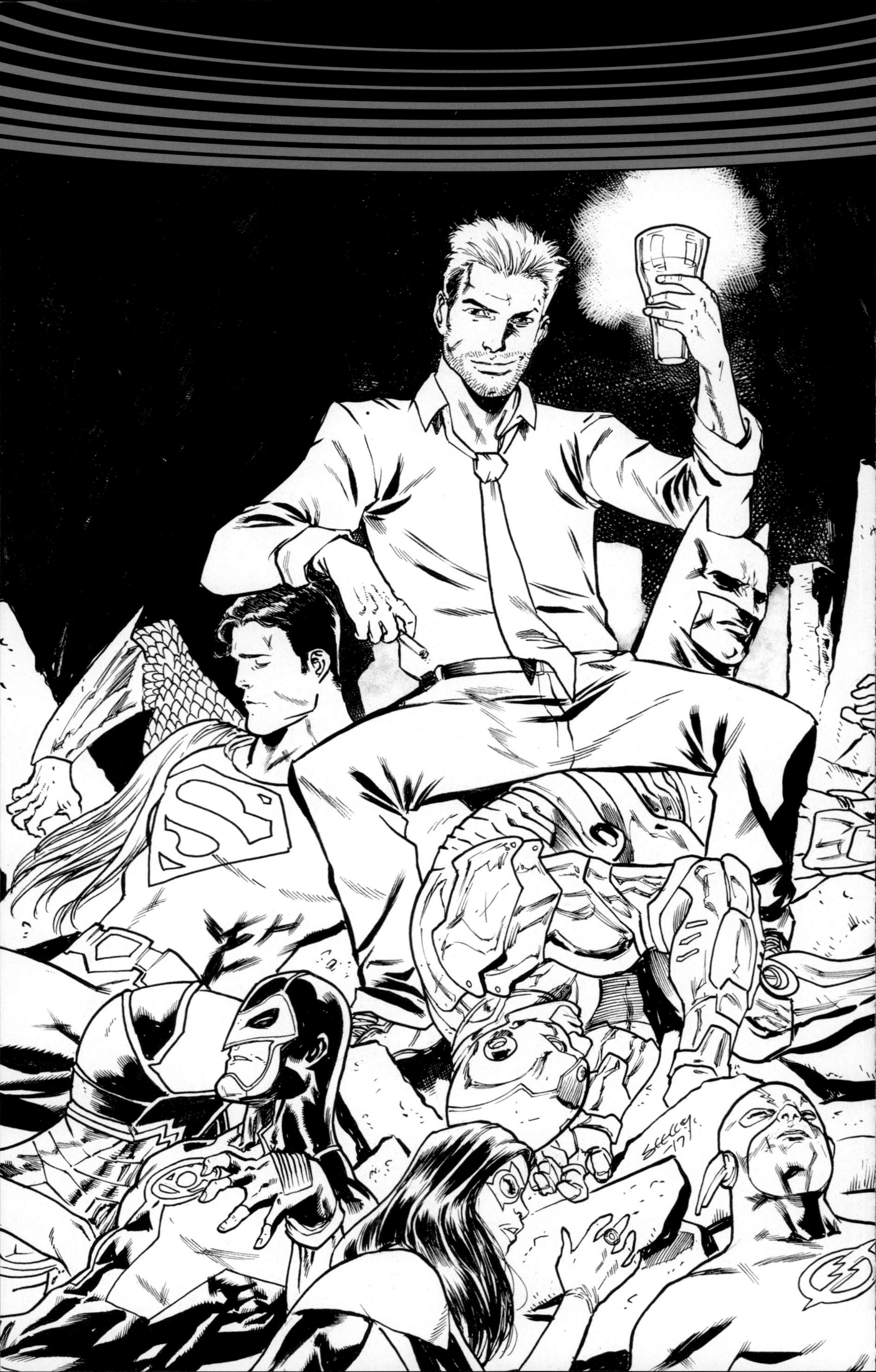

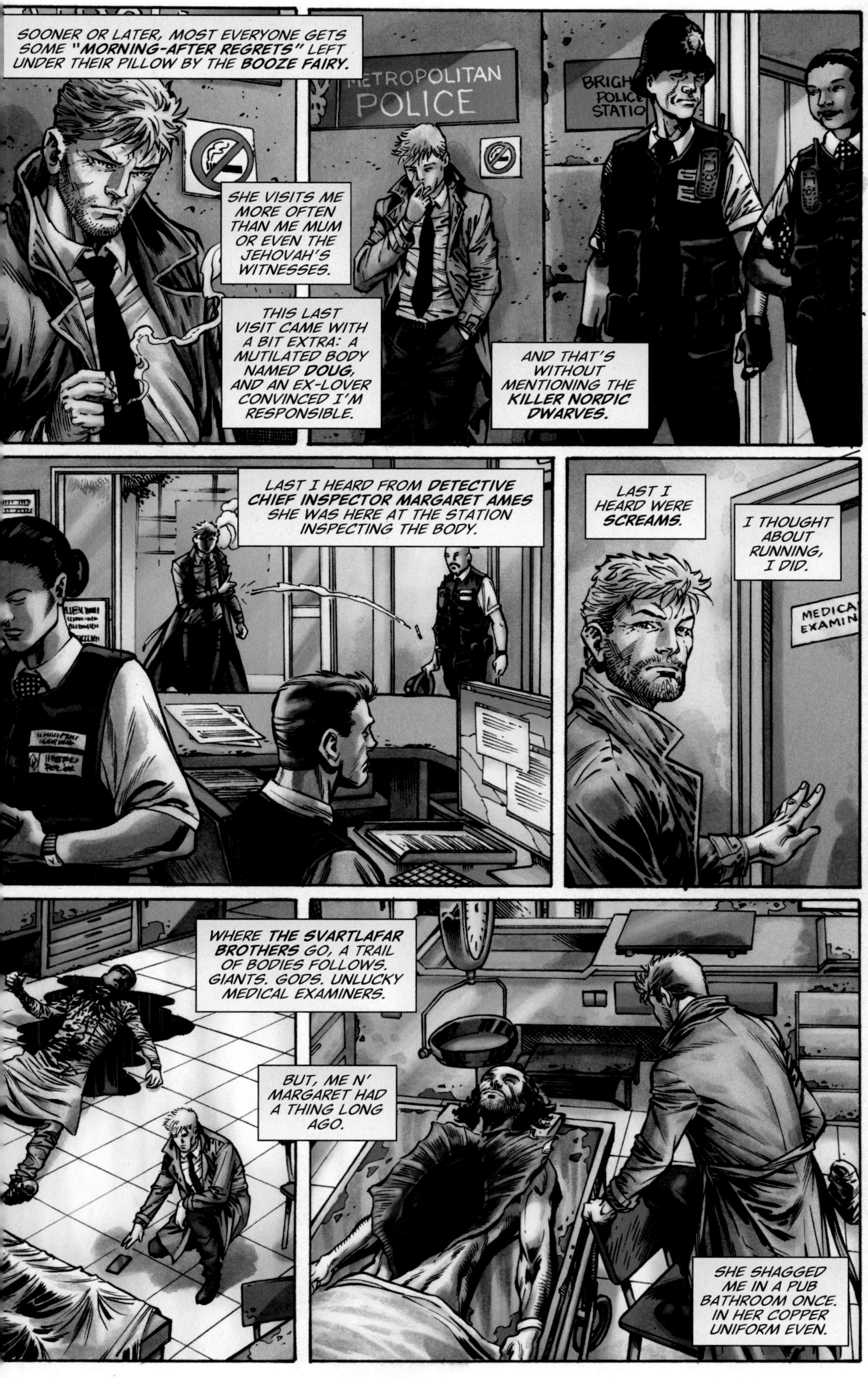
SOONER OR LATER, MOST EVERYONE GETS SOME "MORNING-AFTER REGRETS" LEFT UNDER THEIR PILLOW BY THE BOOZE FAIRY.
METROPOLITAN POLICE
SHE VISITS ME MORE OFTEN THAN ME MUM OR EVEN THE JEHOVAH'S WITNESSES.
THIS LAST VISIT CAME WITH A BIT EXTRA: A MUTILATED BODY NAMED DOUG, AND AN EX-LOVER CONVINCED I'M RESPONSIBLE.
AND THAT'S WITHOUT MENTIONING THE KILLER NORDIC DWARVES.
LAST I HEARD FROM DETECTIVE CHIEF INSPECTOR MARGARET AMES SHE WAS HERE AT THE STATION INSPECTING THE BODY.
LAST I HEARD WERE SCREAMS.
I THOUGHT ABOUT RUNNING, I DID.
WHERE THE SVARTLAFAR BROTHERS GO, A TRAIL OF BODIES FOLLOWS. GIANTS. GODS. UNLUCKY MEDICAL EXAMINERS.
BUT, ME N' MARGARET HAD A THING LONG AGO.
SHE SHAGGED ME IN A PUB BATHROOM ONCE. IN HER COPPER UNIFORM EVEN.

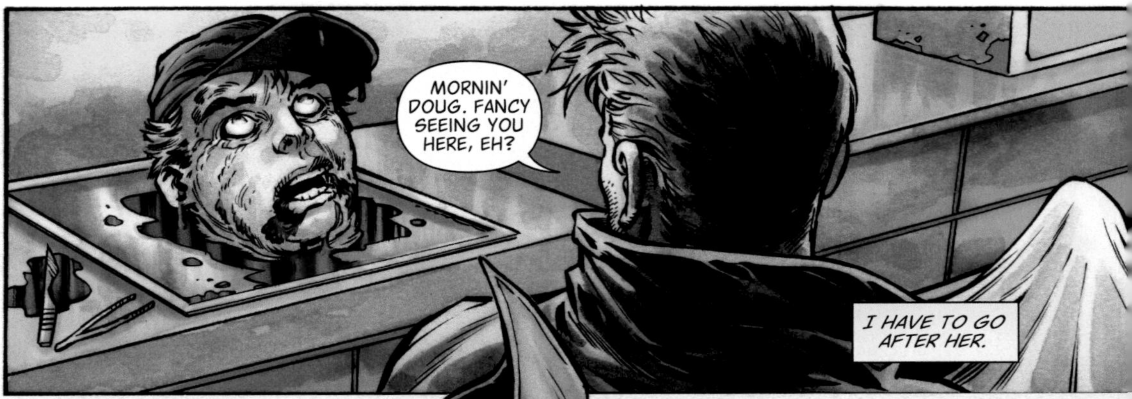
MORNIN' DOUG. FANCY SEEING YOU HERE, EH?
I HAVE TO GO AFTER HER.

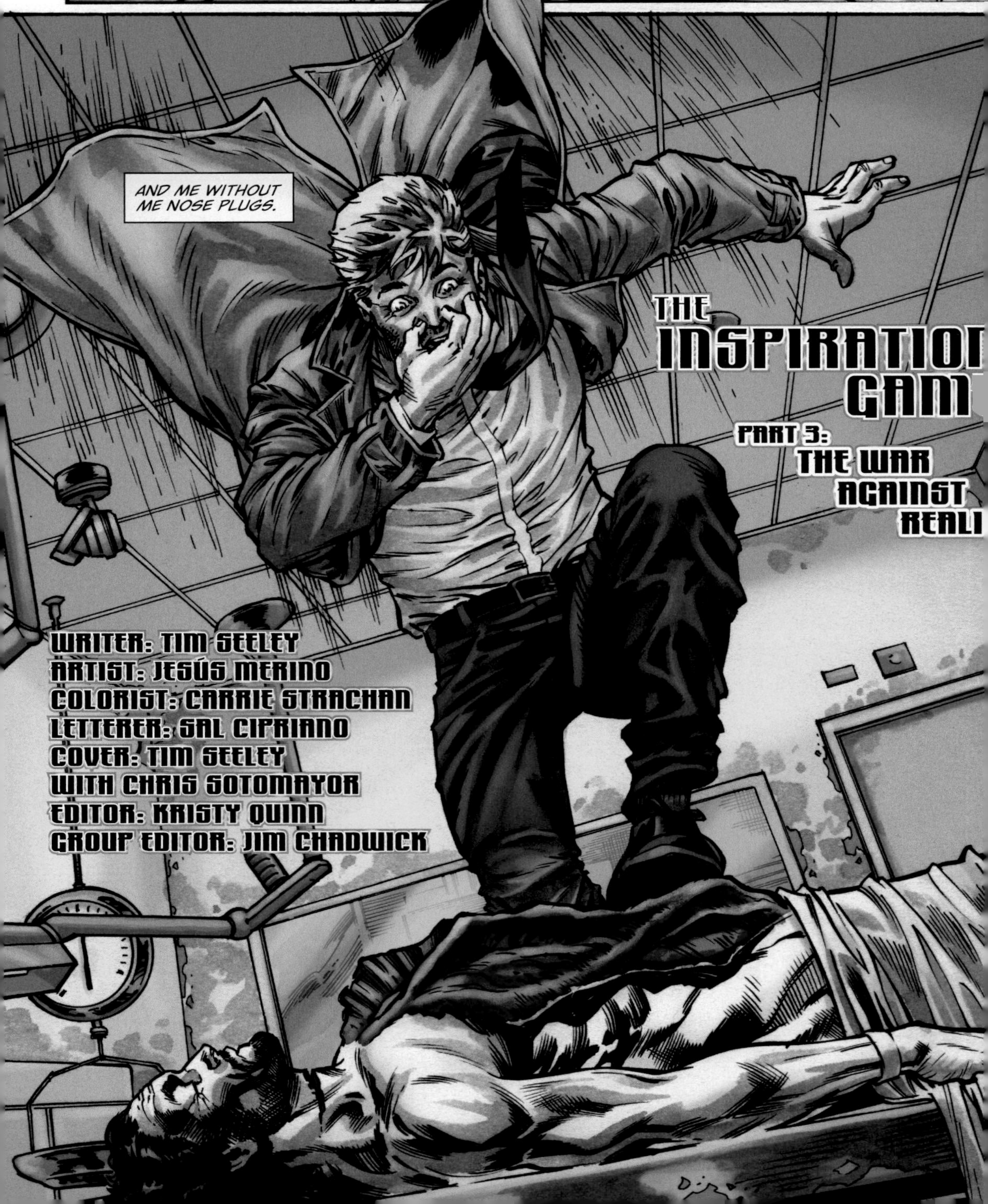
AND ME WITHOUT ME NOSE PLUGS.
THE INSPIRATIO
GAM
PART 3:
THE WAR AGAINST REALI
WRITER: TIM SEELEY
ARTIST: JESÚS MERINO
COLORIST: CARRIE STRACHAN
LETTERER: SAL CIPRIANO
COVER: TIM SEELEY WITH CHRIS SOTOMAYOR
EDITOR: KRISTY QUINN
GROUP EDITOR: JIM CHADWICK

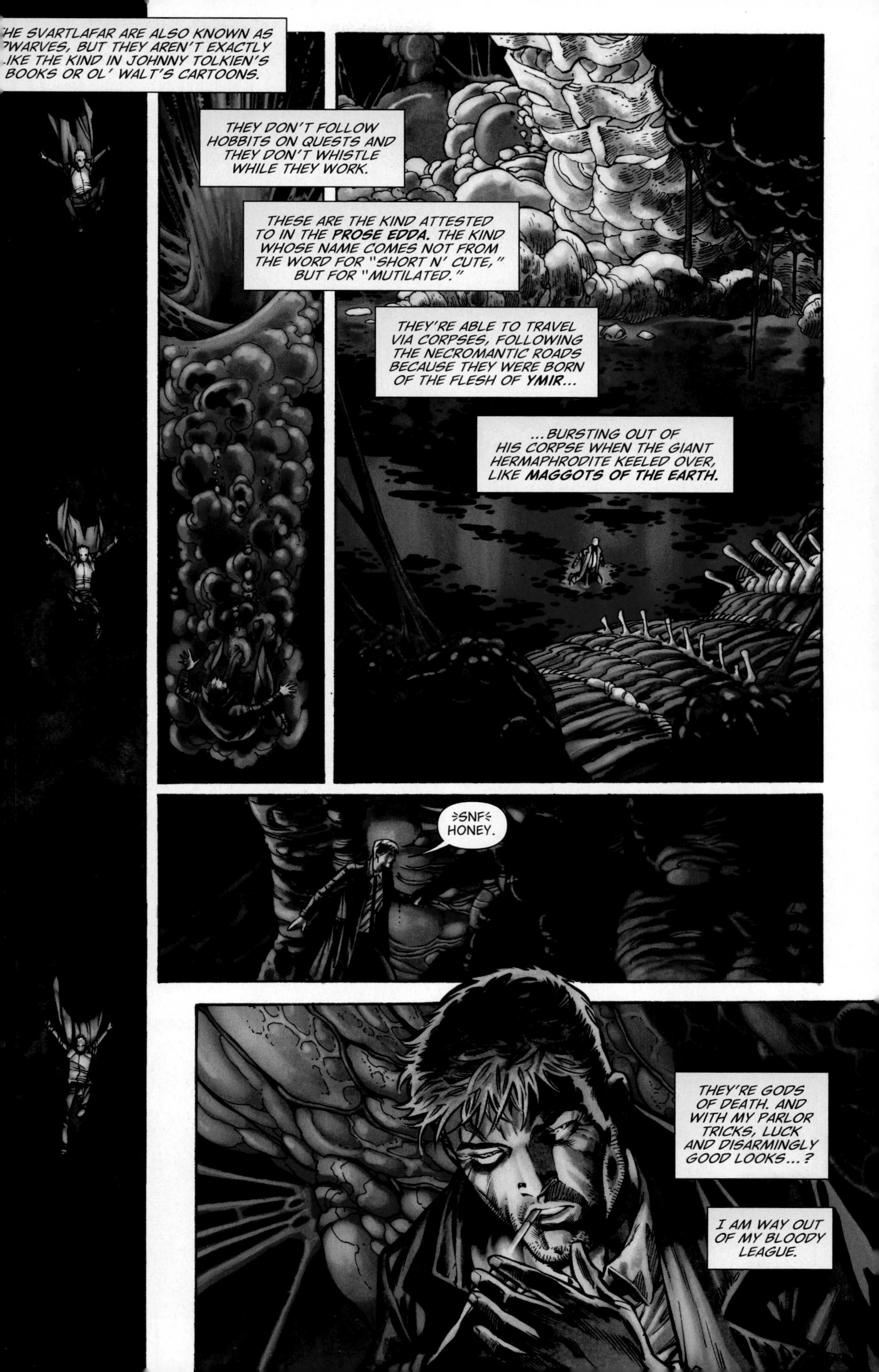

THE SVARTLAFAR ARE ALSO KNOWN AS DWARVES, BUT THEY AREN'T EXACTLY LIKE THE KIND IN JOHNNY TOLKIEN'S BOOKS OR OL' WALT'S CARTOONS.
THEY DON'T FOLLOW HOBBITS ON QUESTS AND THEY DON'T WHISTLE WHILE THEY WORK.
THESE ARE THE KIND ATTESTED TO IN THE PROSE EDDA. THE KIND WHOSE NAME COMES NOT FROM THE WORD FOR "SHORT N' CUTE," BUT FOR "MUTILATED."
THEY'RE ABLE TO TRAVEL VIA CORPSES, FOLLOWING THE NECROMANTIC ROADS BECAUSE THEY WERE BORN OF THE FLESH OF YMIR...
...BURSTING OUT OF HIS CORPSE WHEN THE GIANT HERMAPHRODITE KEELED OVER, LIKE MAGGOTS OF THE EARTH.
SNF HONEY.
THEY'RE GODS OF DEATH. AND WITH MY PARLOR TRICKS, LUCK AND DISARMINGLY GOOD LOOKS...?
I AM WAY OUT OF MY BLOODY LEAGUE.

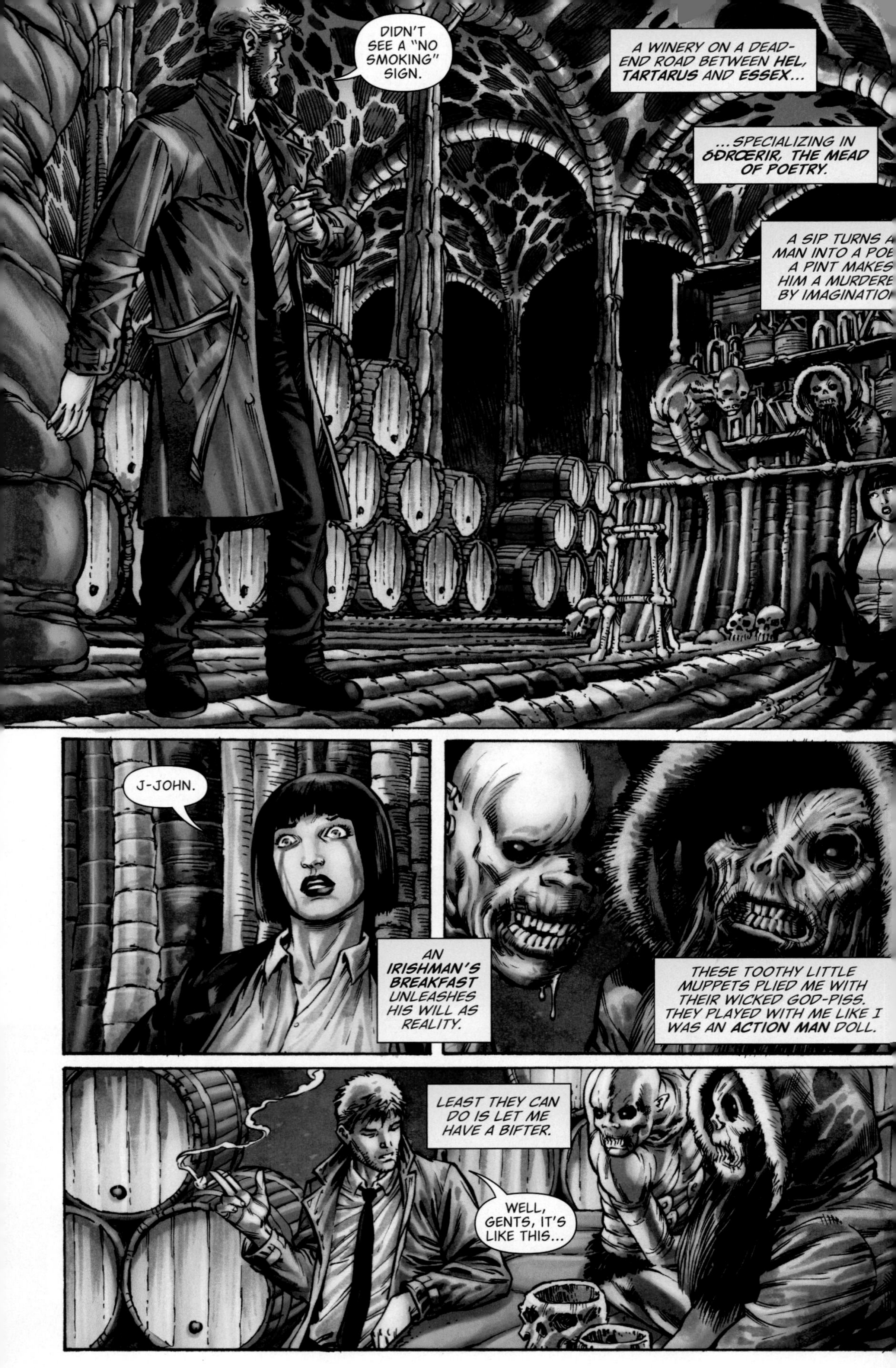

A WINERY ON A DEAD-END ROAD BETWEEN **HEL**, **TARTARUS** AND **ESSEX**...
DIDN'T SEE A "NO SMOKING" SIGN.
...SPECIALIZING IN **ÓÐRŒRIR, THE MEAD OF POETRY.**
A SIP TURNS A MAN INTO A POE A PINT MAKES HIM A MURDERE BY IMAGINATIO
J-JOHN.
AN **IRISHMAN'S BREAKFAST** UNLEASHES HIS WILL AS REALITY.
THESE TOOTHY LITTLE MUPPETS PLIED ME WITH THEIR WICKED GOD-PISS. THEY PLAYED WITH ME LIKE I WAS AN **ACTION MAN** DOLL.
LEAST THEY CAN DO IS LET ME HAVE A BIFTER.
WELL, GENTS, IT'S LIKE THIS...

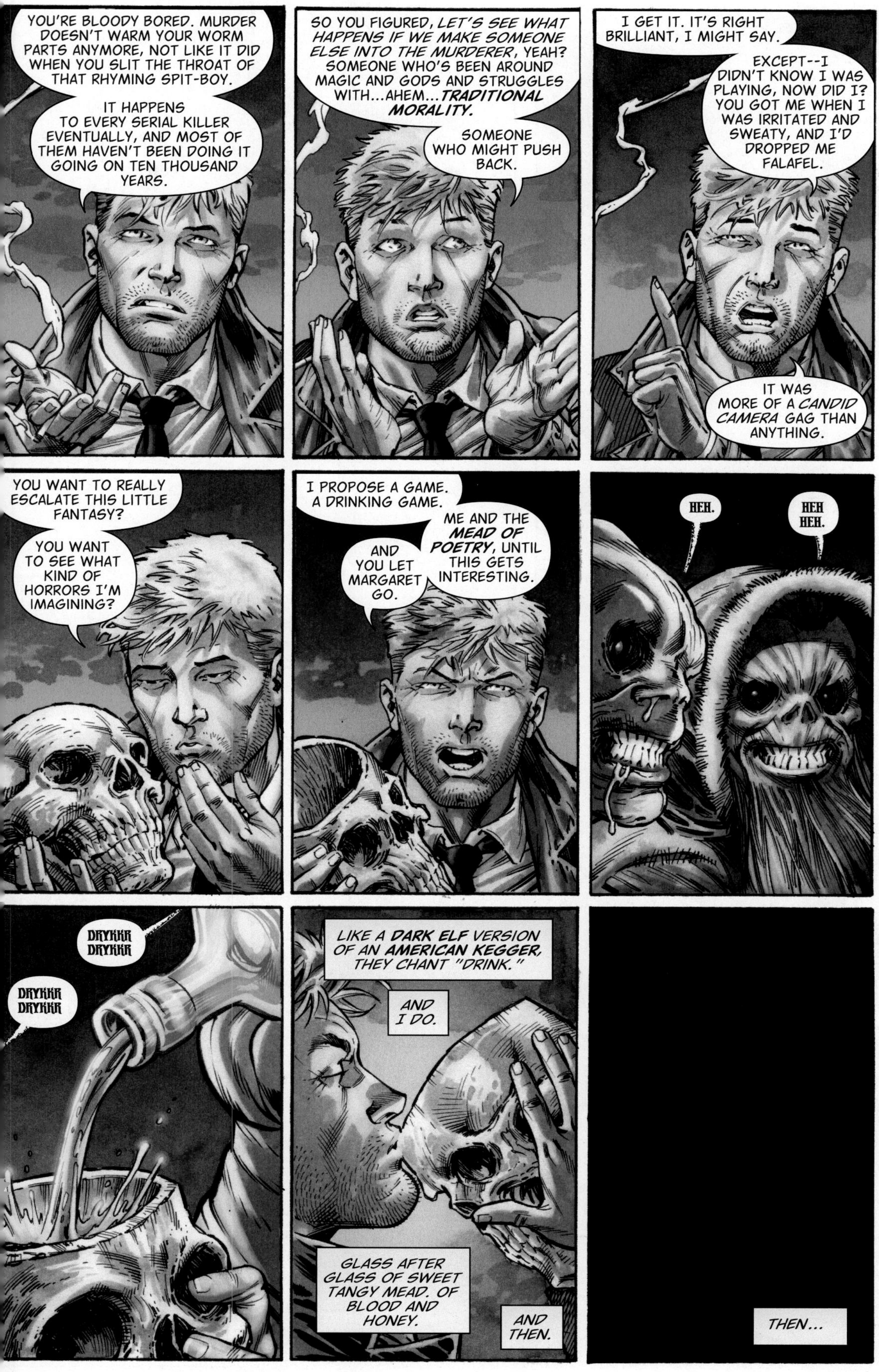
YOU'RE BLOODY BORED. MURDER DOESN'T WARM YOUR WORM PARTS ANYMORE, NOT LIKE IT DID WHEN YOU SLIT THE THROAT OF THAT RHYMING SPIT-BOY.
IT HAPPENS TO EVERY SERIAL KILLER EVENTUALLY, AND MOST OF THEM HAVEN'T BEEN DOING IT GOING ON TEN THOUSAND YEARS.
SO YOU FIGURED, LET'S SEE WHAT HAPPENS IF WE MAKE SOMEONE ELSE INTO THE MURDERER, YEAH? SOMEONE WHO'S BEEN AROUND MAGIC AND GODS AND STRUGGLES WITH...AHEM...TRADITIONAL MORALITY.
SOMEONE WHO MIGHT PUSH BACK.
I GET IT. IT'S RIGHT BRILLIANT, I MIGHT SAY.
EXCEPT--I DIDN'T KNOW I WAS PLAYING, NOW DID I? YOU GOT ME WHEN I WAS IRRITATED AND SWEATY, AND I'D DROPPED ME FALAFEL.
IT WAS MORE OF A CANDID CAMERA GAG THAN ANYTHING.
YOU WANT TO REALLY ESCALATE THIS LITTLE FANTASY?
YOU WANT TO SEE WHAT KIND OF HORRORS I'M IMAGINING?
I PROPOSE A GAME. A DRINKING GAME.
ME AND THE MEAD OF POETRY, UNTIL THIS GETS INTERESTING.
AND YOU LET MARGARET GO.
HEH.
HEH HEH.
DRYKKR DRYKKR
DRYKKR DRYKKR
LIKE A DARK ELF VERSION OF AN AMERICAN KEGGER, THEY CHANT "DRINK."
AND I DO.
GLASS AFTER GLASS OF SWEET TANGY MEAD. OF BLOOD AND HONEY.
AND THEN.
THEN...

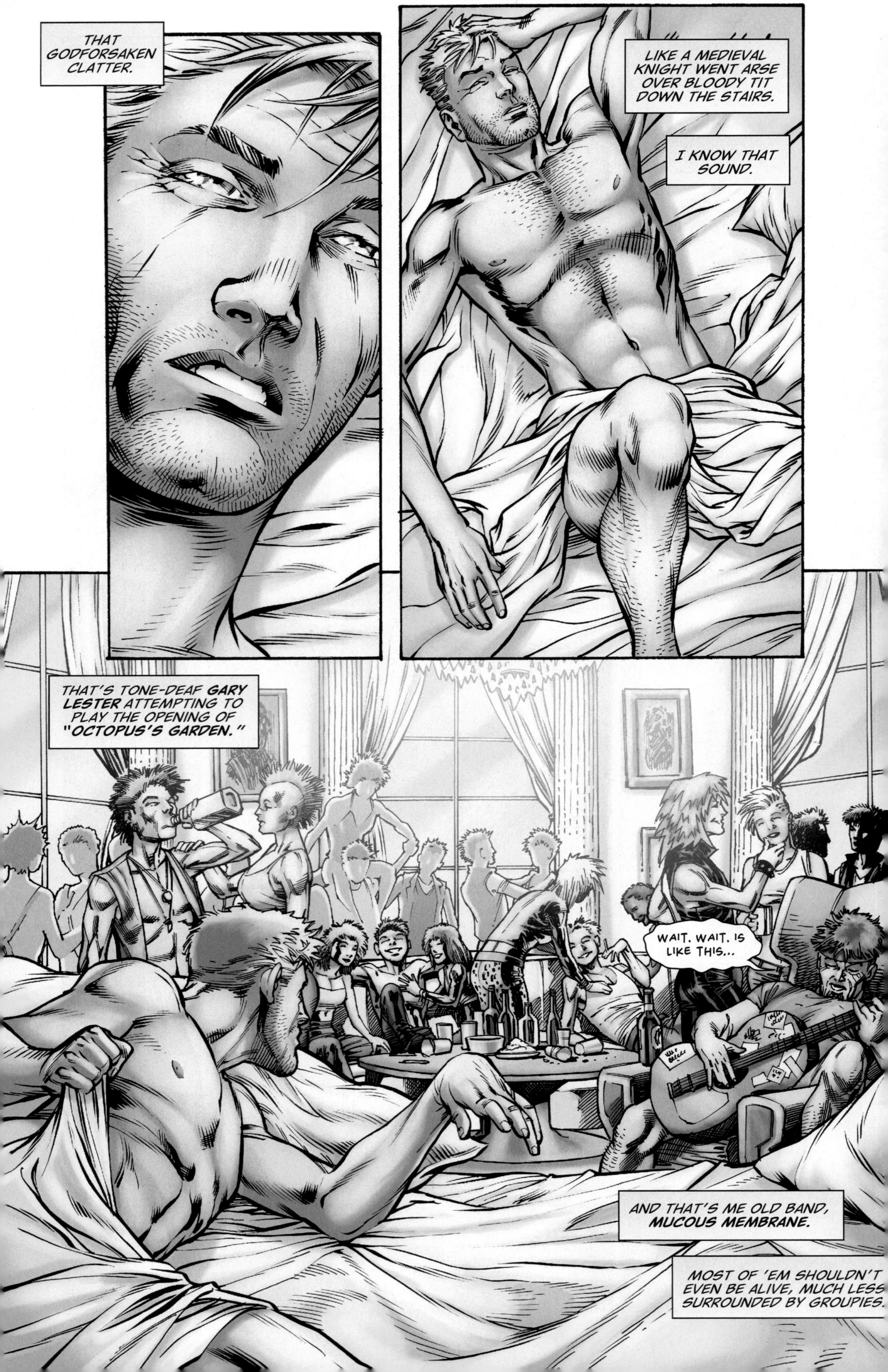
THAT GODFORSAKEN CLATTER.
LIKE A MEDIEVAL KNIGHT WENT ARSE OVER BLOODY TIT DOWN THE STAIRS.
I KNOW THAT SOUND.
THAT'S TONE-DEAF GARY LESTER ATTEMPTING TO PLAY THE OPENING OF "OCTOPUS'S GARDEN."
WAIT. WAIT. IS LIKE THIS...
AND THAT'S ME OLD BAND, MUCOUS MEMBRANE.
MOST OF 'EM SHOULDN'T EVEN BE ALIVE, MUCH LESS SURROUNDED BY GROUPIES.

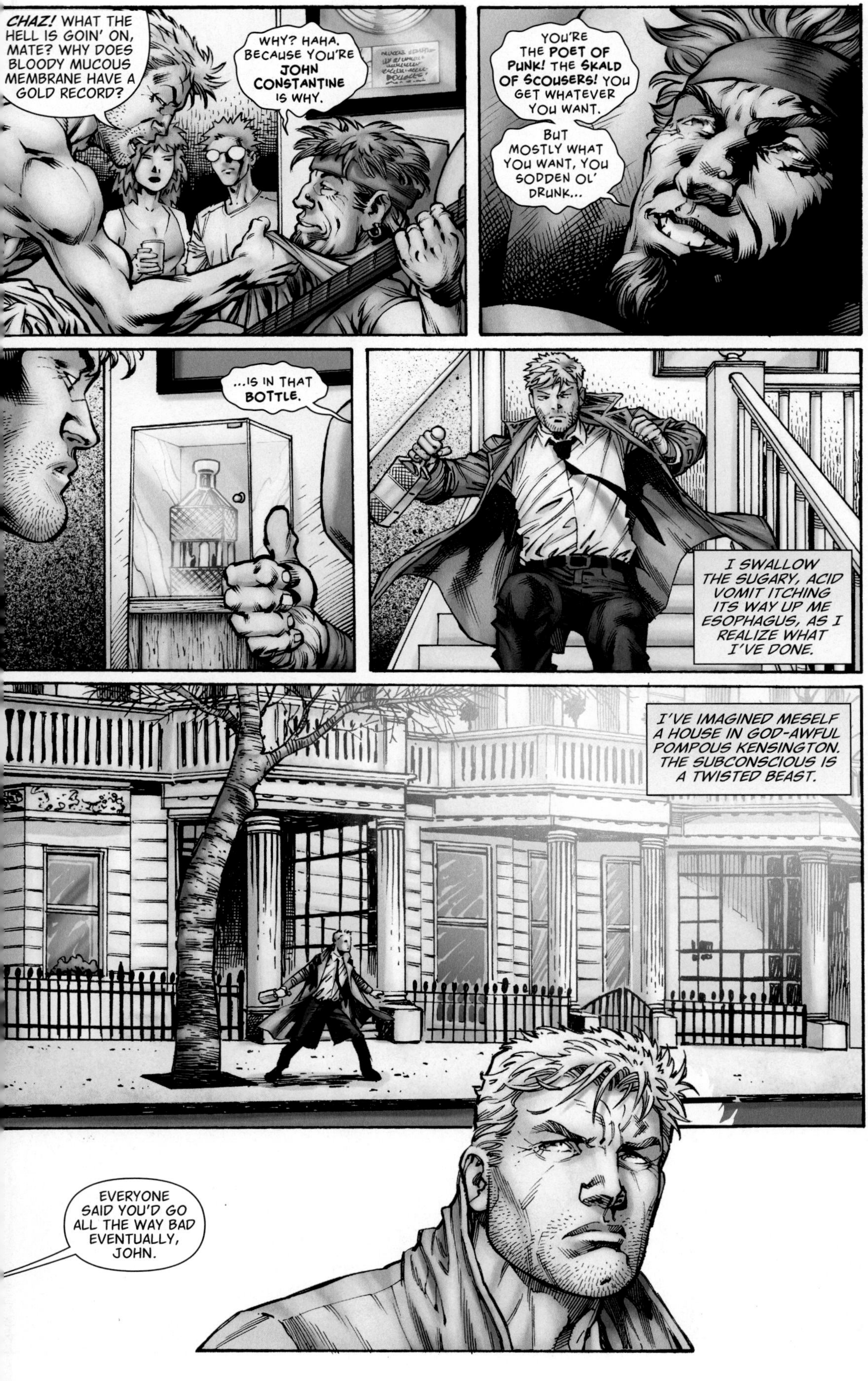
CHAZ! WHAT THE HELL IS GOIN' ON, MATE? WHY DOES BLOODY MUCOUS MEMBRANE HAVE A GOLD RECORD?
WHY? HAHA. BECAUSE YOU'RE JOHN CONSTANTINE IS WHY.
YOU'RE THE POET OF PUNK! THE SKALD OF SCOUSERS! YOU GET WHATEVER YOU WANT.
BUT MOSTLY WHAT YOU WANT, YOU SODDEN OL' DRUNK...
...IS IN THAT BOTTLE.
I SWALLOW THE SUGARY, ACID VOMIT ITCHING ITS WAY UP ME ESOPHAGUS, AS I REALIZE WHAT I'VE DONE.
I'VE IMAGINED MESELF A HOUSE IN GOD-AWFUL POMPOUS KENSINGTON. THE SUBCONSCIOUS IS A TWISTED BEAST.
EVERYONE SAID YOU'D GO ALL THE WAY BAD EVENTUALLY, JOHN.

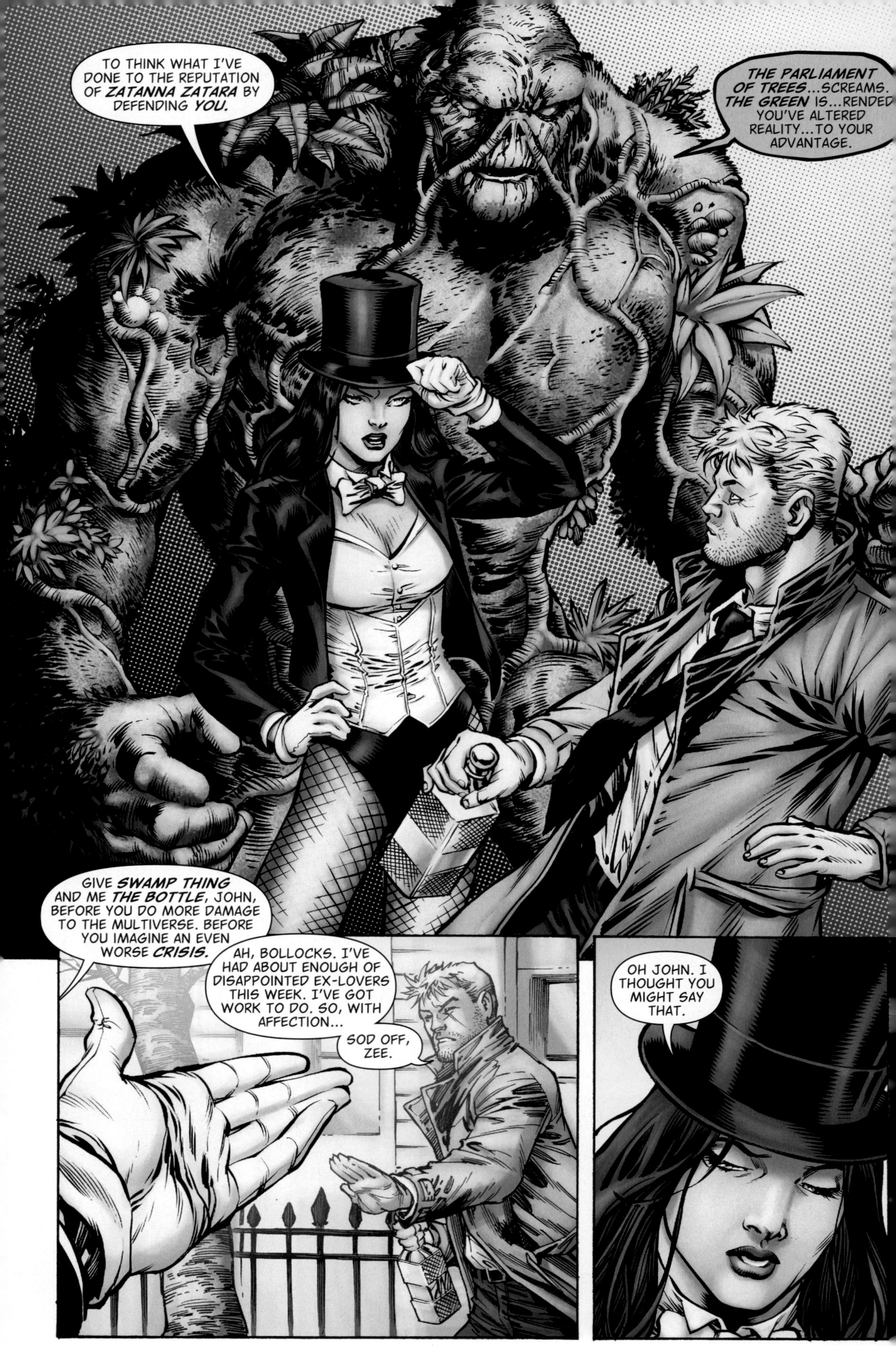
TO THINK WHAT I'VE DONE TO THE REPUTATION OF ZATANNA ZATARA BY DEFENDING YOU.
THE PARLIAMENT OF TREES...SCREAMS. THE GREEN IS...RENDED. YOU'VE ALTERED REALITY...TO YOUR ADVANTAGE.
GIVE SWAMP THING AND ME THE BOTTLE, JOHN, BEFORE YOU DO MORE DAMAGE TO THE MULTIVERSE. BEFORE YOU IMAGINE AN EVEN WORSE CRISIS.
AH, BOLLOCKS. I'VE HAD ABOUT ENOUGH OF DISAPPOINTED EX-LOVERS THIS WEEK. I'VE GOT WORK TO DO. SO, WITH AFFECTION...
SOD OFF, ZEE.
OH JOHN. I THOUGHT YOU MIGHT SAY THAT.

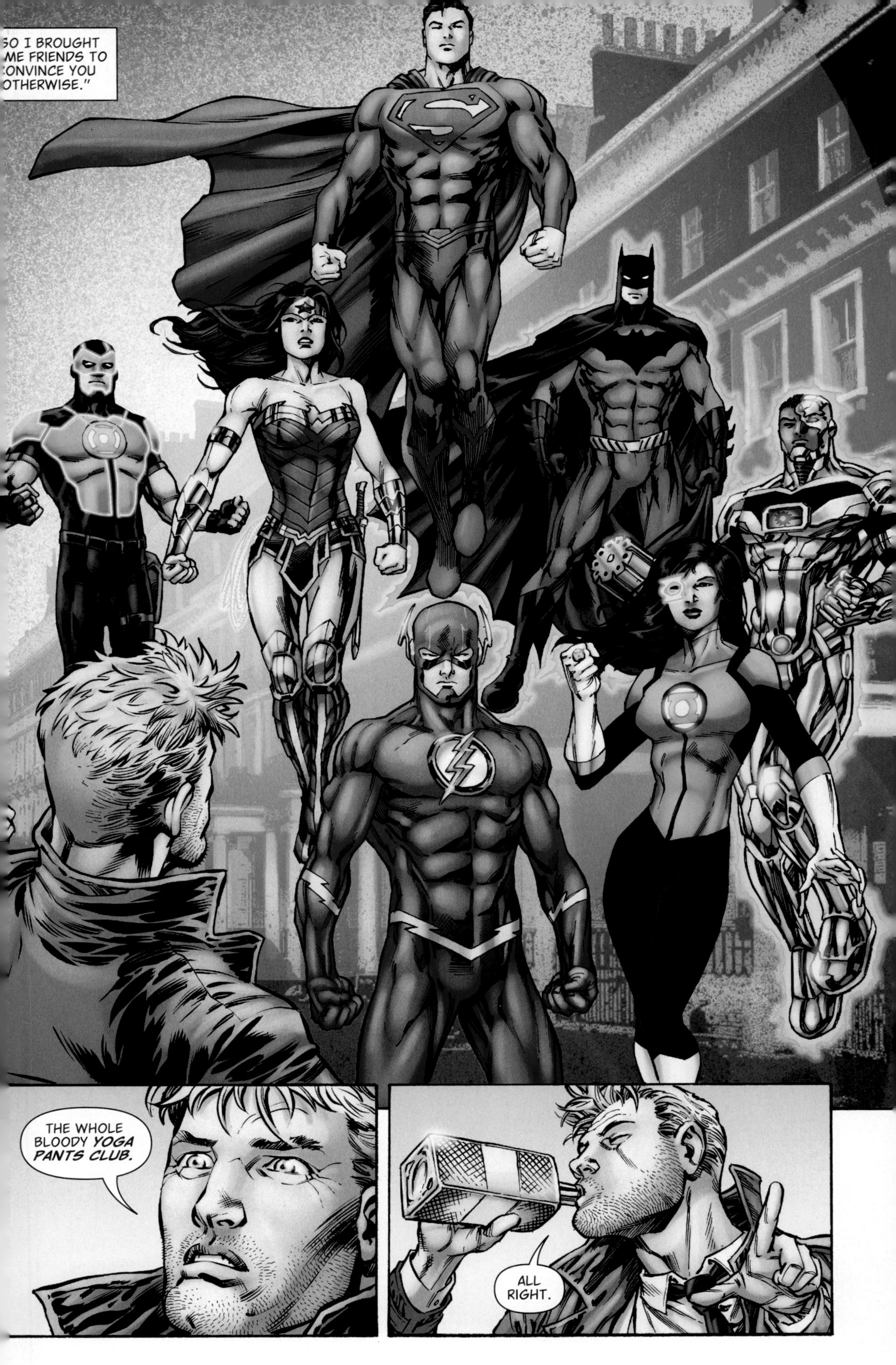
SO I BROUGHT
ME FRIENDS TO
ONVINCE YOU
OTHERWISE."
THE WHOLE BLOODY YOGA PANTS CLUB.
ALL RIGHT.

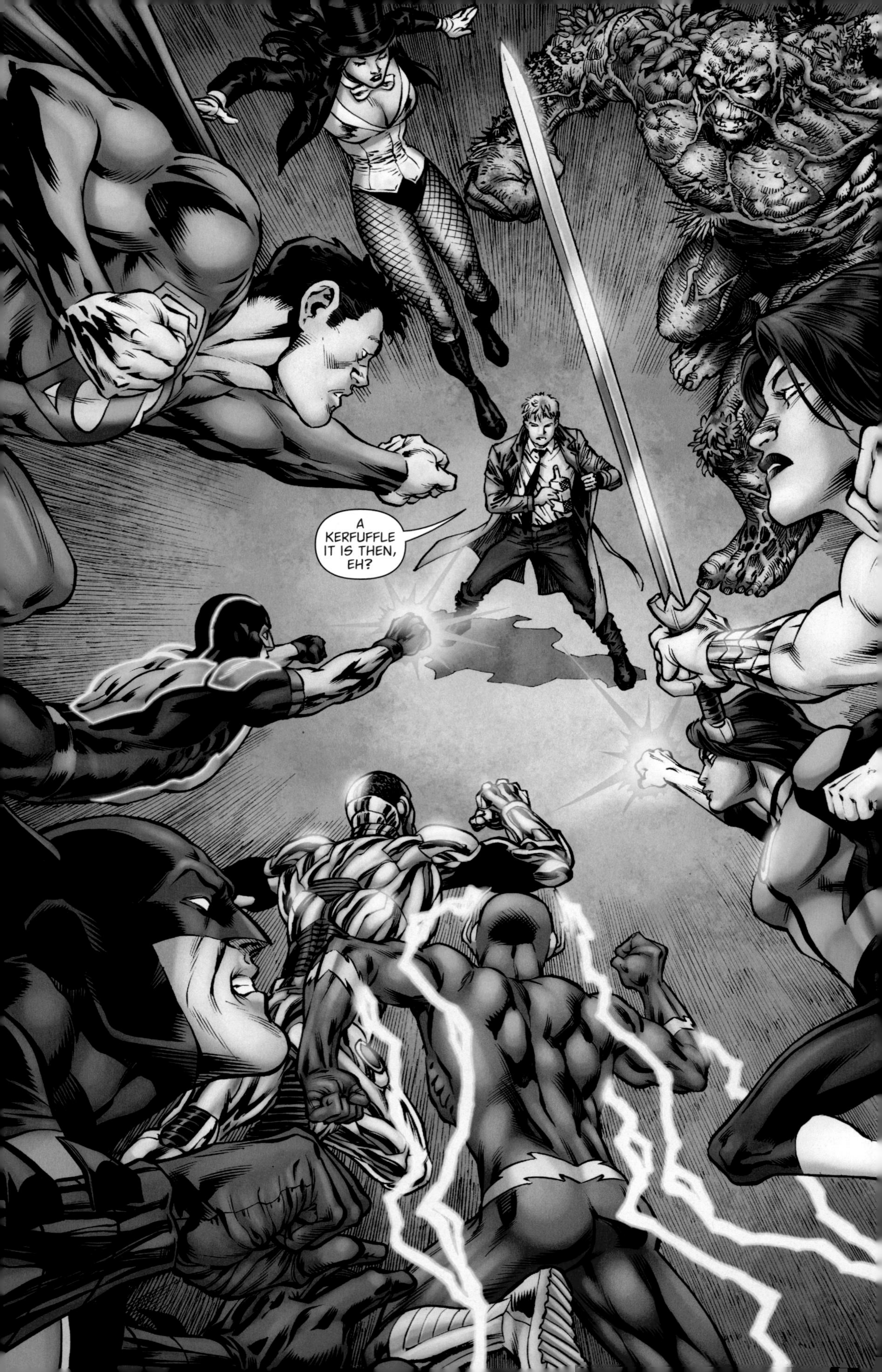
A KERFUFFLE IT IS THEN, EH?

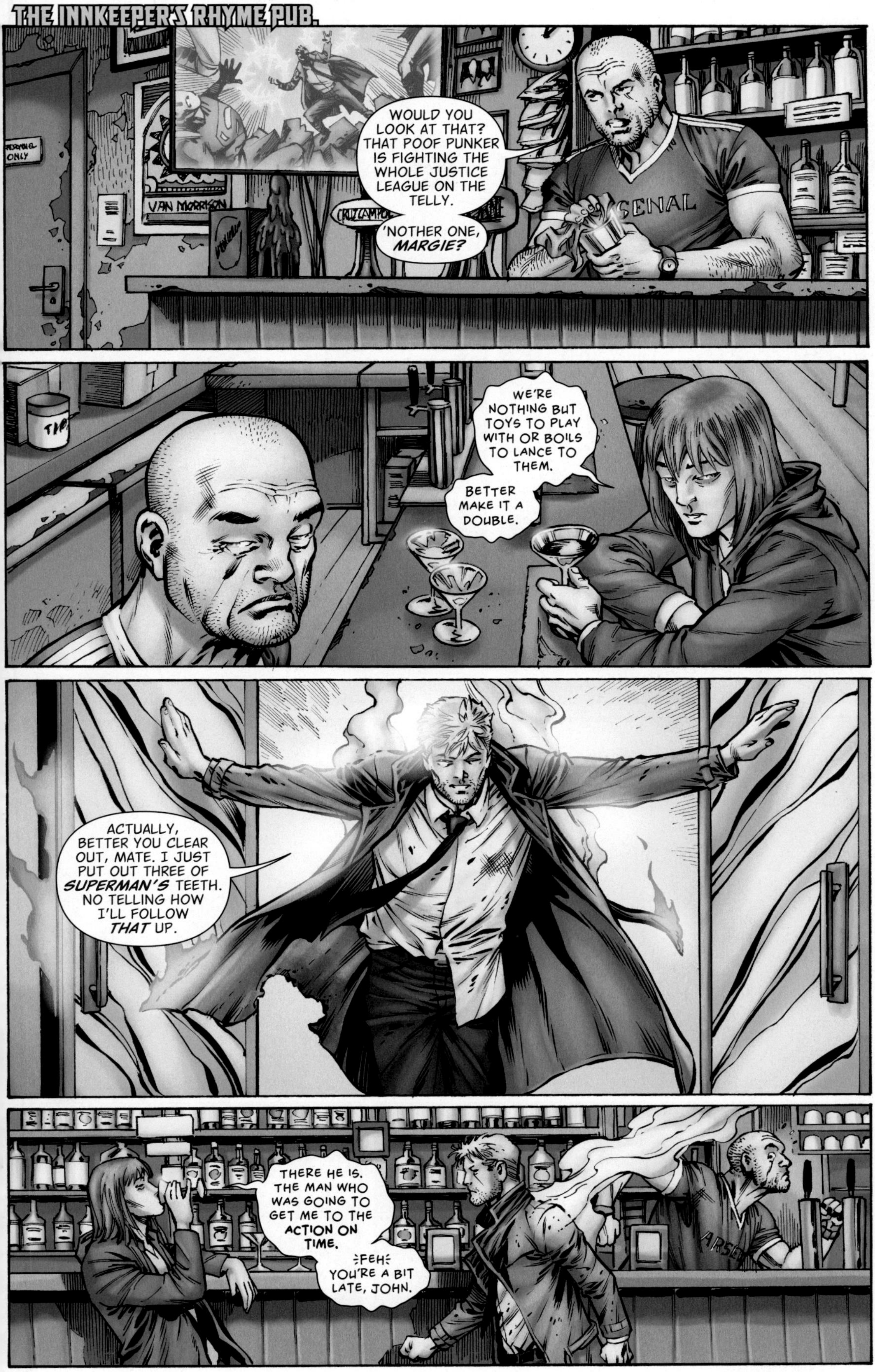
THE INNKEEPER'S RHYME PUB.
WOULD YOU LOOK AT THAT? THAT POOF PUNKER IS FIGHTING THE WHOLE JUSTICE LEAGUE ON THE TELLY.
'NOTHER ONE, MARGIE?
VAN MORRISON
WE'RE NOTHING BUT TOYS TO PLAY WITH OR BOILS TO LANCE TO THEM.
BETTER MAKE IT A DOUBLE.
ACTUALLY, BETTER YOU CLEAR OUT, MATE. I JUST PUT OUT THREE OF SUPERMAN'S TEETH. NO TELLING HOW I'LL FOLLOW THAT UP.
THERE HE IS. THE MAN WHO WAS GOING TO GET ME TO THE ACTION ON TIME.
FEH
YOU'RE A BIT LATE, JOHN.

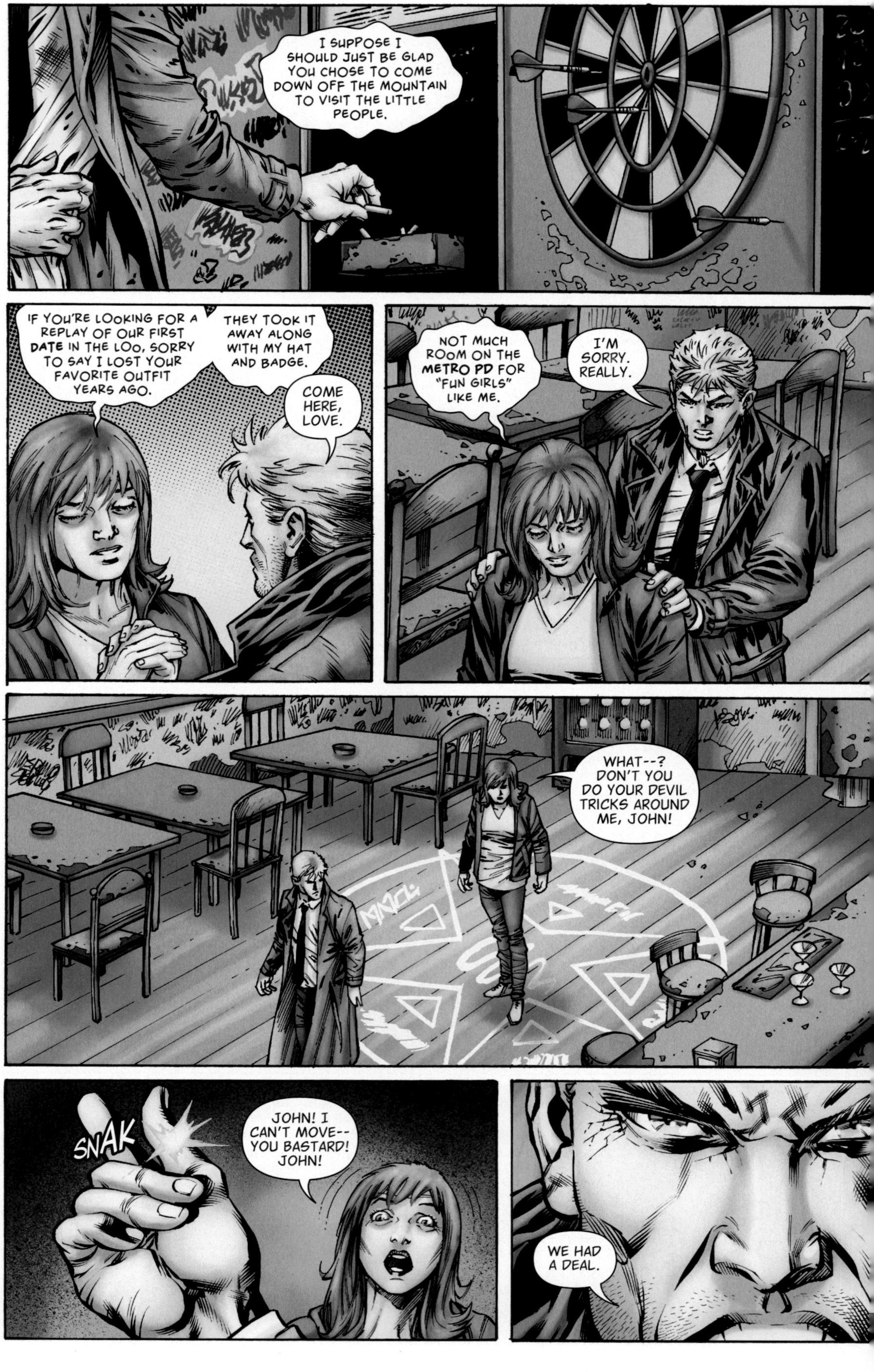
I SUPPOSE I SHOULD JUST BE GLAD YOU CHOSE TO COME DOWN OFF THE MOUNTAIN TO VISIT THE LITTLE PEOPLE.
IF YOU'RE LOOKING FOR A REPLAY OF OUR FIRST DATE IN THE LOO, SORRY TO SAY I LOST YOUR FAVORITE OUTFIT YEARS AGO.
THEY TOOK IT AWAY ALONG WITH MY HAT AND BADGE.
COME HERE, LOVE.
NOT MUCH ROOM ON THE METRO PD FOR "FUN GIRLS" LIKE ME.
I'M SORRY. REALLY.
WHAT--? DON'T YOU DO YOUR DEVIL TRICKS AROUND ME, JOHN!
SNAK
JOHN! I CAN'T MOVE-- YOU BASTARD! JOHN!
WE HAD A DEAL.

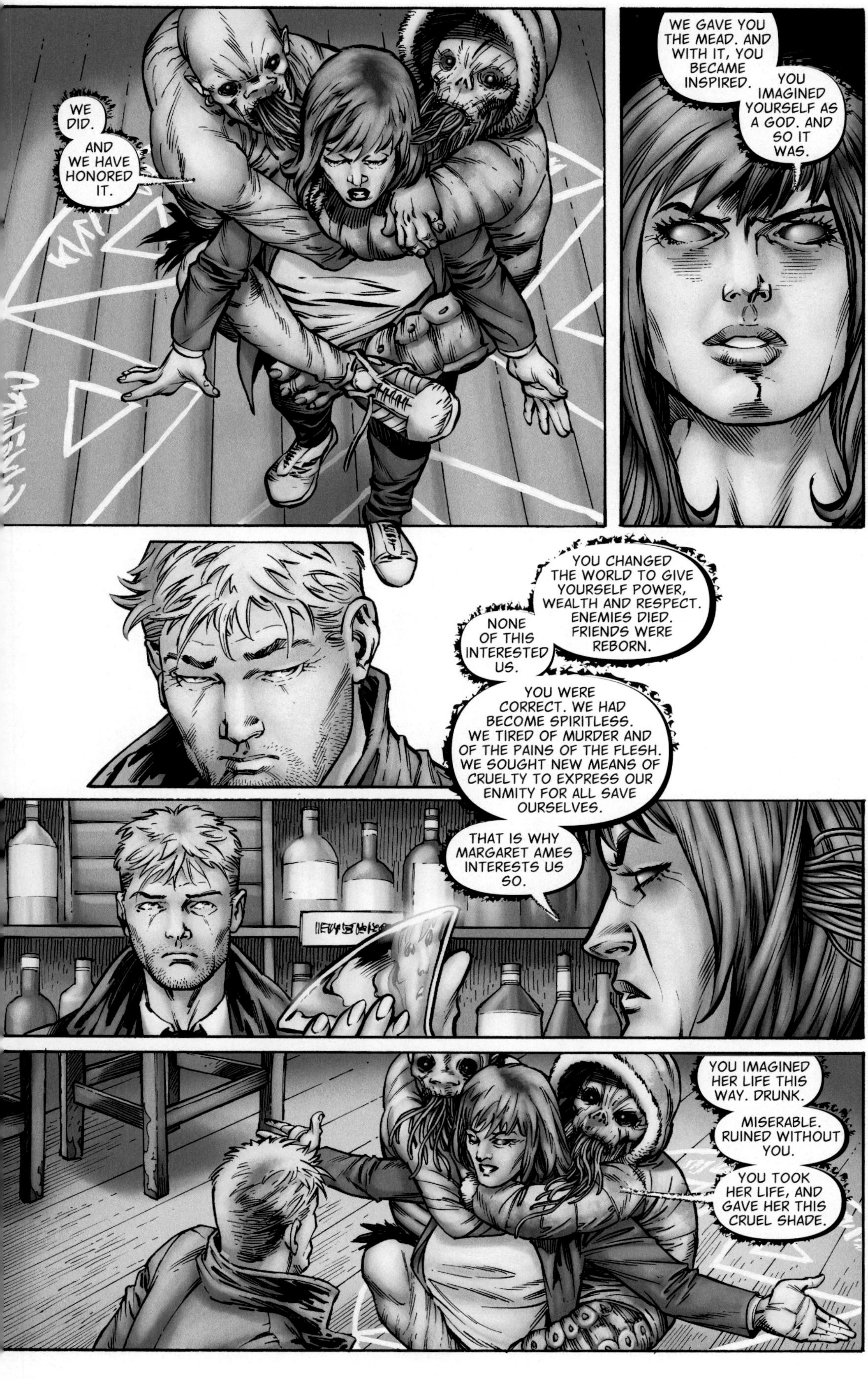
WE DID.
AND WE HAVE HONORED IT.
WE GAVE YOU THE MEAD. AND WITH IT, YOU BECAME INSPIRED.
YOU IMAGINED YOURSELF AS A GOD. AND SO IT WAS.
YOU CHANGED THE WORLD TO GIVE YOURSELF POWER, WEALTH AND RESPECT. ENEMIES DIED. FRIENDS WERE REBORN.
NONE OF THIS INTERESTED US.
YOU WERE CORRECT. WE HAD BECOME SPIRITLESS. WE TIRED OF MURDER AND OF THE PAINS OF THE FLESH. WE SOUGHT NEW MEANS OF CRUELTY TO EXPRESS OUR ENMITY FOR ALL SAVE OURSELVES.
THAT IS WHY MARGARET AMES INTERESTS US SO.
YOU IMAGINED HER LIFE THIS WAY. DRUNK.
MISERABLE. RUINED WITHOUT YOU.
YOU TOOK HER LIFE, AND GAVE HER THIS CRUEL SHADE.

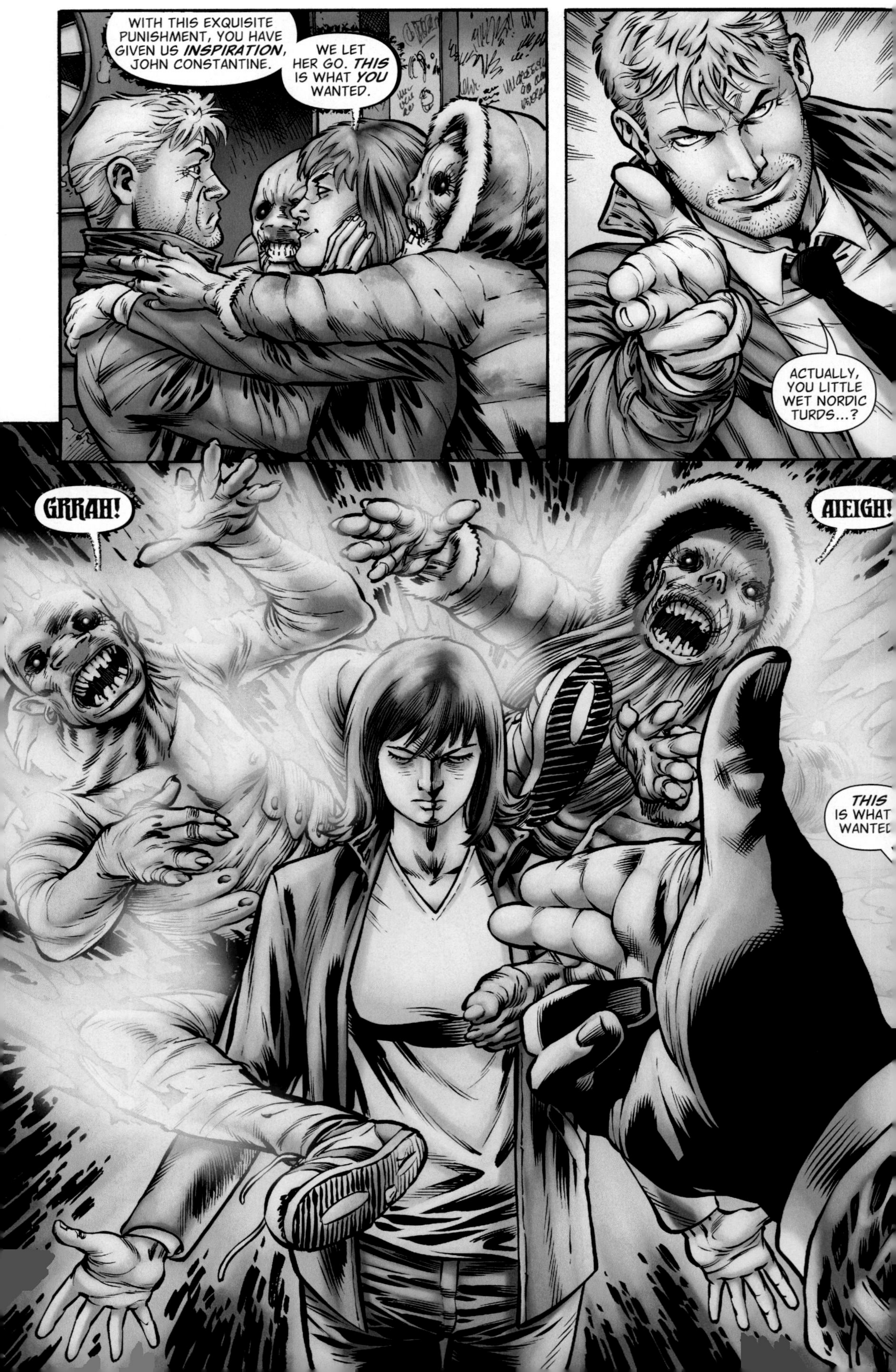

WITH THIS EXQUISITE PUNISHMENT, YOU HAVE GIVEN US INSPIRATION, JOHN CONSTANTINE.
WE LET HER GO. THIS IS WHAT YOU WANTED.
ACTUALLY, YOU LITTLE WET NORDIC TURDS...?
GRRAH!
AIEIGH!
THIS IS WHAT WANTED

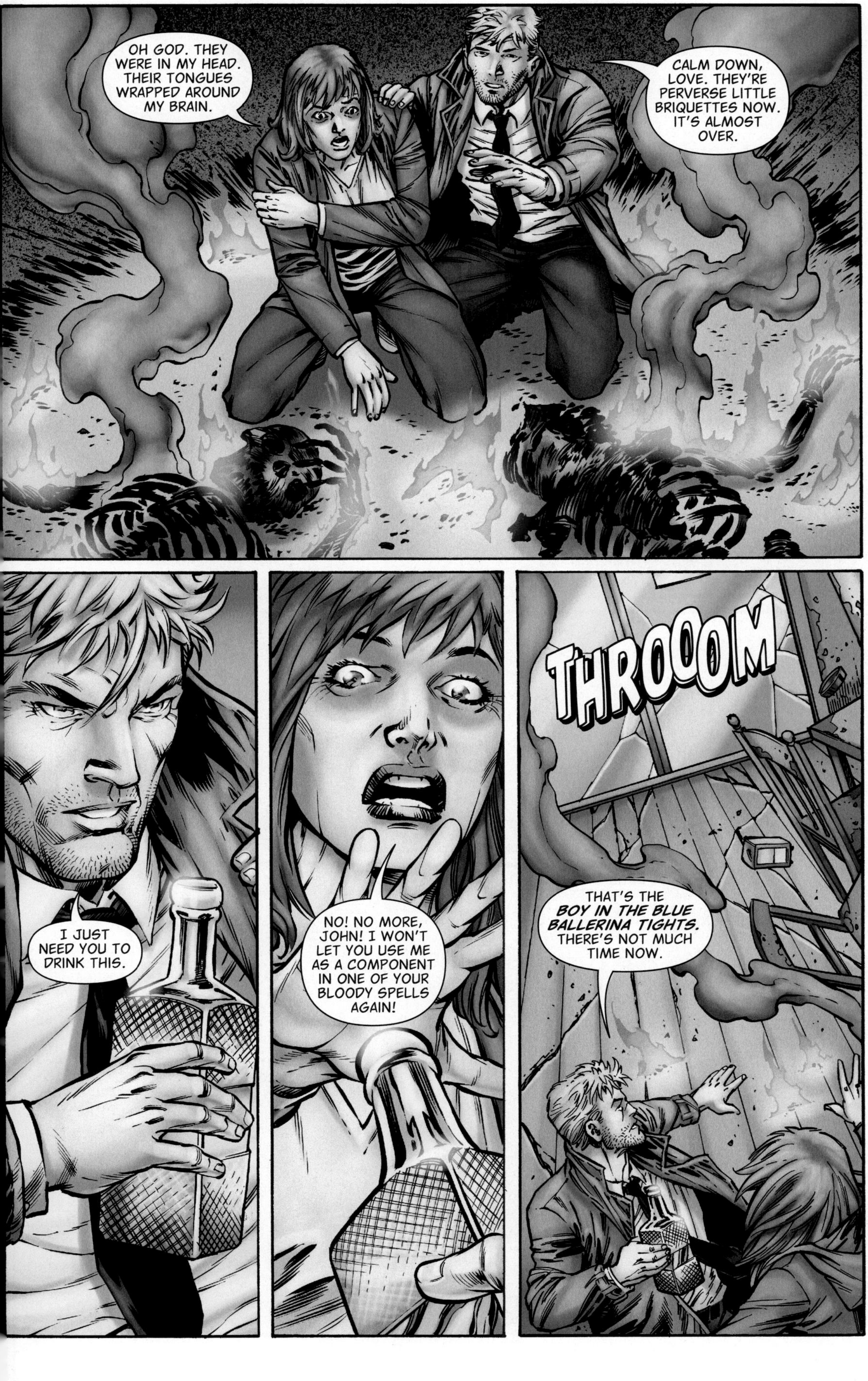
OH GOD. THEY WERE IN MY HEAD. THEIR TONGUES WRAPPED AROUND MY BRAIN.
CALM DOWN, LOVE. THEY'RE PERVERSE LITTLE BRIQUETTES NOW. IT'S ALMOST OVER.
I JUST NEED YOU TO DRINK THIS.
NO! NO MORE, JOHN! I WON'T LET YOU USE ME AS A COMPONENT IN ONE OF YOUR BLOODY SPELLS AGAIN!
THROOOM
THAT'S THE *BOY IN THE BLUE BALLERINA TIGHTS.* THERE'S NOT MUCH TIME NOW.

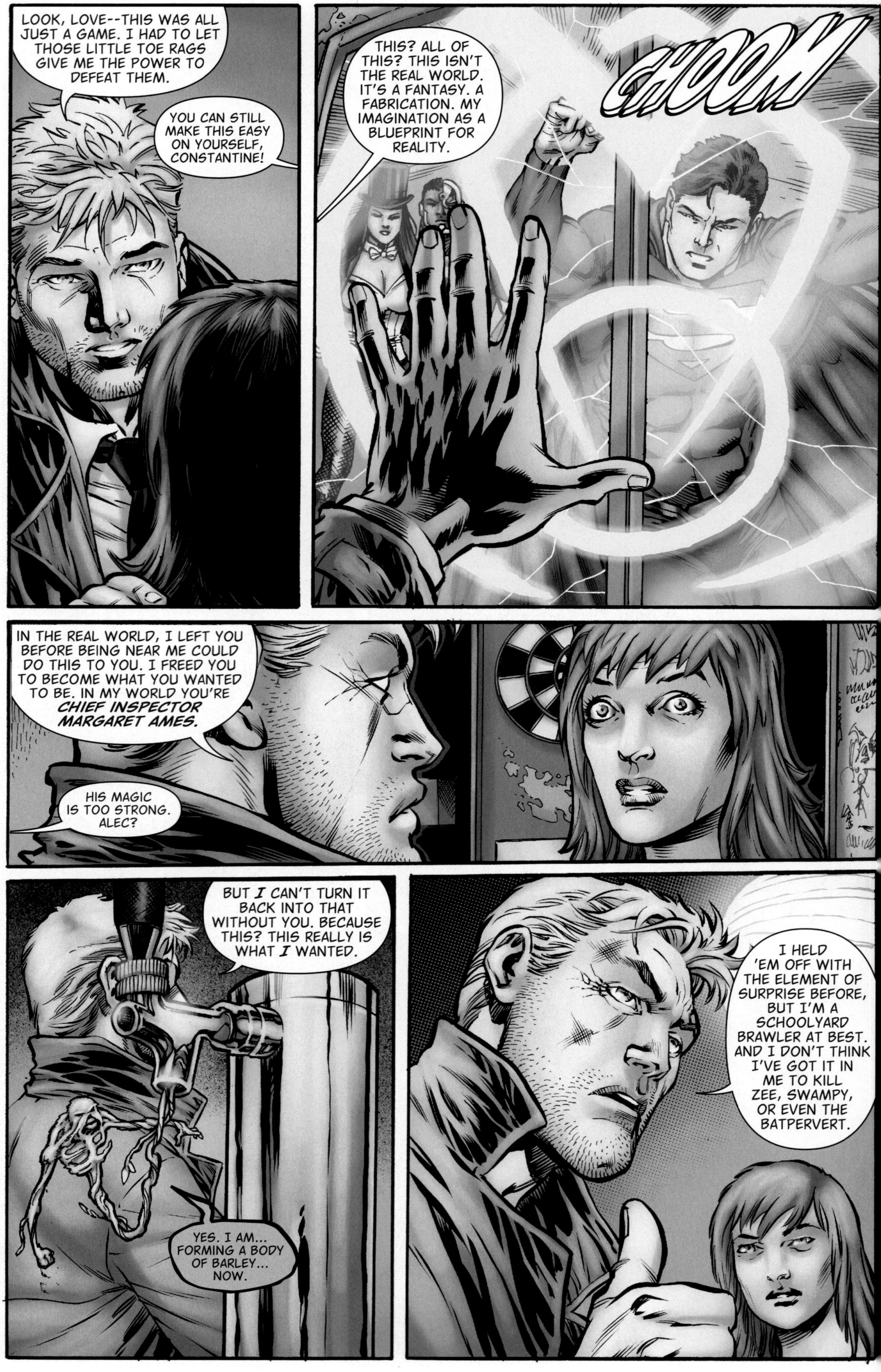

LOOK, LOVE--THIS WAS ALL JUST A GAME. I HAD TO LET THOSE LITTLE TOE RAGS GIVE ME THE POWER TO DEFEAT THEM.
YOU CAN STILL MAKE THIS EASY ON YOURSELF, CONSTANTINE!
THIS? ALL OF THIS? THIS ISN'T THE REAL WORLD. IT'S A FANTASY. A FABRICATION. MY IMAGINATION AS A BLUEPRINT FOR REALITY.
CHOOM
IN THE REAL WORLD, I LEFT YOU BEFORE BEING NEAR ME COULD DO THIS TO YOU. I FREED YOU TO BECOME WHAT YOU WANTED TO BE. IN MY WORLD YOU'RE *CHIEF INSPECTOR MARGARET AMES.*
HIS MAGIC IS TOO STRONG. ALEC?
BUT *I* CAN'T TURN IT BACK INTO THAT WITHOUT YOU. BECAUSE THIS? THIS REALLY IS WHAT *I* WANTED.
YES. I AM... FORMING A BODY OF BARLEY... NOW.
I HELD 'EM OFF WITH THE ELEMENT OF SURPRISE BEFORE, BUT I'M A SCHOOLYARD BRAWLER AT BEST. AND I DON'T THINK I'VE GOT IT IN ME TO KILL ZEE, SWAMPY, OR EVEN THE BATPERVERT.

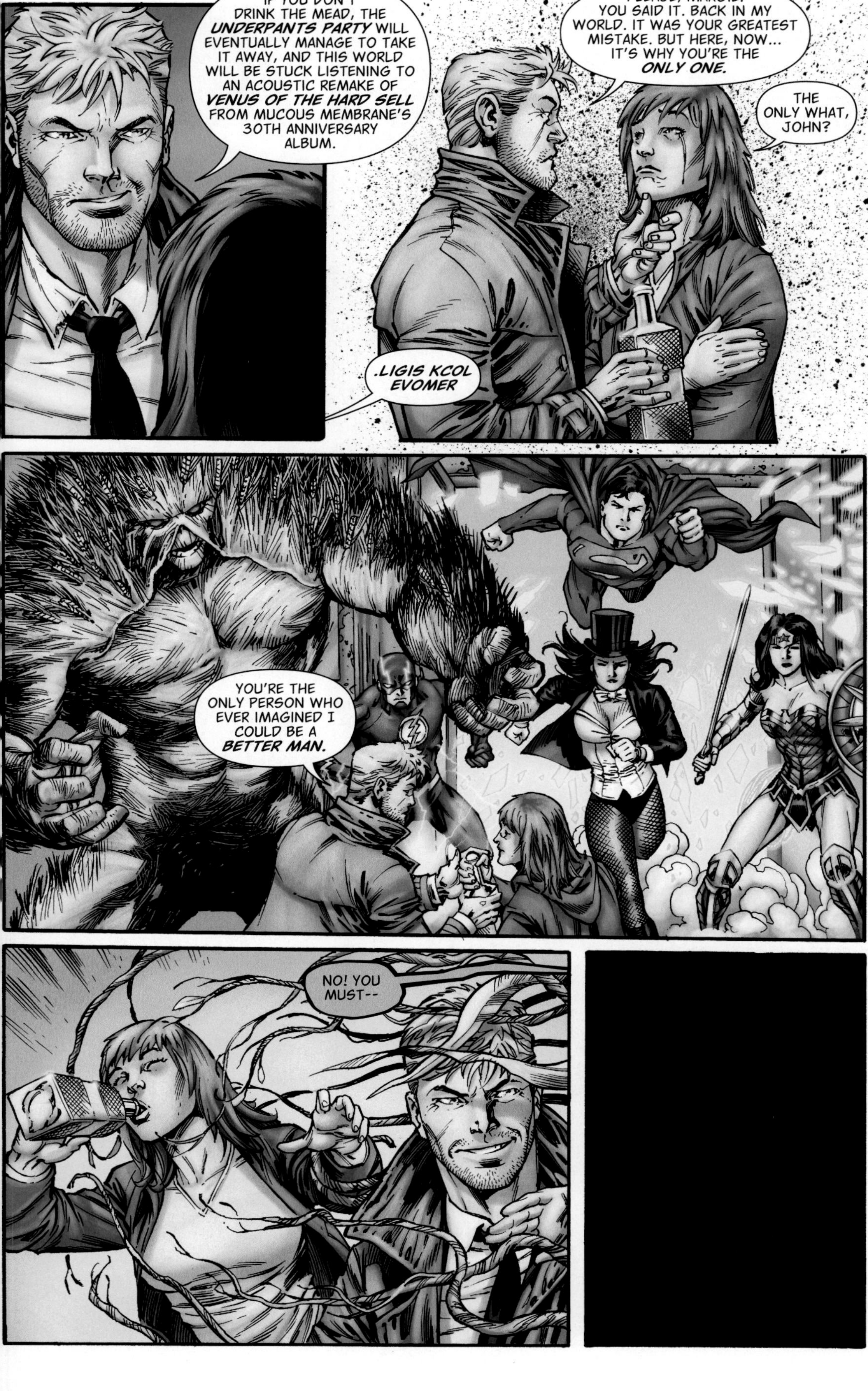
IF YOU DON'T DRINK THE MEAD, THE UNDERPANTS PARTY WILL EVENTUALLY MANAGE TO TAKE IT AWAY, AND THIS WORLD WILL BE STUCK LISTENING TO AN ACOUSTIC REMAKE OF VENUS OF THE HARD SELL FROM MUCOUS MEMBRANE'S 30TH ANNIVERSARY ALBUM.
.LIGIS KCOL EVOMER
PLEASE, MARGIE. YOU SAID IT. BACK IN MY WORLD. IT WAS YOUR GREATEST MISTAKE. BUT HERE, NOW... IT'S WHY YOU'RE THE ONLY ONE.
THE ONLY WHAT, JOHN?
YOU'RE THE ONLY PERSON WHO EVER IMAGINED I COULD BE A BETTER MAN.
NO! YOU MUST--

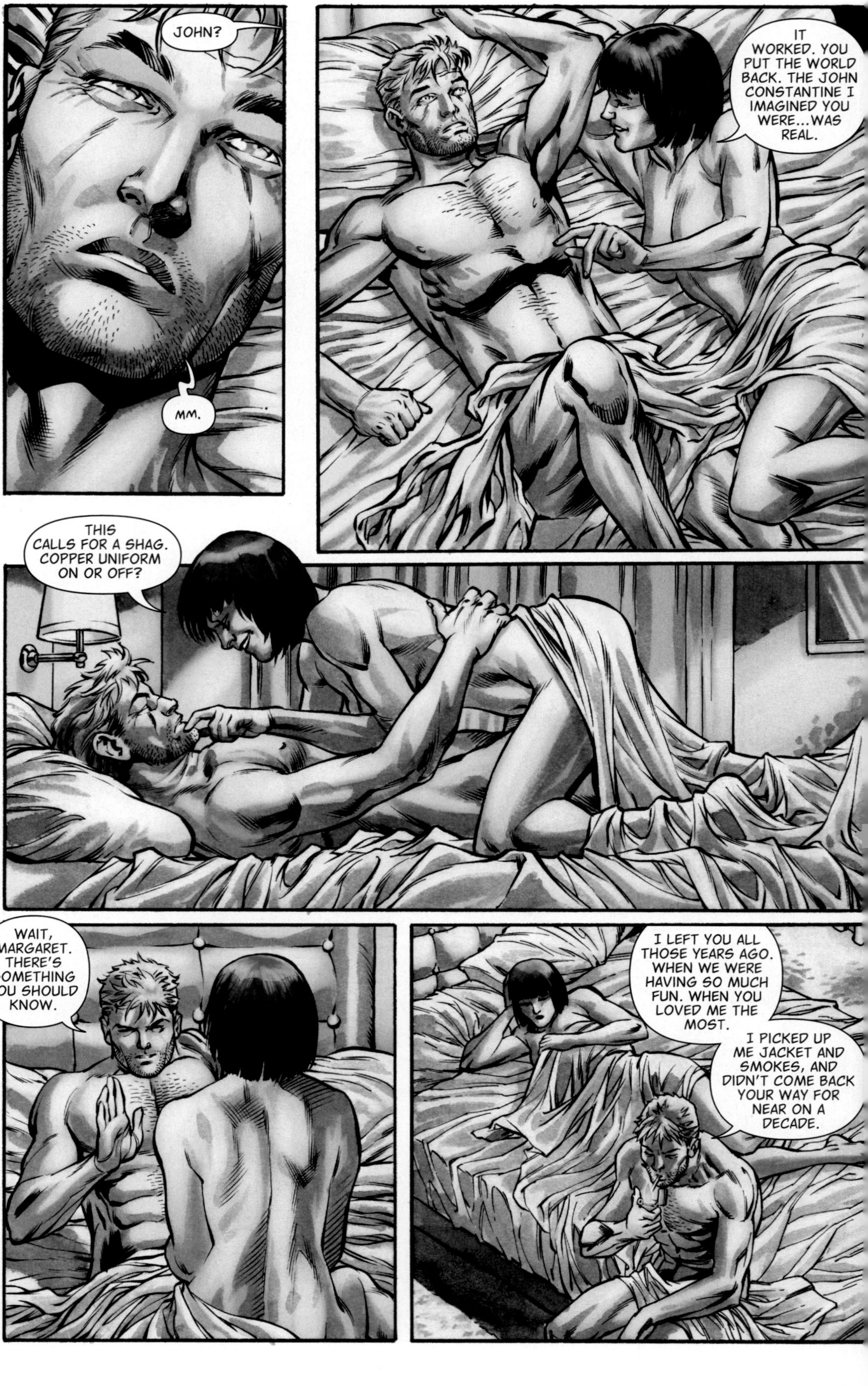
JOHN?
MM.
IT WORKED. YOU PUT THE WORLD BACK. THE JOHN CONSTANTINE I IMAGINED YOU WERE...WAS REAL.
THIS CALLS FOR A SHAG. COPPER UNIFORM ON OR OFF?
WAIT, MARGARET. THERE'S SOMETHING YOU SHOULD KNOW.
I LEFT YOU ALL THOSE YEARS AGO. WHEN WE WERE HAVING SO MUCH FUN. WHEN YOU LOVED ME THE MOST.
I PICKED UP ME JACKET AND SMOKES, AND DIDN'T COME BACK YOUR WAY FOR NEAR ON A DECADE.

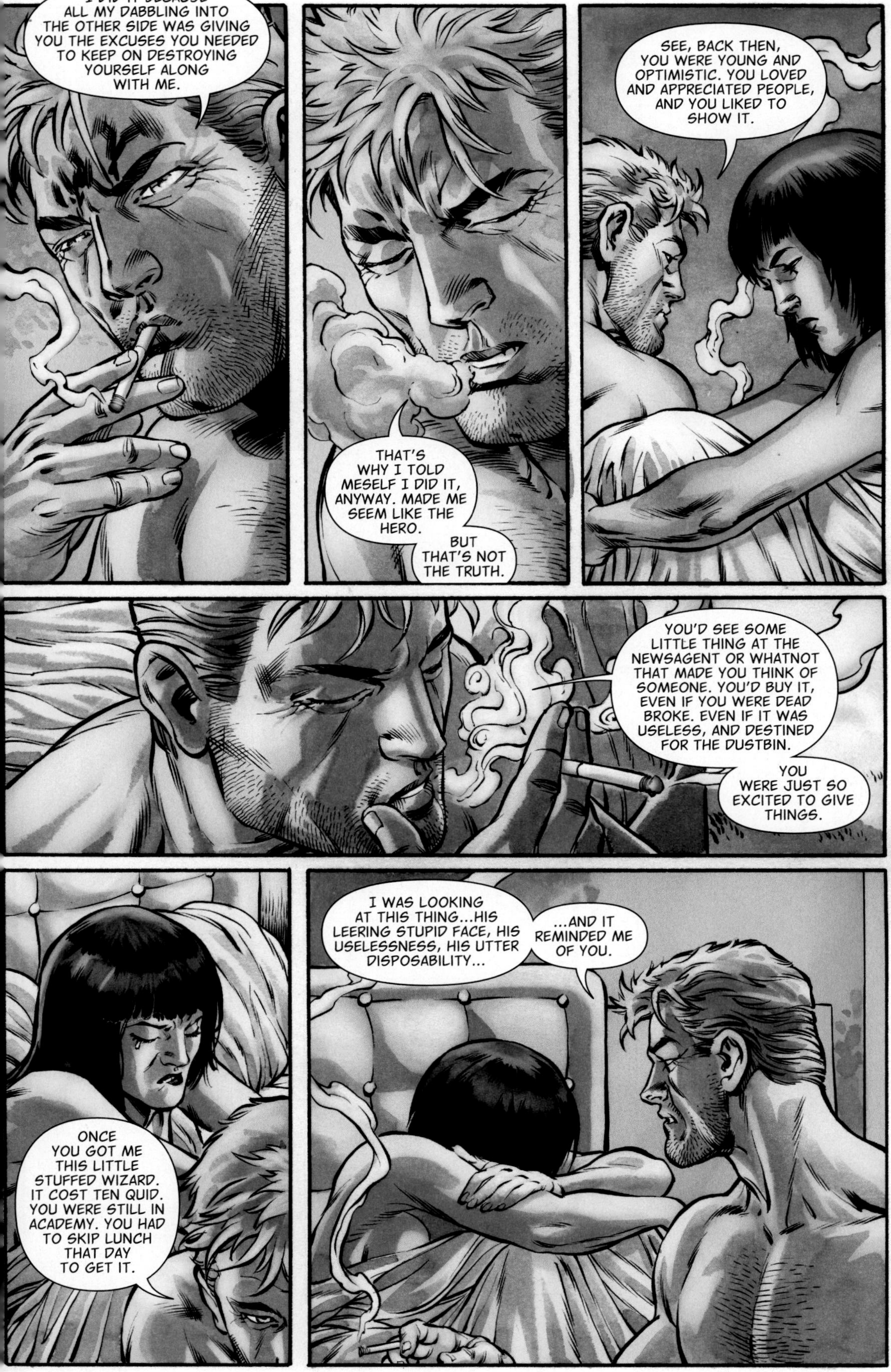
I DID IT BECAUSE ALL MY DABBLING INTO THE OTHER SIDE WAS GIVING YOU THE EXCUSES YOU NEEDED TO KEEP ON DESTROYING YOURSELF ALONG WITH ME.
THAT'S WHY I TOLD MESELF I DID IT, ANYWAY. MADE ME SEEM LIKE THE HERO.
BUT THAT'S NOT THE TRUTH.
SEE, BACK THEN, YOU WERE YOUNG AND OPTIMISTIC. YOU LOVED AND APPRECIATED PEOPLE, AND YOU LIKED TO SHOW IT.
YOU'D SEE SOME LITTLE THING AT THE NEWSAGENT OR WHATNOT THAT MADE YOU THINK OF SOMEONE. YOU'D BUY IT, EVEN IF YOU WERE DEAD BROKE. EVEN IF IT WAS USELESS, AND DESTINED FOR THE DUSTBIN.
YOU WERE JUST SO EXCITED TO GIVE THINGS.
ONCE YOU GOT ME THIS LITTLE STUFFED WIZARD. IT COST TEN QUID. YOU WERE STILL IN ACADEMY. YOU HAD TO SKIP LUNCH THAT DAY TO GET IT.
I WAS LOOKING AT THIS THING...HIS LEERING STUPID FACE, HIS USELESSNESS, HIS UTTER DISPOSABILITY...
...AND IT REMINDED ME OF YOU.

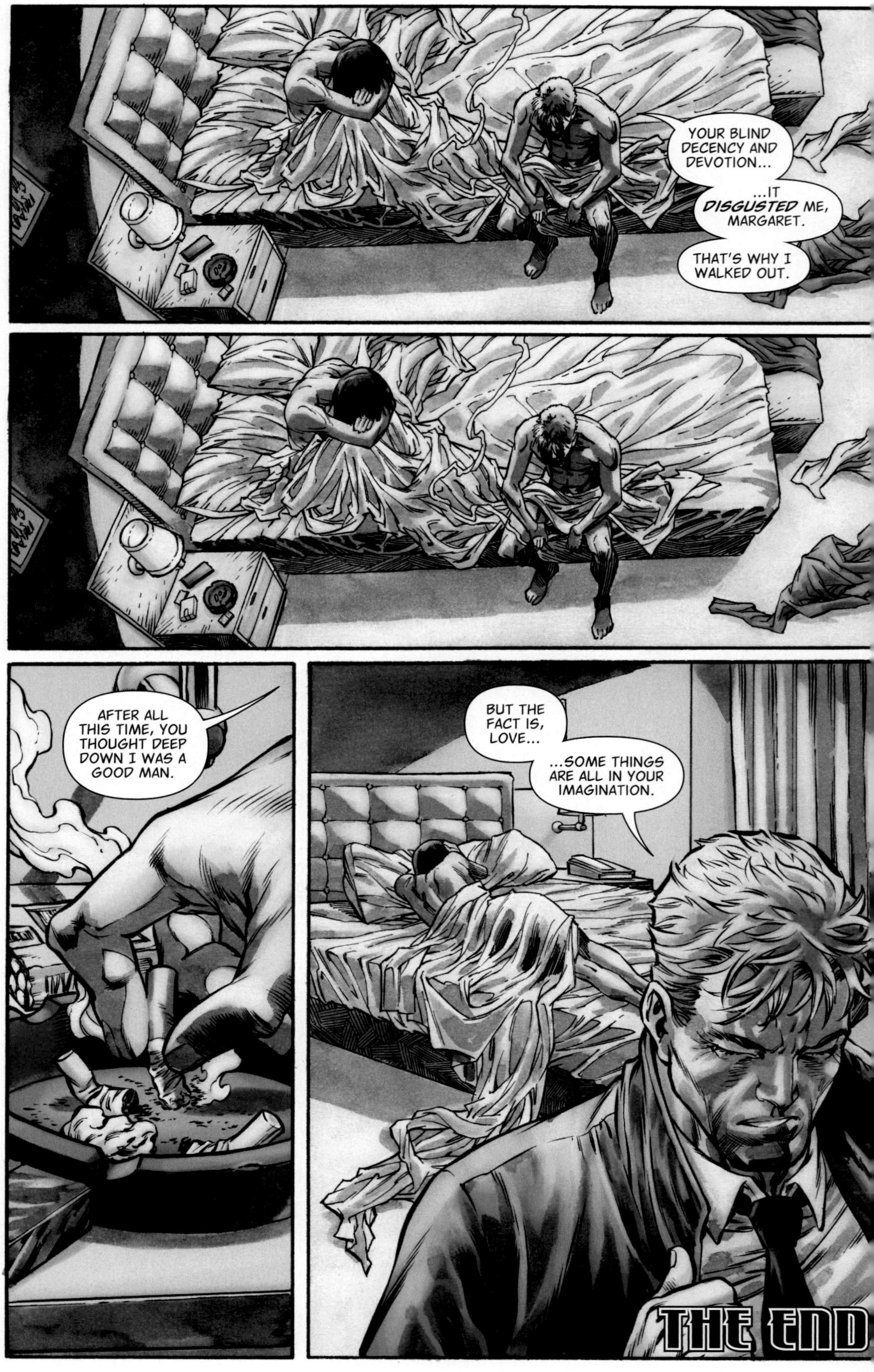
YOUR BLIND DECENCY AND DEVOTION...
...IT DISGUSTED ME, MARGARET.
THAT'S WHY I WALKED OUT.
AFTER ALL THIS TIME, YOU THOUGHT DEEP DOWN I WAS A GOOD MAN.
BUT THE FACT IS, LOVE...
...SOME THINGS ARE ALL IN YOUR IMAGINATION.
THE END

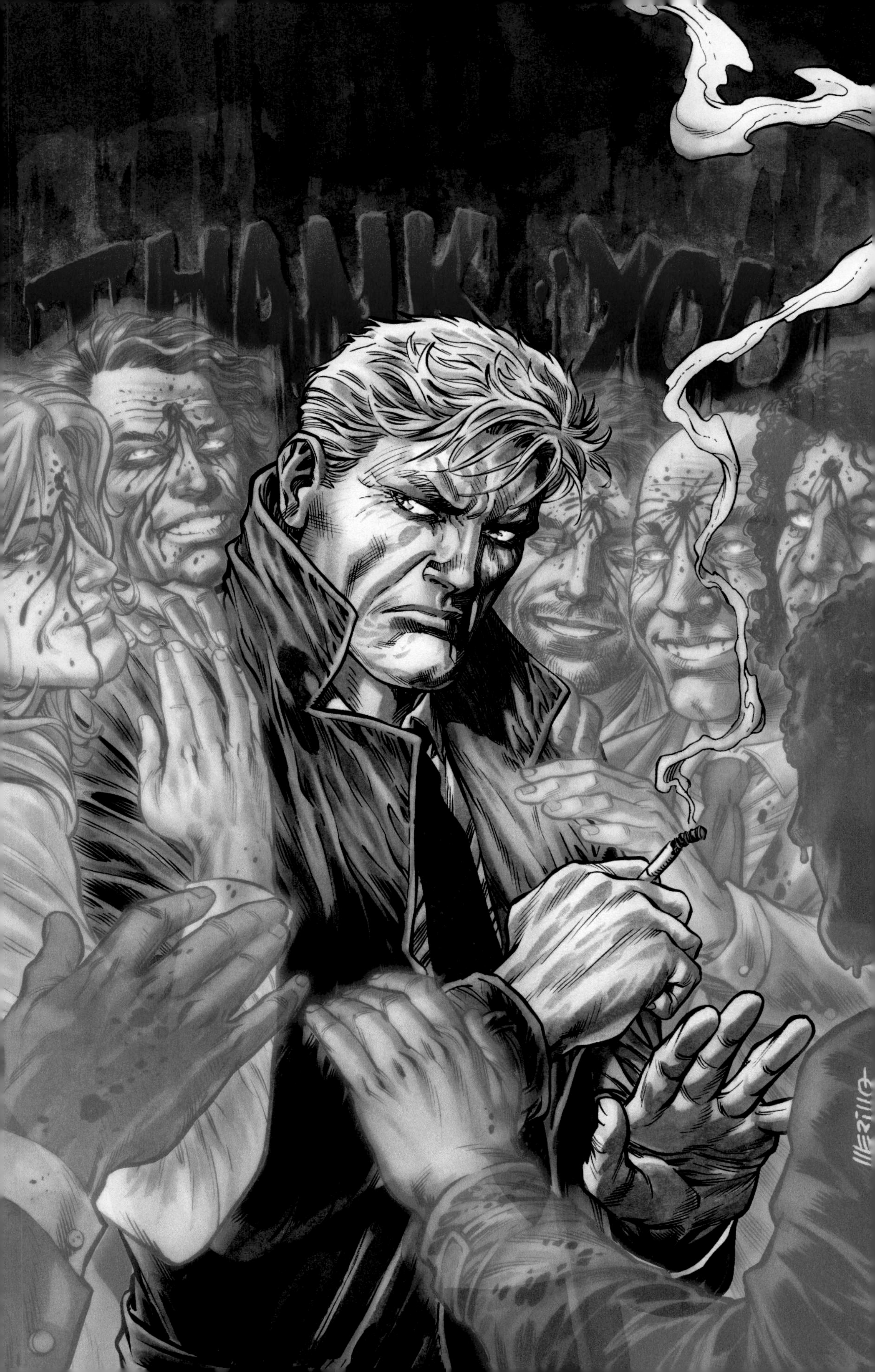
THANK YOU

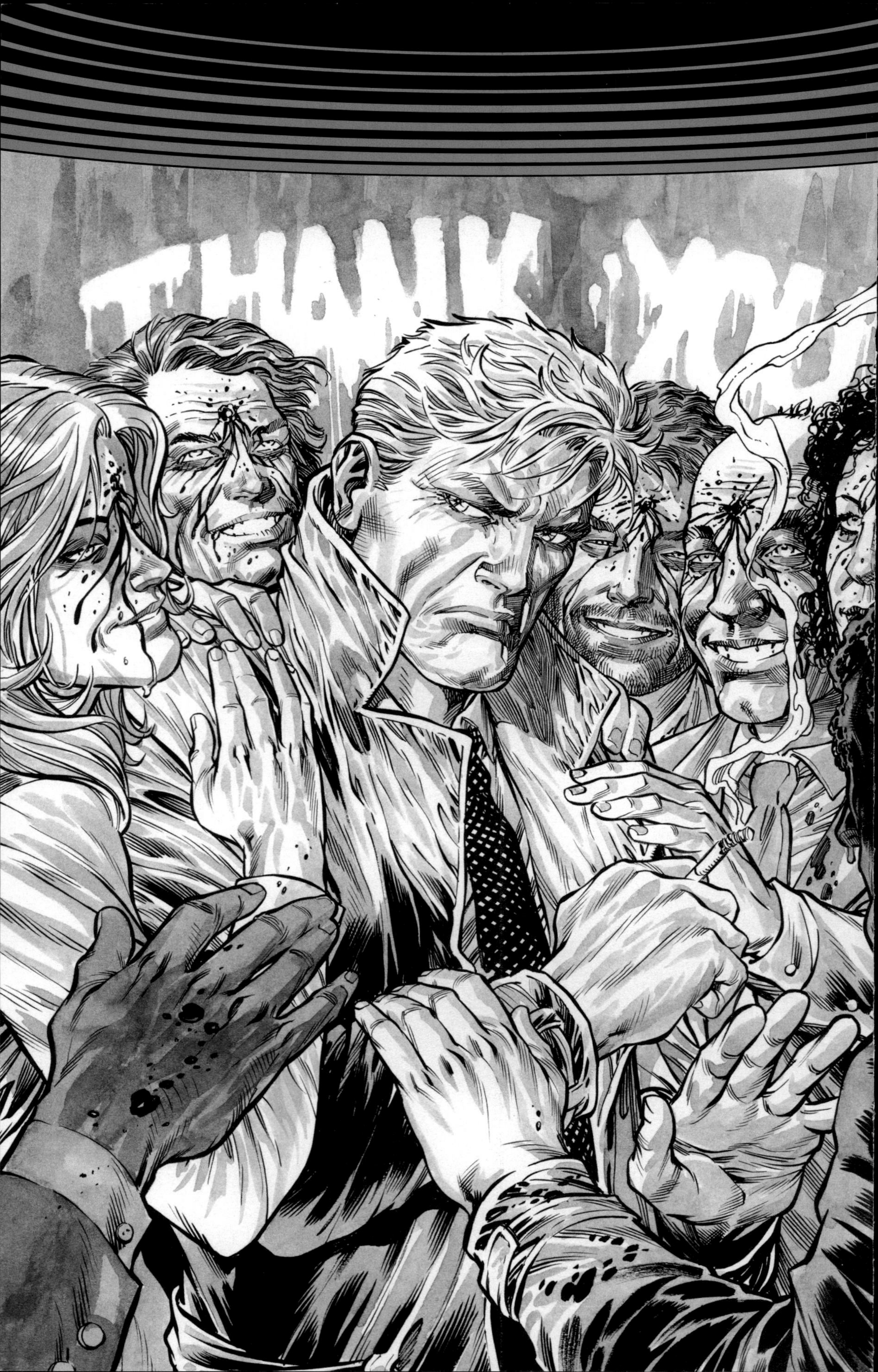

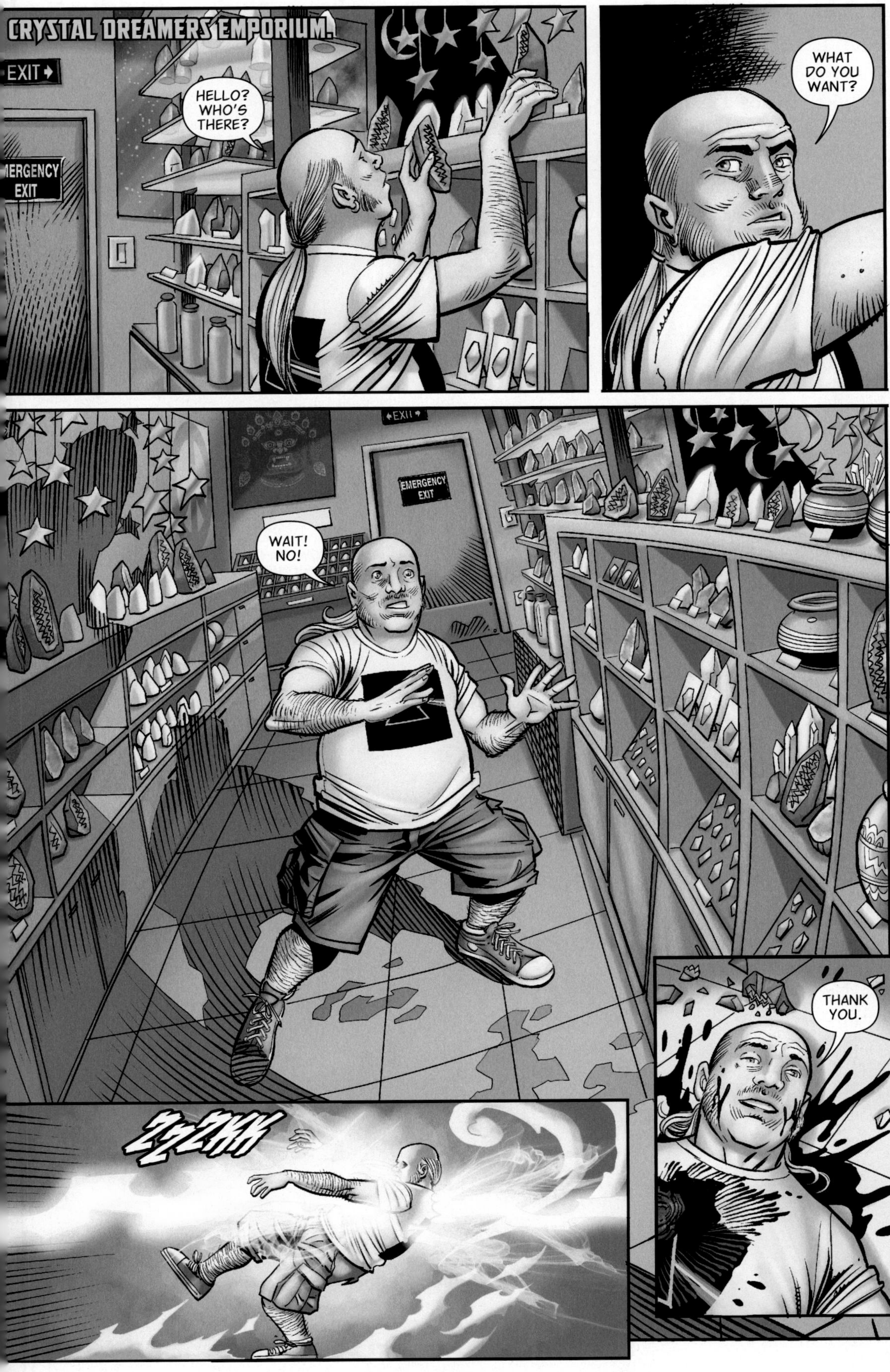
CRYSTAL DREAMERS EMPORIUM.
EXIT
EMERGENCY EXIT
HELLO? WHO'S THERE?
WHAT DO YOU WANT?
EXIT
EMERGENCY EXIT
WAIT! NO!
THANK YOU.
ZZZKK

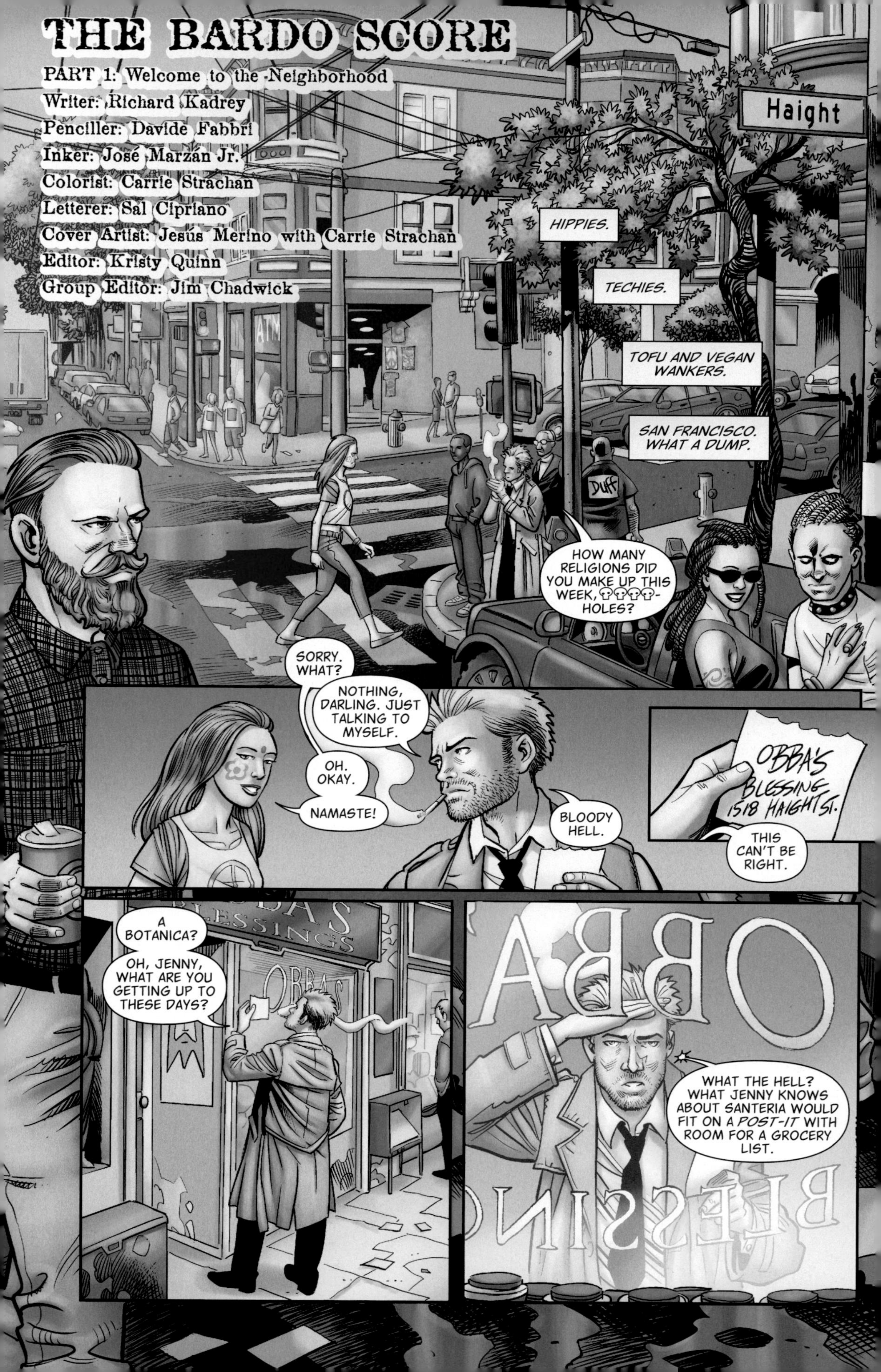
THE BARDO SCORE
PART 1: Welcome to the Neighborhood
Writer: Richard Kadrey
Penciller: Davide Fabbri
Inker: José Marzán Jr.
Colorist: Carrie Strachan
Letterer: Sal Cipriano
Cover Artist: Jesús Merino with Carrie Strachan
Editor: Kristy Quinn
Group Editor: Jim Chadwick
Haight
HIPPIES.
TECHIES.
TOFU AND VEGAN WANKERS.
SAN FRANCISCO. WHAT A DUMP.
HOW MANY RELIGIONS DID YOU MAKE UP THIS WEEK, ☠☠☠☠-HOLES?
SORRY. WHAT?
NOTHING, DARLING. JUST TALKING TO MYSELF.
OH. OKAY.
NAMASTE!
BLOODY HELL.
OBBA'S BLESSING 1518 HAIGHT ST.
THIS CAN'T BE RIGHT.
A BOTANICA?
OH, JENNY, WHAT ARE YOU GETTING UP TO THESE DAYS?
WHAT THE HELL? WHAT JENNY KNOWS ABOUT SANTERIA WOULD FIT ON A POST-IT WITH ROOM FOR A GROCERY LIST.

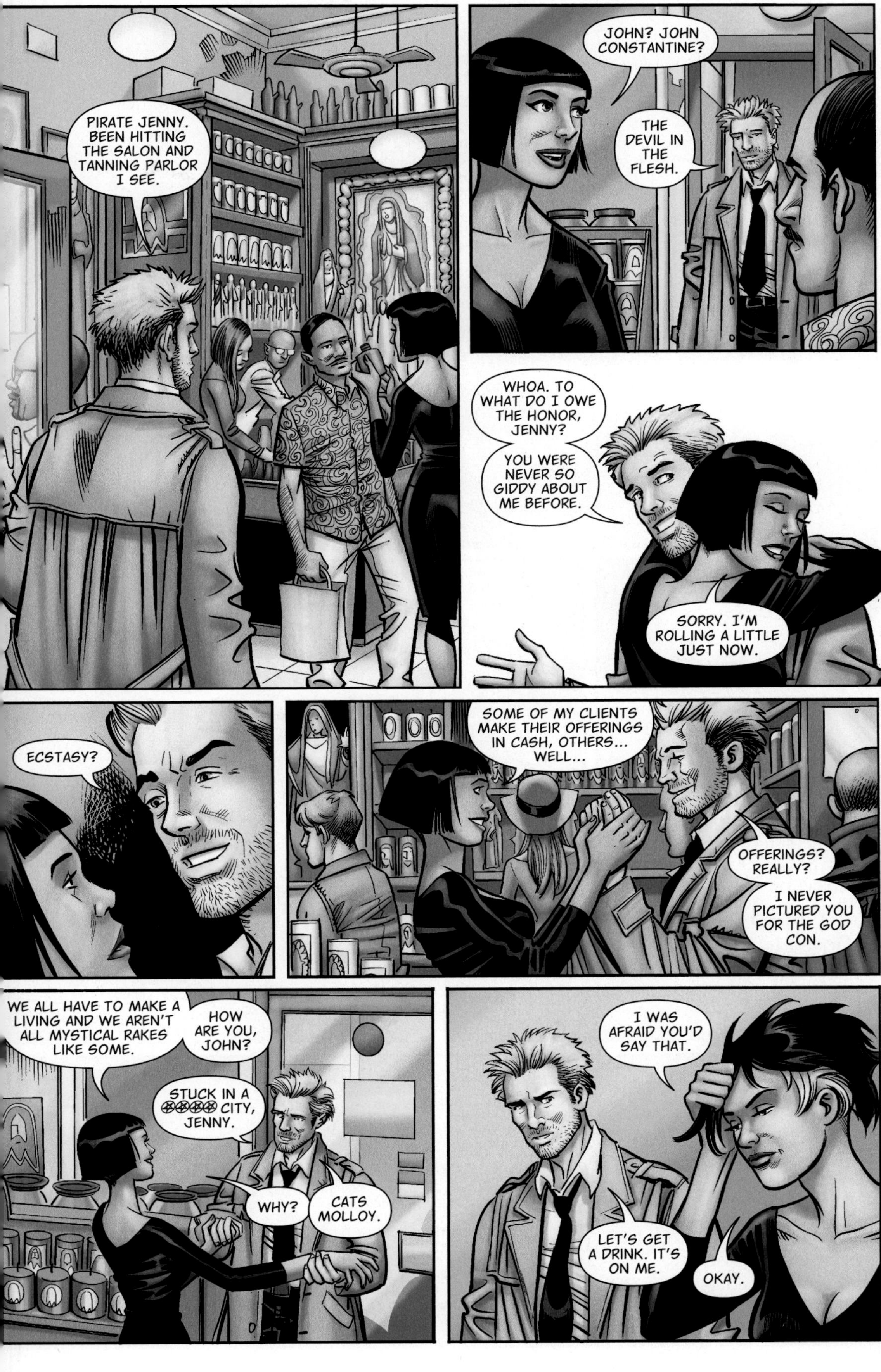
PIRATE JENNY. BEEN HITTING THE SALON AND TANNING PARLOR I SEE.
JOHN? JOHN CONSTANTINE?
THE DEVIL IN THE FLESH.
WHOA. TO WHAT DO I OWE THE HONOR, JENNY?
YOU WERE NEVER SO GIDDY ABOUT ME BEFORE.
SORRY. I'M ROLLING A LITTLE JUST NOW.
ECSTASY?
SOME OF MY CLIENTS MAKE THEIR OFFERINGS IN CASH, OTHERS... WELL...
OFFERINGS? REALLY?
I NEVER PICTURED YOU FOR THE GOD CON.
WE ALL HAVE TO MAKE A LIVING AND WE AREN'T ALL MYSTICAL RAKES LIKE SOME.
HOW ARE YOU, JOHN?
STUCK IN A ⛤⛤⛤⛤ CITY, JENNY.
WHY?
CATS MOLLOY.
I WAS AFRAID YOU'D SAY THAT.
LET'S GET A DRINK. IT'S ON ME.
OKAY.

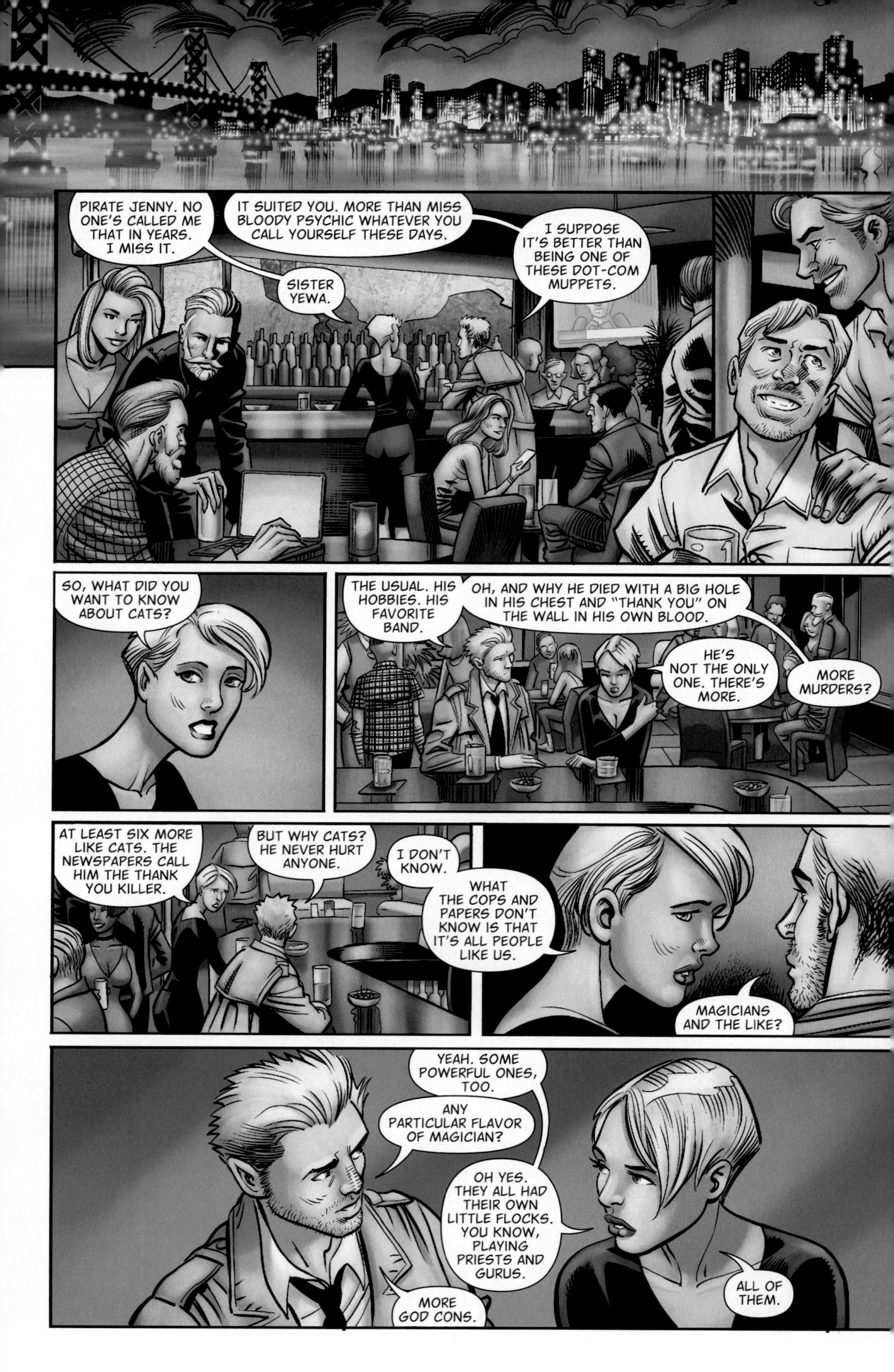
PIRATE JENNY. NO ONE'S CALLED ME THAT IN YEARS. I MISS IT.
IT SUITED YOU. MORE THAN MISS BLOODY PSYCHIC WHATEVER YOU CALL YOURSELF THESE DAYS.
SISTER YEWA.
I SUPPOSE IT'S BETTER THAN BEING ONE OF THESE DOT-COM MUPPETS.
SO, WHAT DID YOU WANT TO KNOW ABOUT CATS?
THE USUAL. HIS HOBBIES. HIS FAVORITE BAND.
OH, AND WHY HE DIED WITH A BIG HOLE IN HIS CHEST AND "THANK YOU" ON THE WALL IN HIS OWN BLOOD.
HE'S NOT THE ONLY ONE. THERE'S MORE.
MORE MURDERS?
AT LEAST SIX MORE LIKE CATS. THE NEWSPAPERS CALL HIM THE THANK YOU KILLER.
BUT WHY CATS? HE NEVER HURT ANYONE.
I DON'T KNOW.
WHAT THE COPS AND PAPERS DON'T KNOW IS THAT IT'S ALL PEOPLE LIKE US.
MAGICIANS AND THE LIKE?
YEAH. SOME POWERFUL ONES, TOO.
ANY PARTICULAR FLAVOR OF MAGICIAN?
OH YES. THEY ALL HAD THEIR OWN LITTLE FLOCKS. YOU KNOW, PLAYING PRIESTS AND GURUS.
MORE GOD CONS.
ALL OF THEM.

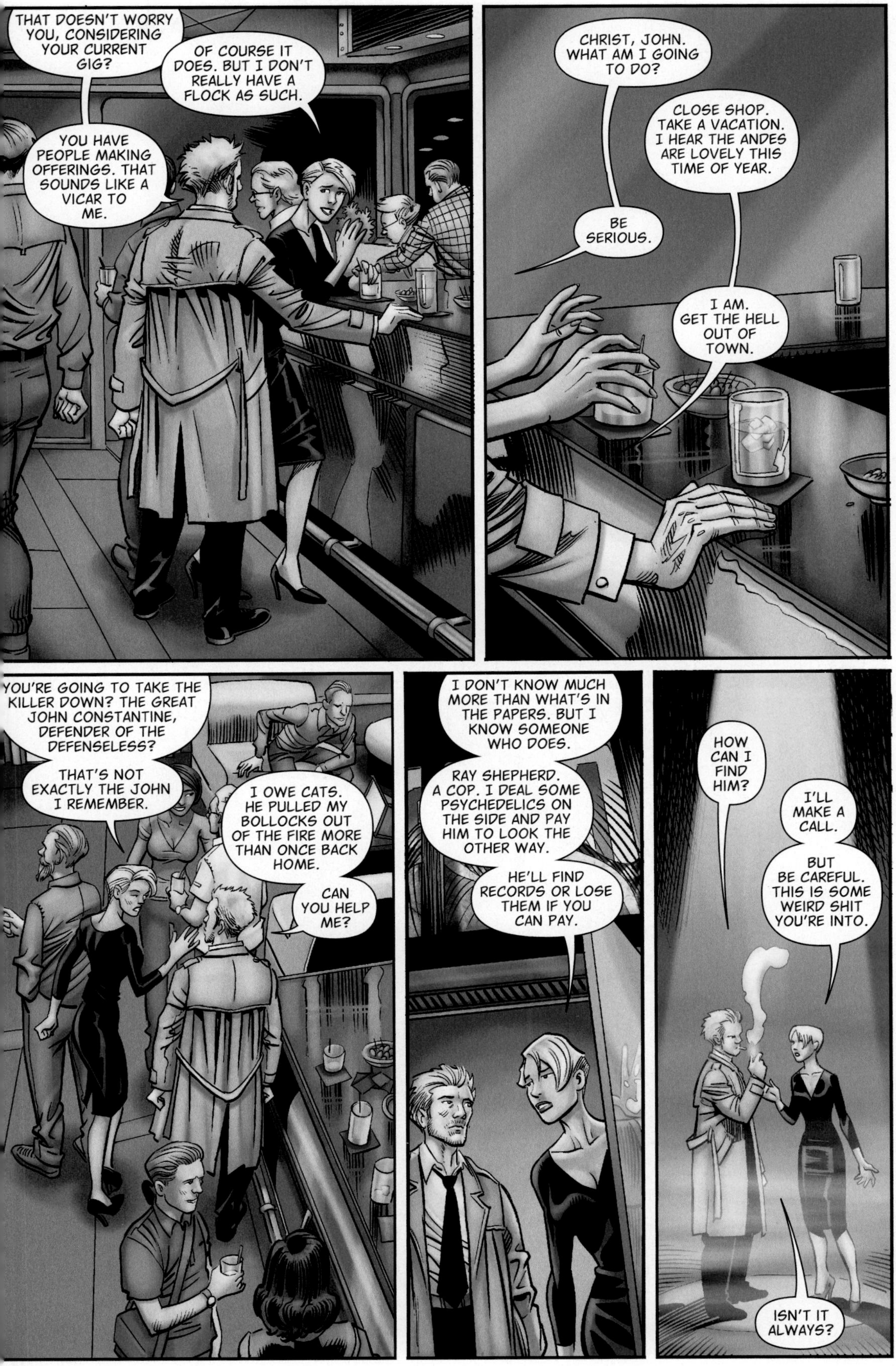
THAT DOESN'T WORRY YOU, CONSIDERING YOUR CURRENT GIG?
OF COURSE IT DOES. BUT I DON'T REALLY HAVE A FLOCK AS SUCH.
YOU HAVE PEOPLE MAKING OFFERINGS. THAT SOUNDS LIKE A VICAR TO ME.
CHRIST, JOHN. WHAT AM I GOING TO DO?
CLOSE SHOP. TAKE A VACATION. I HEAR THE ANDES ARE LOVELY THIS TIME OF YEAR.
BE SERIOUS.
I AM. GET THE HELL OUT OF TOWN.
YOU'RE GOING TO TAKE THE KILLER DOWN? THE GREAT JOHN CONSTANTINE, DEFENDER OF THE DEFENSELESS?
THAT'S NOT EXACTLY THE JOHN I REMEMBER.
I OWE CATS. HE PULLED MY BOLLOCKS OUT OF THE FIRE MORE THAN ONCE BACK HOME.
CAN YOU HELP ME?
I DON'T KNOW MUCH MORE THAN WHAT'S IN THE PAPERS. BUT I KNOW SOMEONE WHO DOES.
RAY SHEPHERD. A COP. I DEAL SOME PSYCHEDELICS ON THE SIDE AND PAY HIM TO LOOK THE OTHER WAY.
HE'LL FIND RECORDS OR LOSE THEM IF YOU CAN PAY.
HOW CAN I FIND HIM?
I'LL MAKE A CALL.
BUT BE CAREFUL. THIS IS SOME WEIRD SHIT YOU'RE INTO.
ISN'T IT ALWAYS?

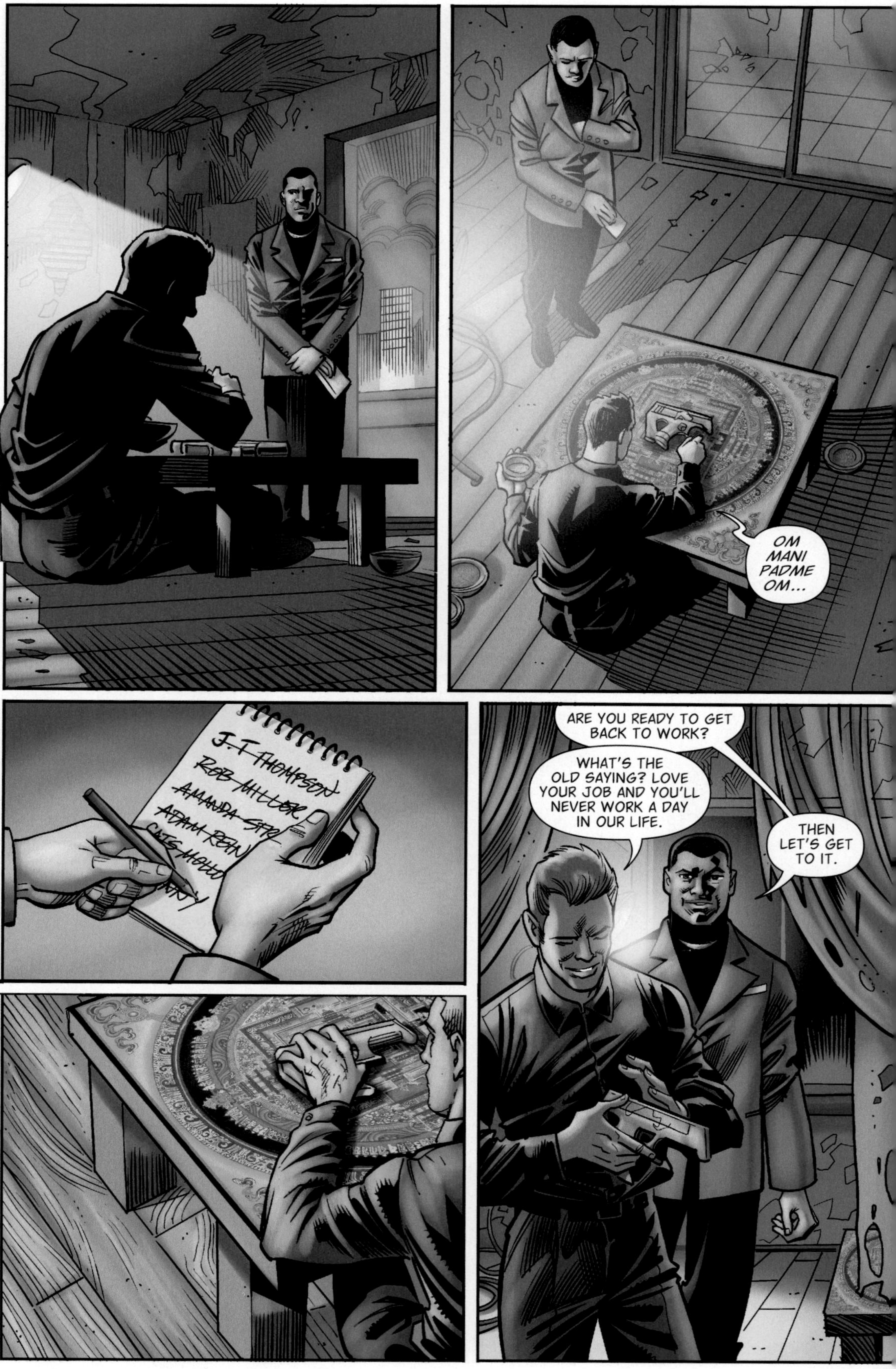
OM MANI PADME OM...
J.T THOMPSON
ROB MILLER
AMANDA STR
ADAM REIN
ARE YOU READY TO GET BACK TO WORK?
WHAT'S THE OLD SAYING? LOVE YOUR JOB AND YOU'LL NEVER WORK A DAY IN OUR LIFE.
THEN LET'S GET TO IT.

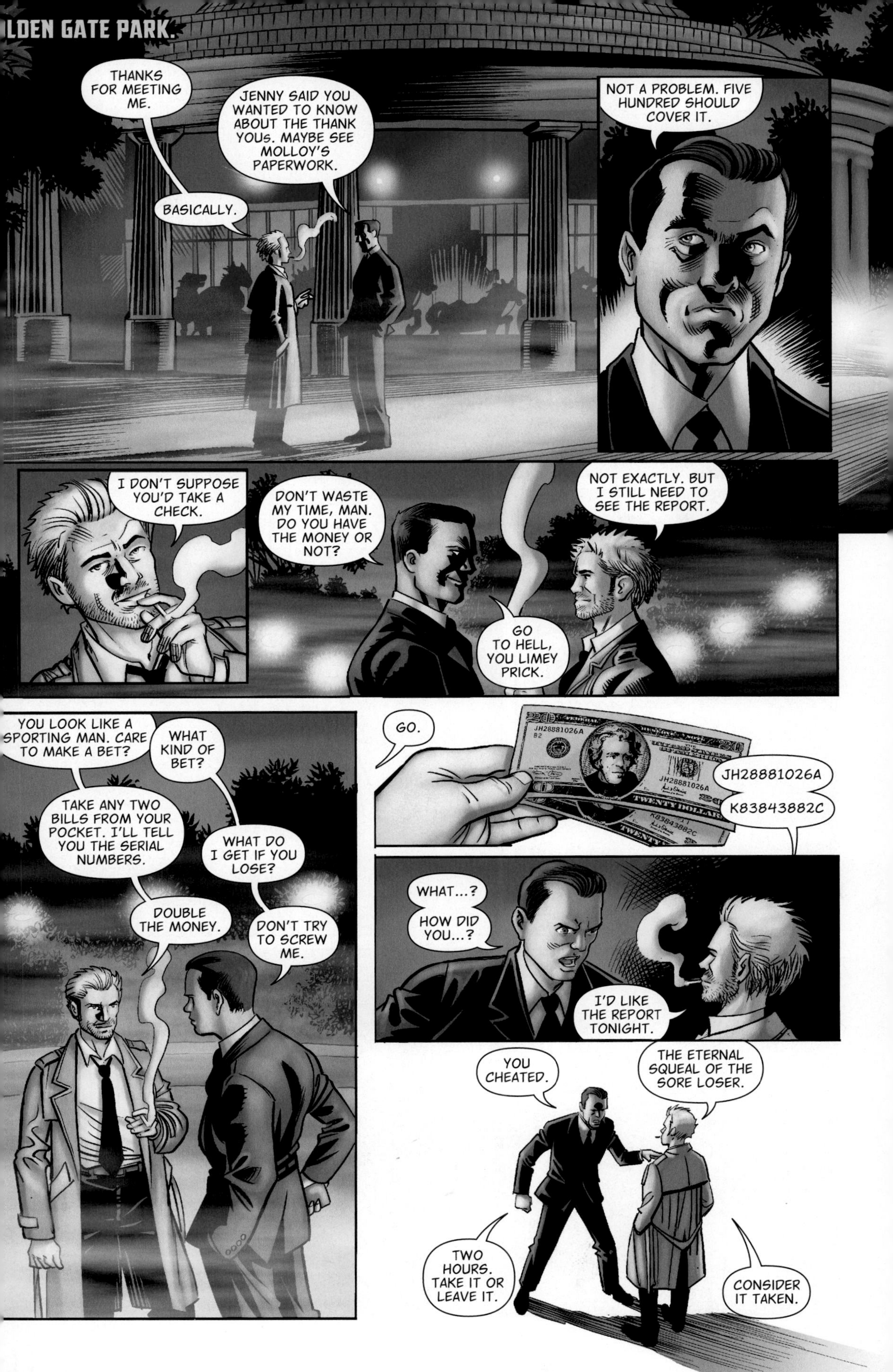
LDEN GATE PARK.
THANKS FOR MEETING ME.
JENNY SAID YOU WANTED TO KNOW ABOUT THE THANK YOUs. MAYBE SEE MOLLOY'S PAPERWORK.
BASICALLY.
NOT A PROBLEM. FIVE HUNDRED SHOULD COVER IT.
I DON'T SUPPOSE YOU'D TAKE A CHECK.
DON'T WASTE MY TIME, MAN. DO YOU HAVE THE MONEY OR NOT?
NOT EXACTLY. BUT I STILL NEED TO SEE THE REPORT.
GO TO HELL, YOU LIMEY PRICK.
YOU LOOK LIKE A SPORTING MAN. CARE TO MAKE A BET?
WHAT KIND OF BET?
TAKE ANY TWO BILLS FROM YOUR POCKET. I'LL TELL YOU THE SERIAL NUMBERS.
WHAT DO I GET IF YOU LOSE?
DOUBLE THE MONEY.
DON'T TRY TO SCREW ME.
GO.
JH28881026A
K83843882C
WHAT...?
HOW DID YOU...?
I'D LIKE THE REPORT TONIGHT.
YOU CHEATED.
THE ETERNAL SQUEAL OF THE SORE LOSER.
TWO HOURS. TAKE IT OR LEAVE IT.
CONSIDER IT TAKEN.

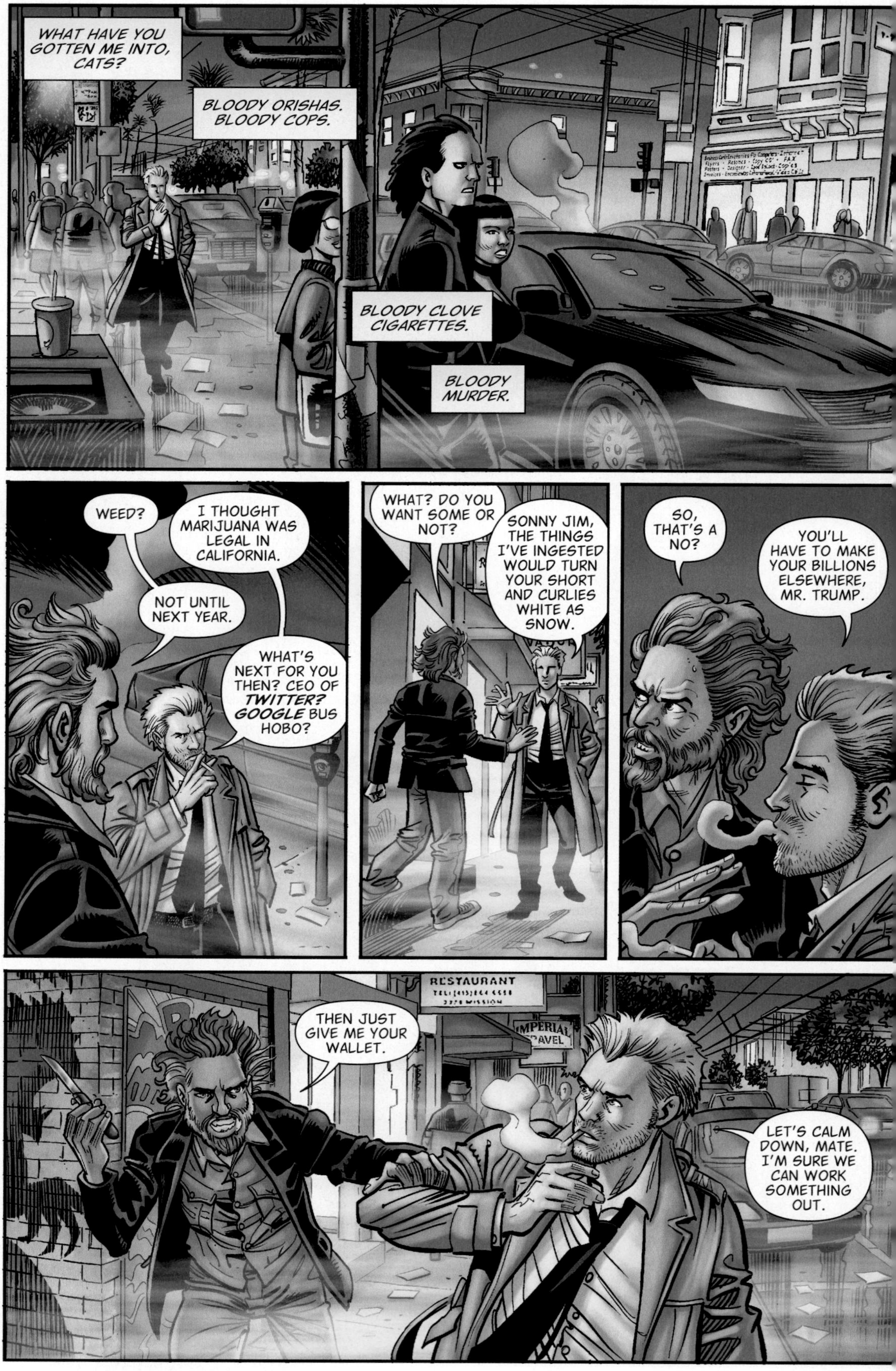
WHAT HAVE YOU GOTTEN ME INTO, CATS?
BLOODY ORISHAS. BLOODY COPS.
BLOODY CLOVE CIGARETTES.
BLOODY MURDER.
WEED?
I THOUGHT MARIJUANA WAS LEGAL IN CALIFORNIA.
NOT UNTIL NEXT YEAR.
WHAT'S NEXT FOR YOU THEN? CEO OF TWITTER? GOOGLE BUS HOBO?
WHAT? DO YOU WANT SOME OR NOT?
SONNY JIM, THE THINGS I'VE INGESTED WOULD TURN YOUR SHORT AND CURLIES WHITE AS SNOW.
SO, THAT'S A NO?
YOU'LL HAVE TO MAKE YOUR BILLIONS ELSEWHERE, MR. TRUMP.
RESTAURANT
IMPERIAL TRAVEL
THEN JUST GIVE ME YOUR WALLET.
LET'S CALM DOWN, MATE. I'M SURE WE CAN WORK SOMETHING OUT.

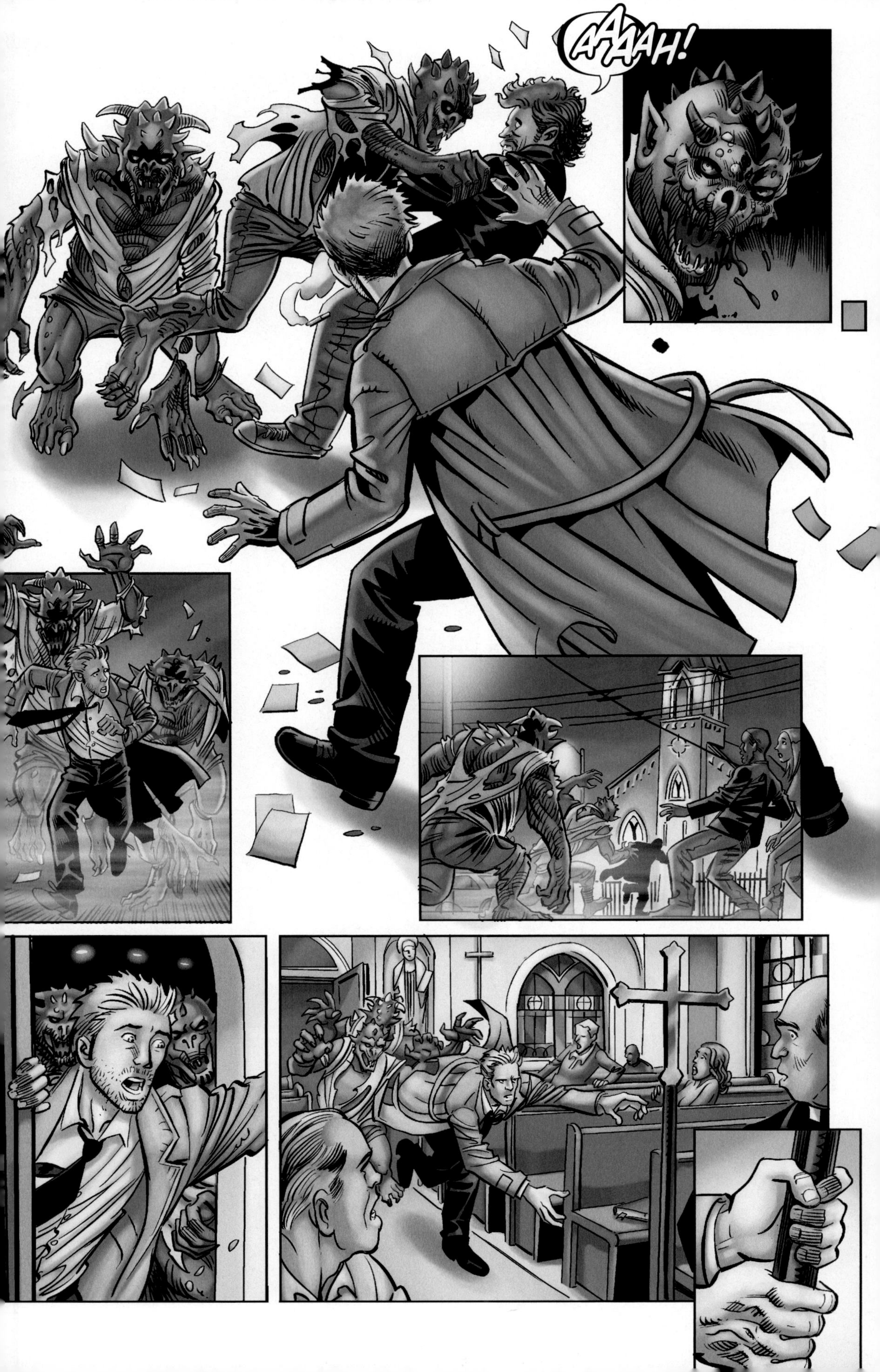
AAAAH!

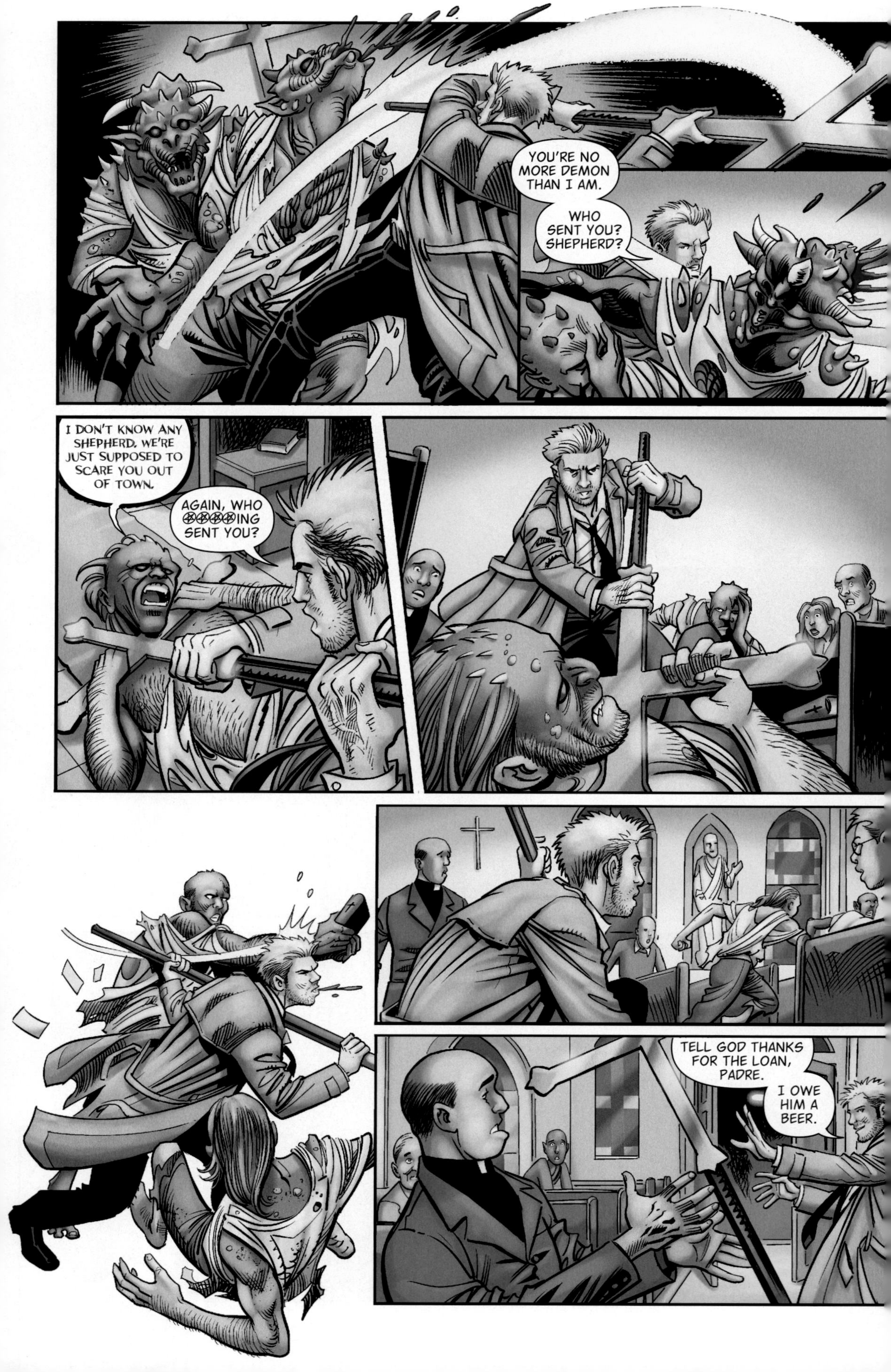
YOU'RE NO MORE DEMON THAN I AM.
WHO SENT YOU? SHEPHERD?
I DON'T KNOW ANY SHEPHERD. WE'RE JUST SUPPOSED TO SCARE YOU OUT OF TOWN.
AGAIN, WHO ⊗⊗⊗⊗ING SENT YOU?
TELL GOD THANKS FOR THE LOAN, PADRE.
I OWE HIM A BEER.

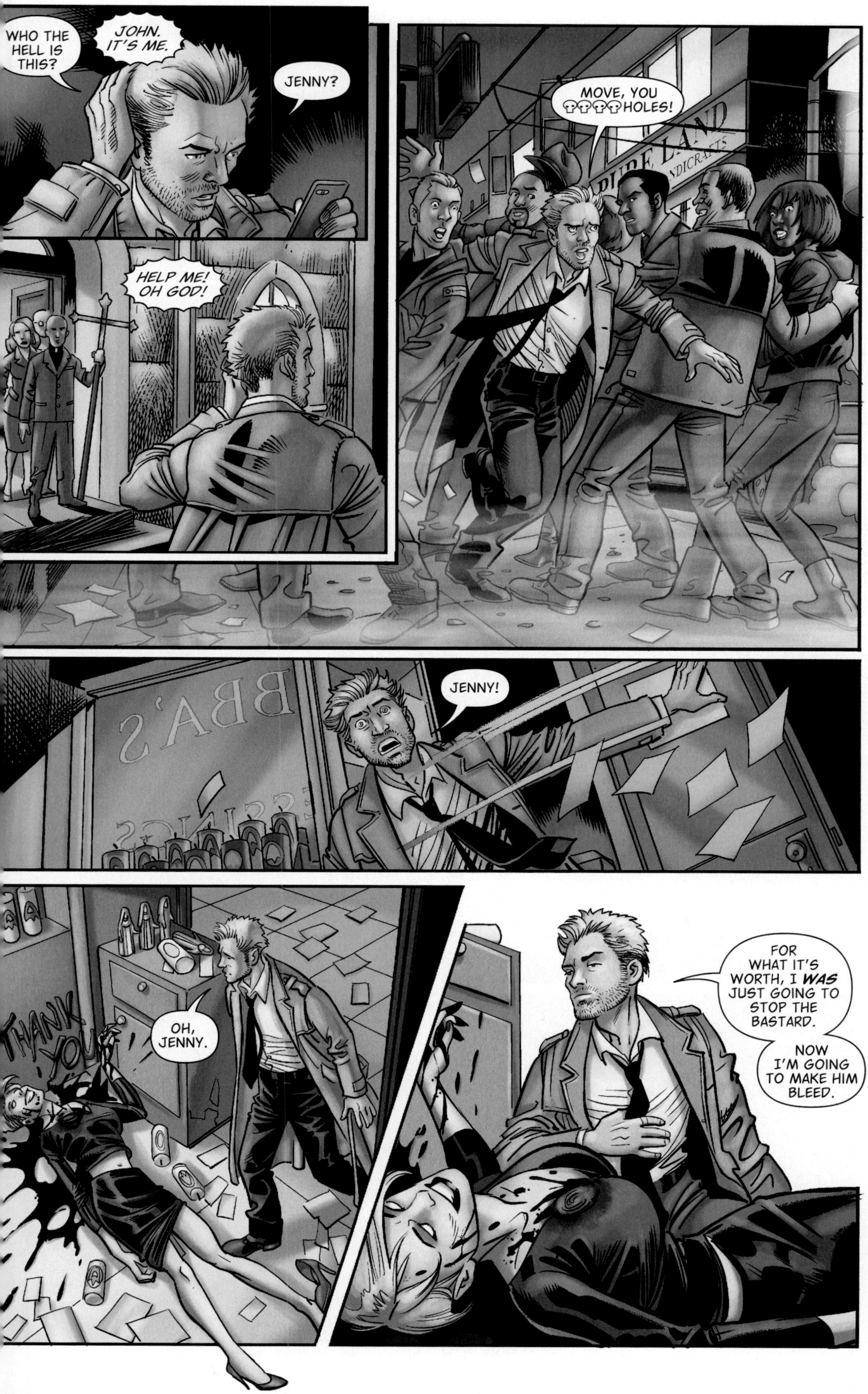

WHO THE HELL IS THIS?
JOHN. IT'S ME.
JENNY?
HELP ME! OH GOD!
MOVE, YOU ☠☠☠HOLES!
PURE LAND
HANDICRAFTS
BBA'S
JENNY!
OH, JENNY.
THANK YOU
FOR WHAT IT'S WORTH, I ***WAS*** JUST GOING TO STOP THE BASTARD.
NOW I'M GOING TO MAKE HIM BLEED.

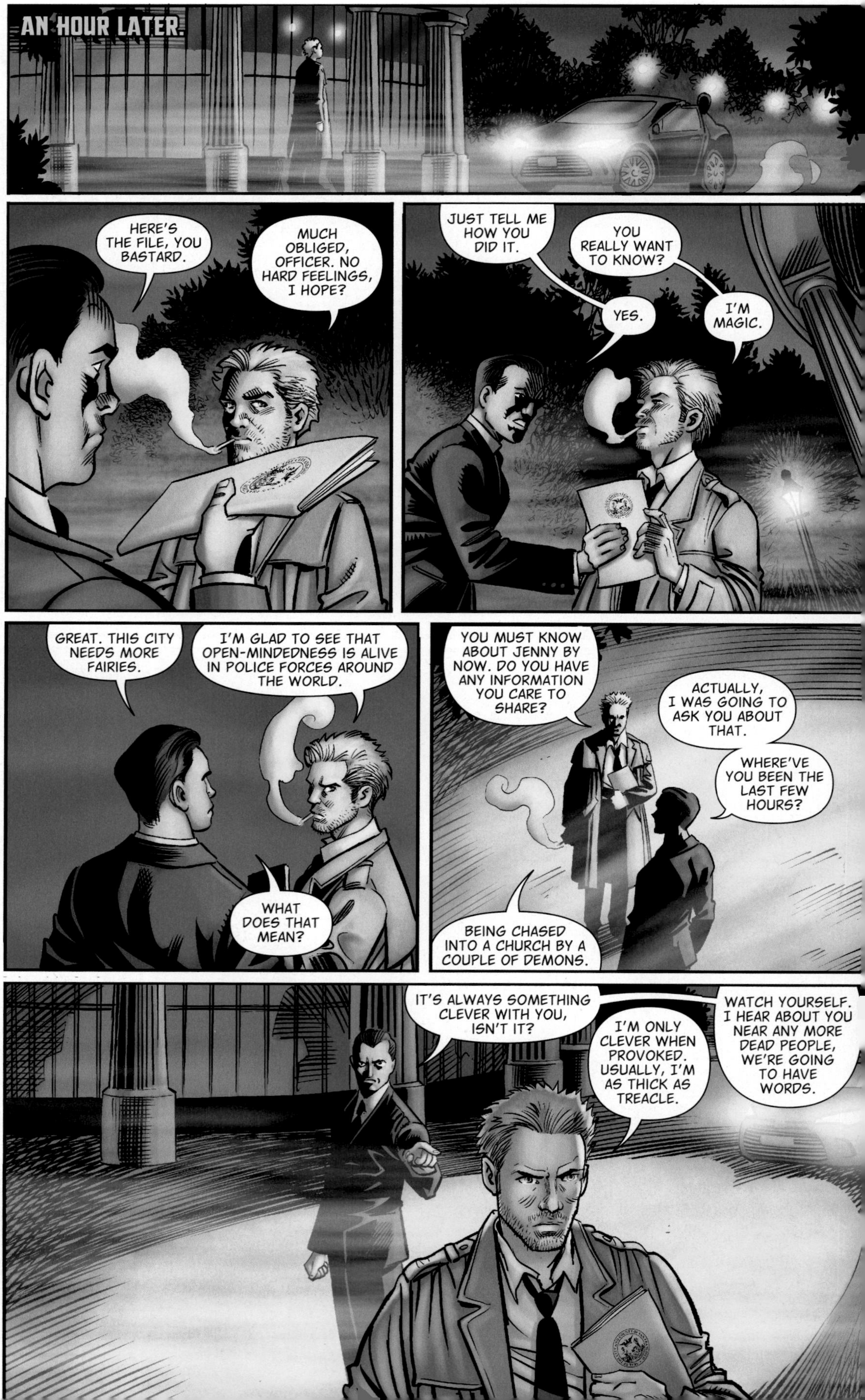
AN HOUR LATER.
HERE'S THE FILE, YOU BASTARD.
MUCH OBLIGED, OFFICER. NO HARD FEELINGS, I HOPE?
JUST TELL ME HOW YOU DID IT.
YOU REALLY WANT TO KNOW?
YES.
I'M MAGIC.
GREAT. THIS CITY NEEDS MORE FAIRIES.
I'M GLAD TO SEE THAT OPEN-MINDEDNESS IS ALIVE IN POLICE FORCES AROUND THE WORLD.
WHAT DOES THAT MEAN?
YOU MUST KNOW ABOUT JENNY BY NOW. DO YOU HAVE ANY INFORMATION YOU CARE TO SHARE?
ACTUALLY, I WAS GOING TO ASK YOU ABOUT THAT.
WHERE'VE YOU BEEN THE LAST FEW HOURS?
BEING CHASED INTO A CHURCH BY A COUPLE OF DEMONS.
IT'S ALWAYS SOMETHING CLEVER WITH YOU, ISN'T IT?
I'M ONLY CLEVER WHEN PROVOKED. USUALLY, I'M AS THICK AS TREACLE.
WATCH YOURSELF. I HEAR ABOUT YOU NEAR ANY MORE DEAD PEOPLE, WE'RE GOING TO HAVE WORDS.

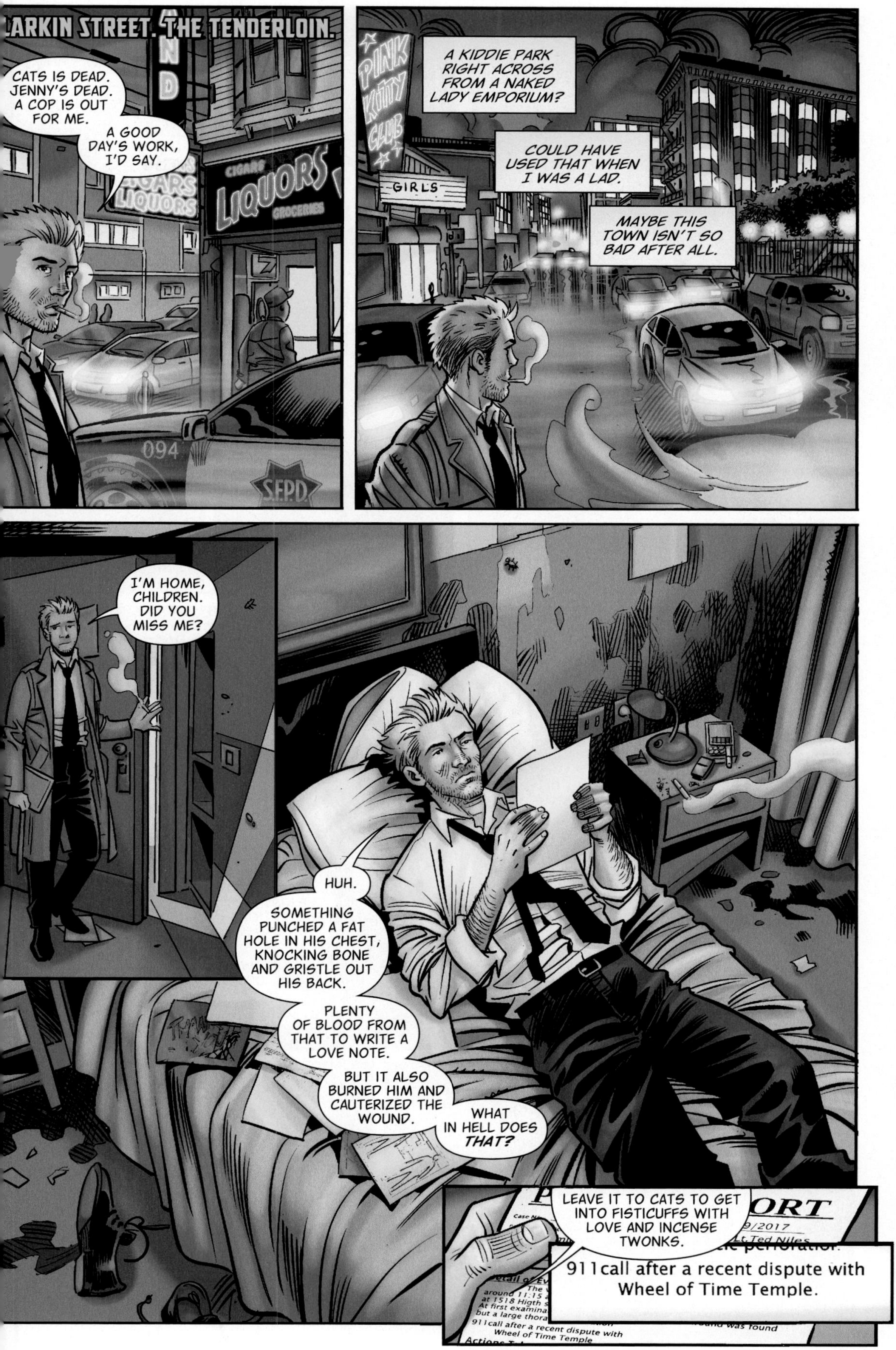
LARKIN STREET. THE TENDERLOIN.
CATS IS DEAD. JENNY'S DEAD. A COP IS OUT FOR ME.
A GOOD DAY'S WORK, I'D SAY.
CIGARS
LIQUORS
GROCERIES
094
S.F.P.D.
PINK KITTY CLUB
GIRLS
A KIDDIE PARK RIGHT ACROSS FROM A NAKED LADY EMPORIUM?
COULD HAVE USED THAT WHEN I WAS A LAD.
MAYBE THIS TOWN ISN'T SO BAD AFTER ALL.
I'M HOME, CHILDREN. DID YOU MISS ME?
HUH.
SOMETHING PUNCHED A FAT HOLE IN HIS CHEST, KNOCKING BONE AND GRISTLE OUT HIS BACK.
PLENTY OF BLOOD FROM THAT TO WRITE A LOVE NOTE.
BUT IT ALSO BURNED HIM AND CAUTERIZED THE WOUND.
WHAT IN HELL DOES *THAT?*
LEAVE IT TO CATS TO GET INTO FISTICUFFS WITH LOVE AND INCENSE TWONKS.
911call after a recent dispute with Wheel of Time Temple.

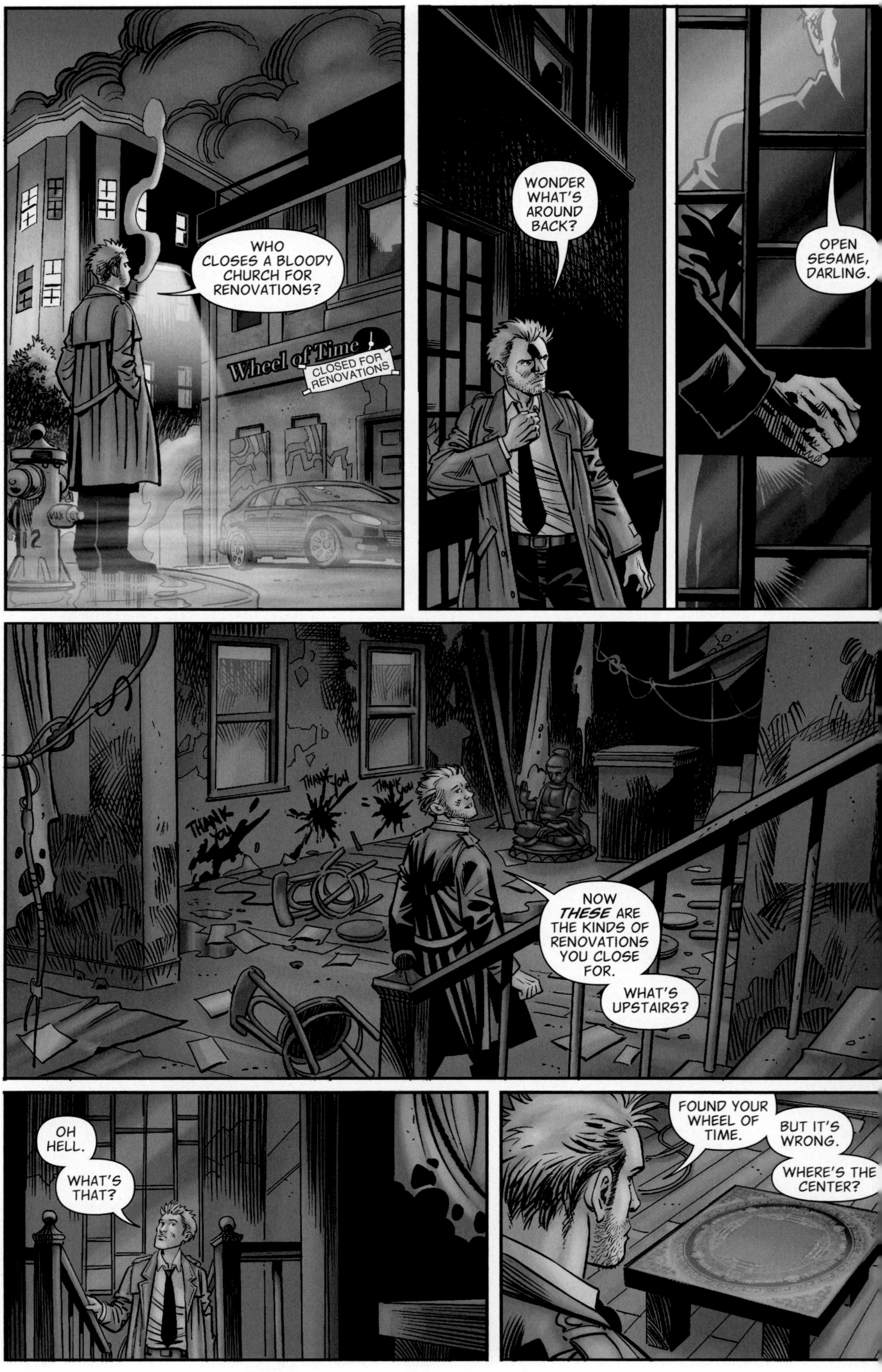
WHO CLOSES A BLOODY CHURCH FOR RENOVATIONS?
Wheel of Time
CLOSED FOR RENOVATIONS
WONDER WHAT'S AROUND BACK?
OPEN SESAME, DARLING.
THANK YOU
THANK YOU
THANK YOU
NOW THESE ARE THE KINDS OF RENOVATIONS YOU CLOSE FOR.
WHAT'S UPSTAIRS?
OH HELL.
WHAT'S THAT?
FOUND YOUR WHEEL OF TIME.
BUT IT'S WRONG.
WHERE'S THE CENTER?

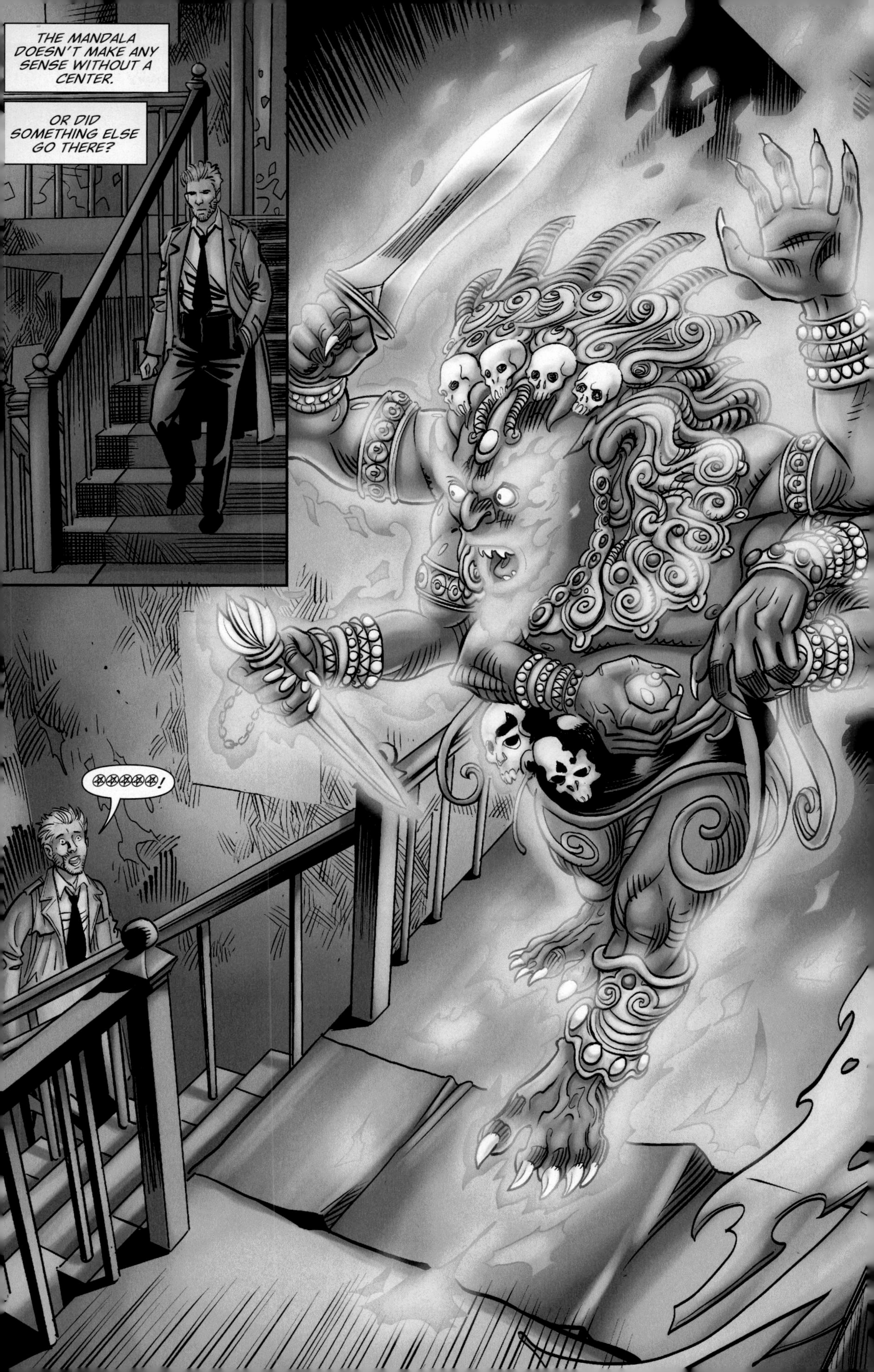

THE MANDALA DOESN'T MAKE ANY SENSE WITHOUT A CENTER.
OR DID SOMETHING ELSE GO THERE?

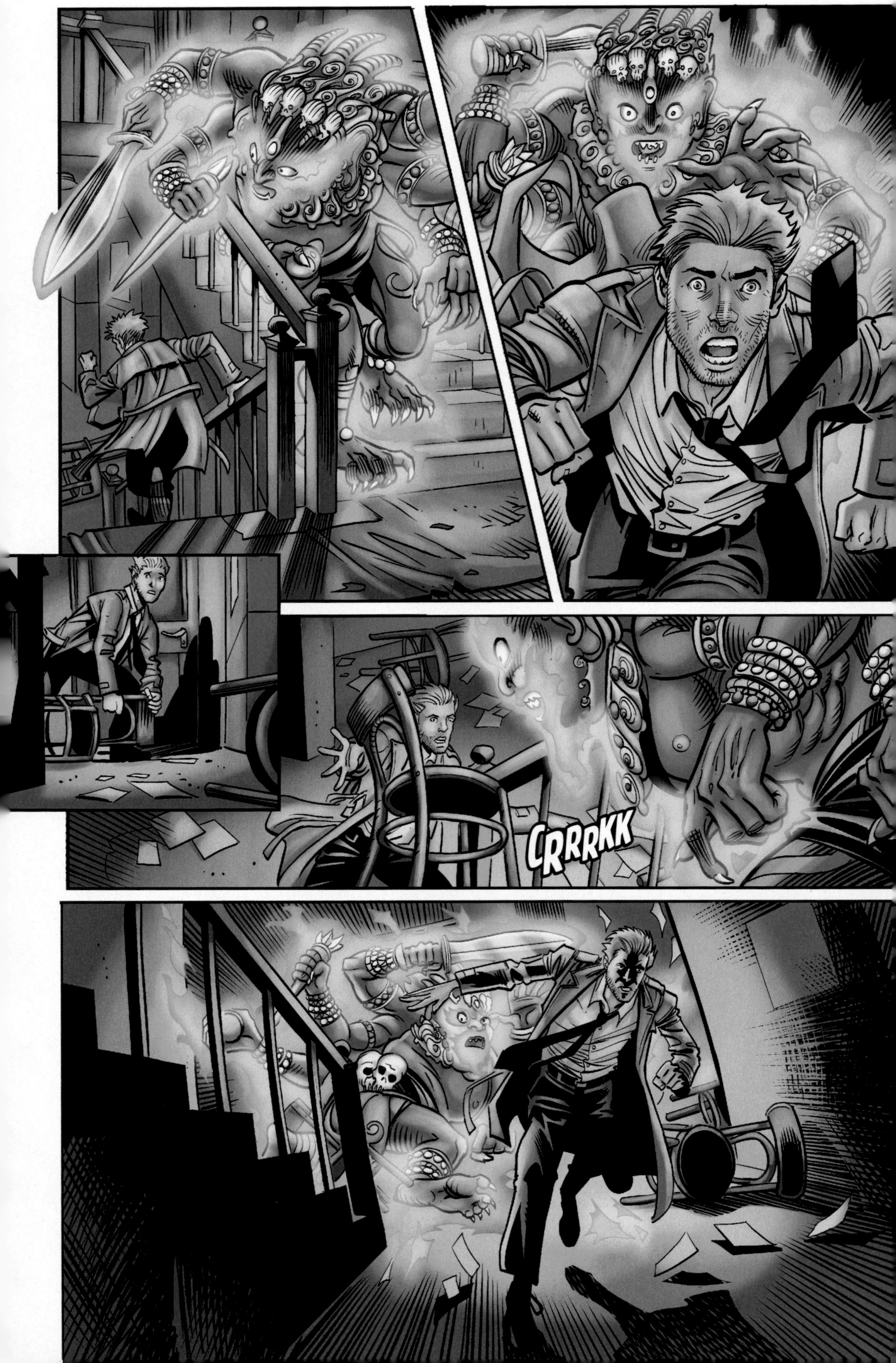
CRRRKK

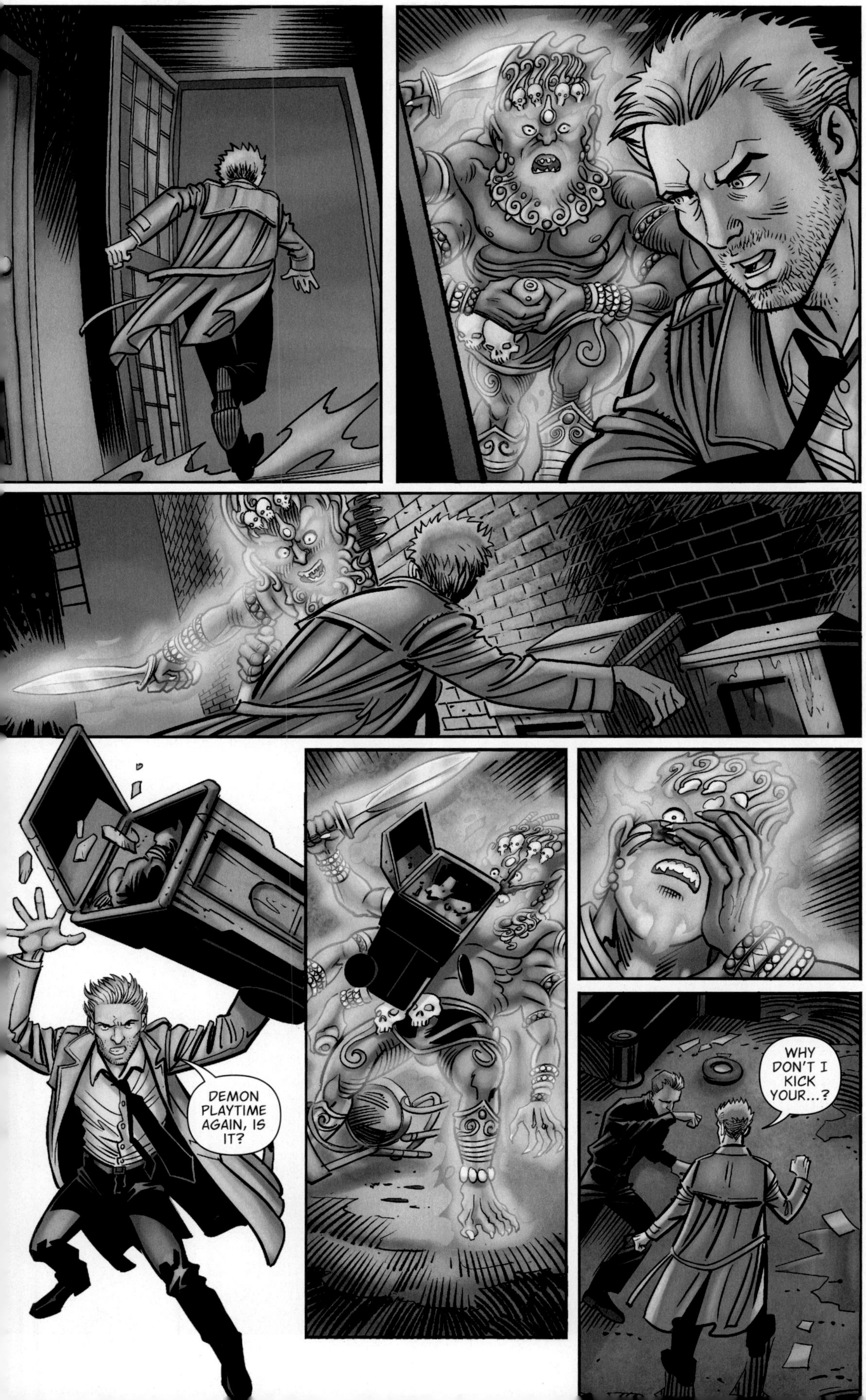
DEMON PLAYTIME AGAIN, IS IT?
WHY DON'T I KICK YOUR...?

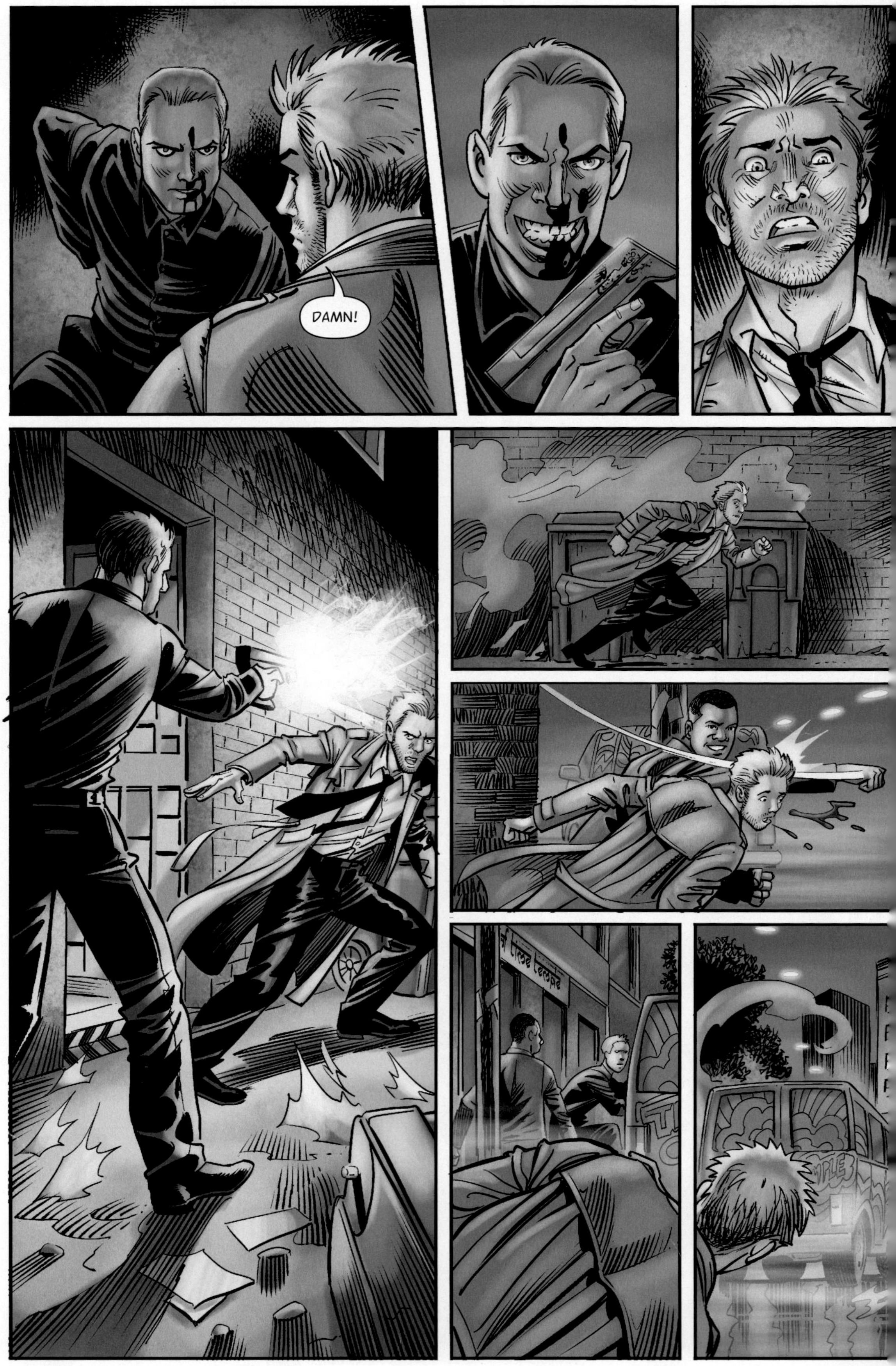
DAMN!

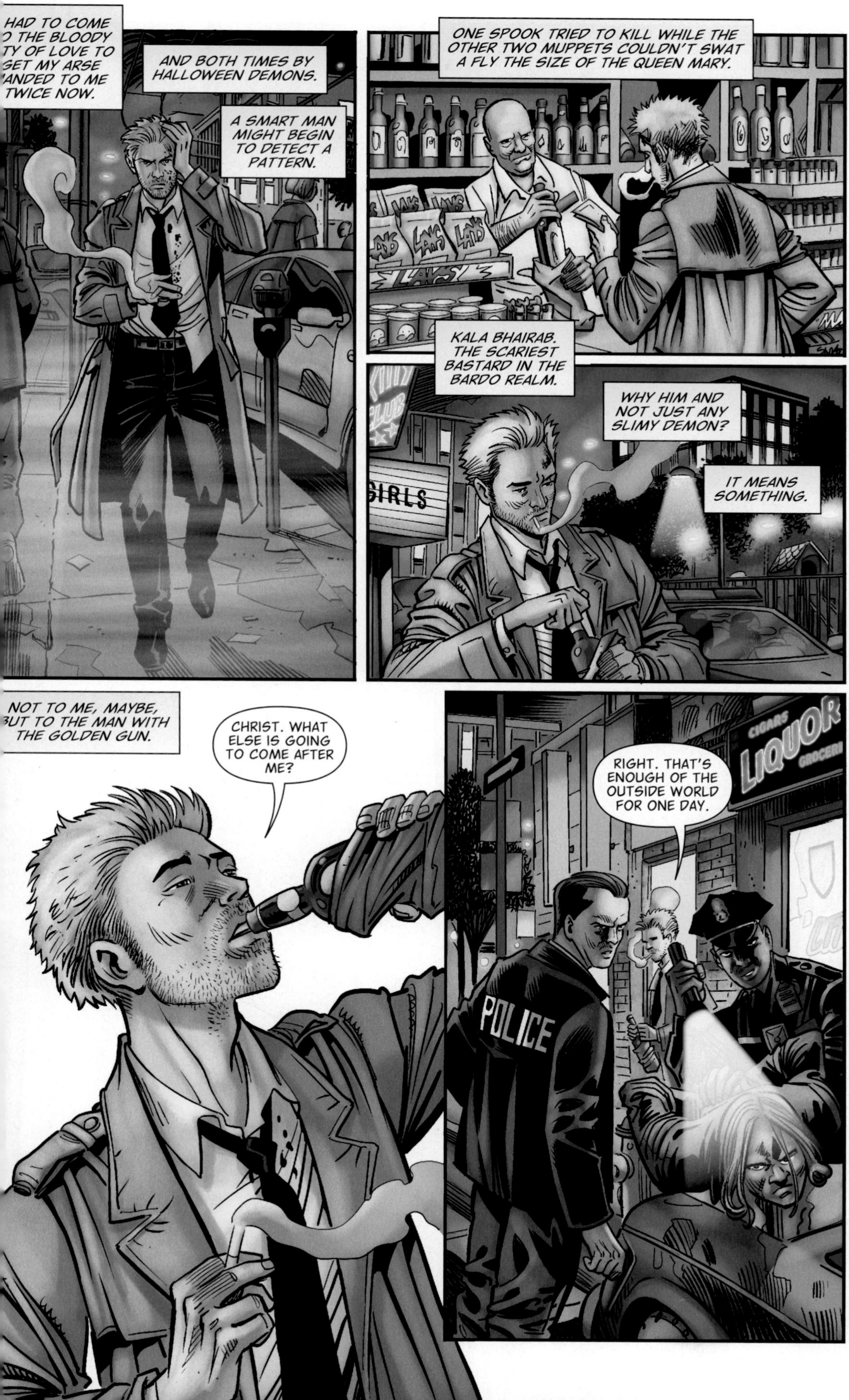
HAD TO COME
TO THE BLOODY
CITY OF LOVE TO
GET MY ARSE
HANDED TO ME
TWICE NOW.
AND BOTH TIMES BY
HALLOWEEN DEMONS.
A SMART MAN
MIGHT BEGIN
TO DETECT A
PATTERN.
ONE SPOOK TRIED TO KILL WHILE THE
OTHER TWO MUPPETS COULDN'T SWAT
A FLY THE SIZE OF THE QUEEN MARY.
KALA BHAIRAB.
THE SCARIEST
BASTARD IN THE
BARDO REALM.
WHY HIM AND
NOT JUST ANY
SLIMY DEMON?
IT MEANS
SOMETHING.
GIRLS
NOT TO ME, MAYBE,
BUT TO THE MAN WITH
THE GOLDEN GUN.
CHRIST. WHAT
ELSE IS GOING
TO COME AFTER
ME?
CIGARS
LIQUOR
RIGHT. THAT'S
ENOUGH OF THE
OUTSIDE WORLD
FOR ONE DAY.
POLICE

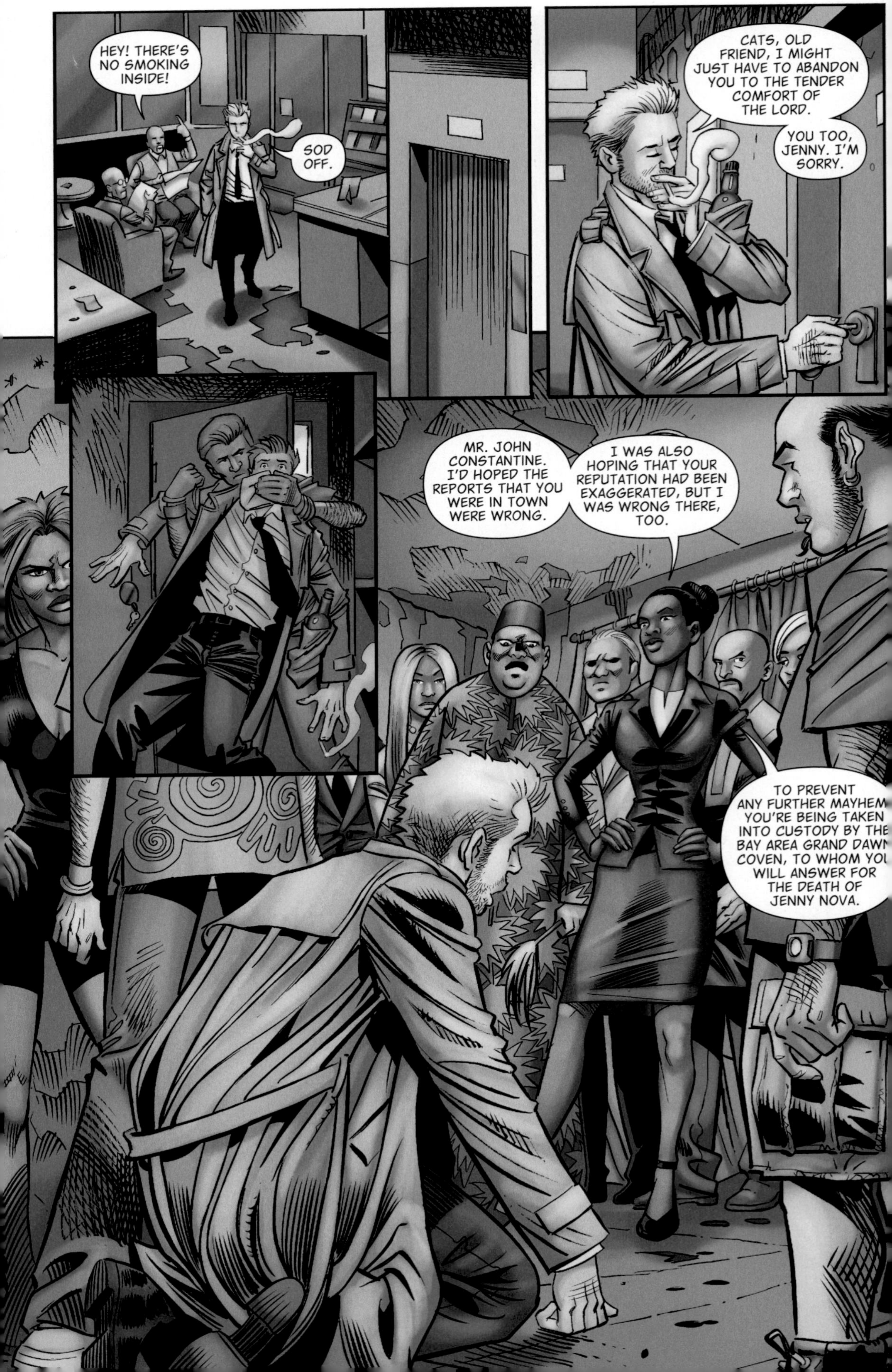
HEY! THERE'S NO SMOKING INSIDE!
SOD OFF.
CATS, OLD FRIEND, I MIGHT JUST HAVE TO ABANDON YOU TO THE TENDER COMFORT OF THE LORD.
YOU TOO, JENNY. I'M SORRY.
MR. JOHN CONSTANTINE. I'D HOPED THE REPORTS THAT YOU WERE IN TOWN WERE WRONG.
I WAS ALSO HOPING THAT YOUR REPUTATION HAD BEEN EXAGGERATED, BUT I WAS WRONG THERE, TOO.
TO PREVENT ANY FURTHER MAYHEM YOU'RE BEING TAKEN INTO CUSTODY BY THE BAY AREA GRAND DAWN COVEN, TO WHOM YOU WILL ANSWER FOR THE DEATH OF JENNY NOVA.

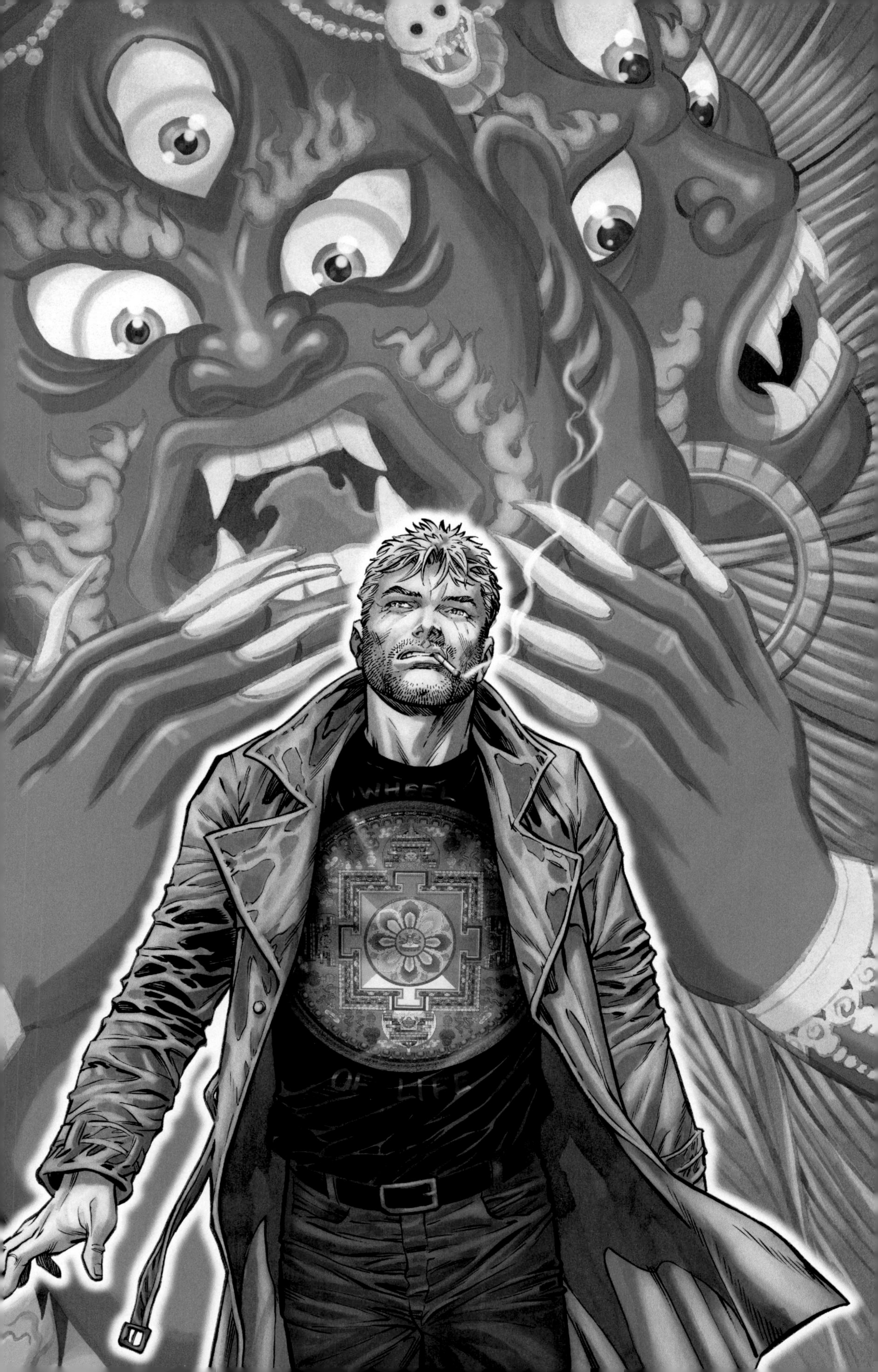
WHEEL
OF LIFE

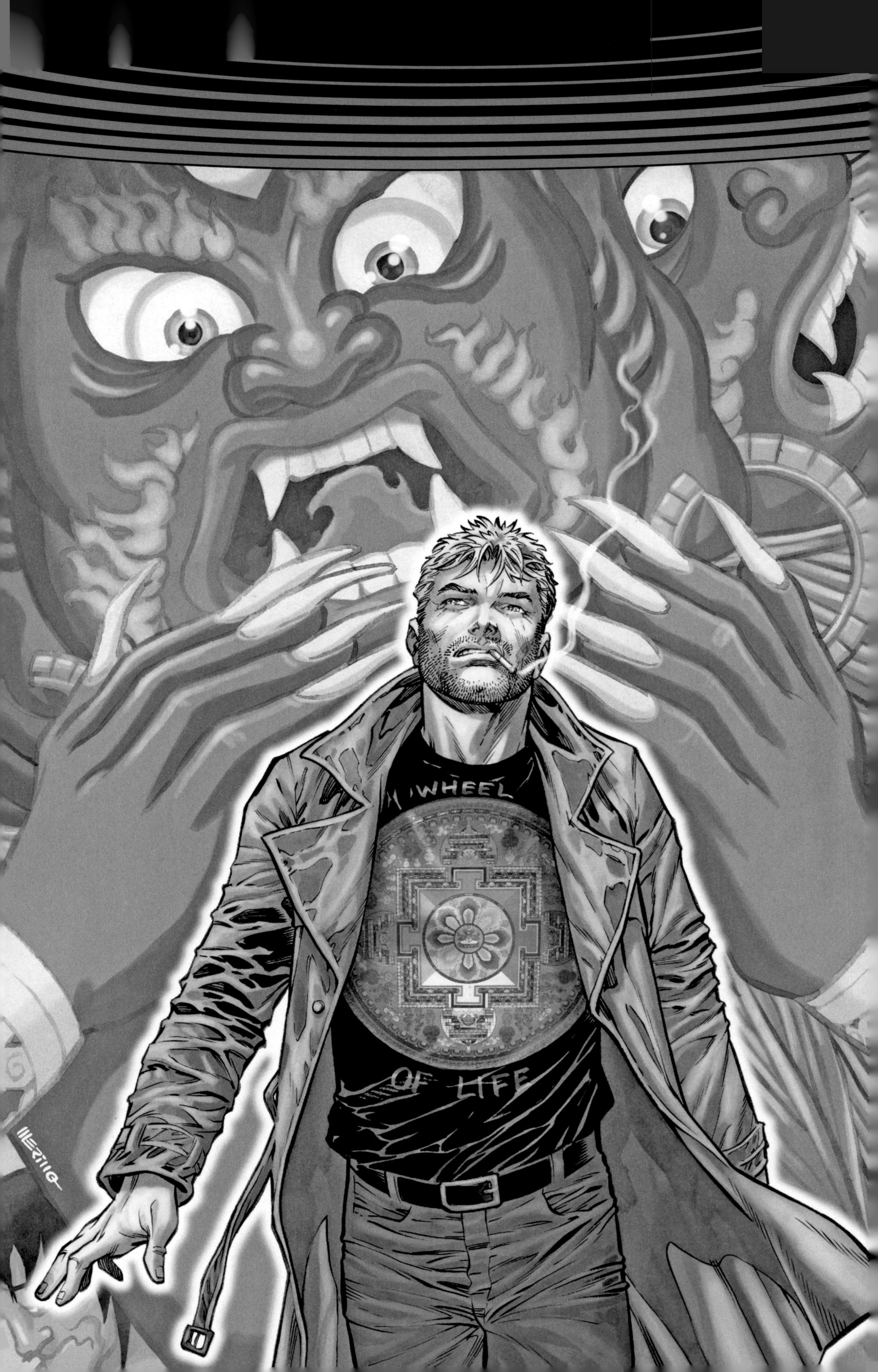
WHEEL
OF LIFE

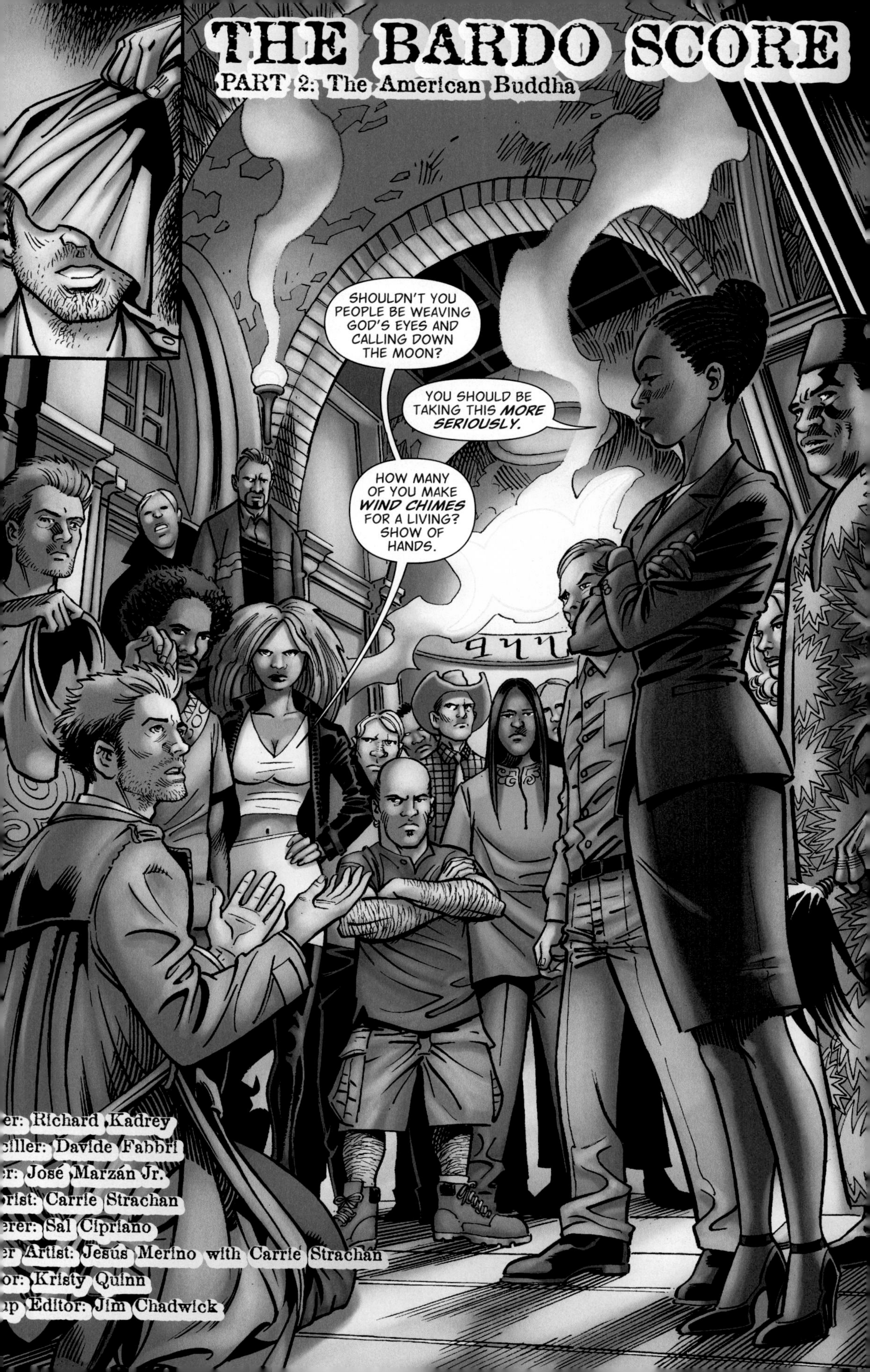
THE BARDO SCORE
PART 2: The American Buddha
SHOULDN'T YOU PEOPLE BE WEAVING GOD'S EYES AND CALLING DOWN THE MOON?
YOU SHOULD BE TAKING THIS MORE SERIOUSLY.
HOW MANY OF YOU MAKE WIND CHIMES FOR A LIVING? SHOW OF HANDS.
er: Richard Kadrey
ciller: Davide Fabbri
er: José Marzán Jr.
orist: Carrie Strachan
erer: Sal Cipriano
er Artist: Jesús Merino with Carrie Strachan
or: Kristy Quinn
up Editor: Jim Chadwick

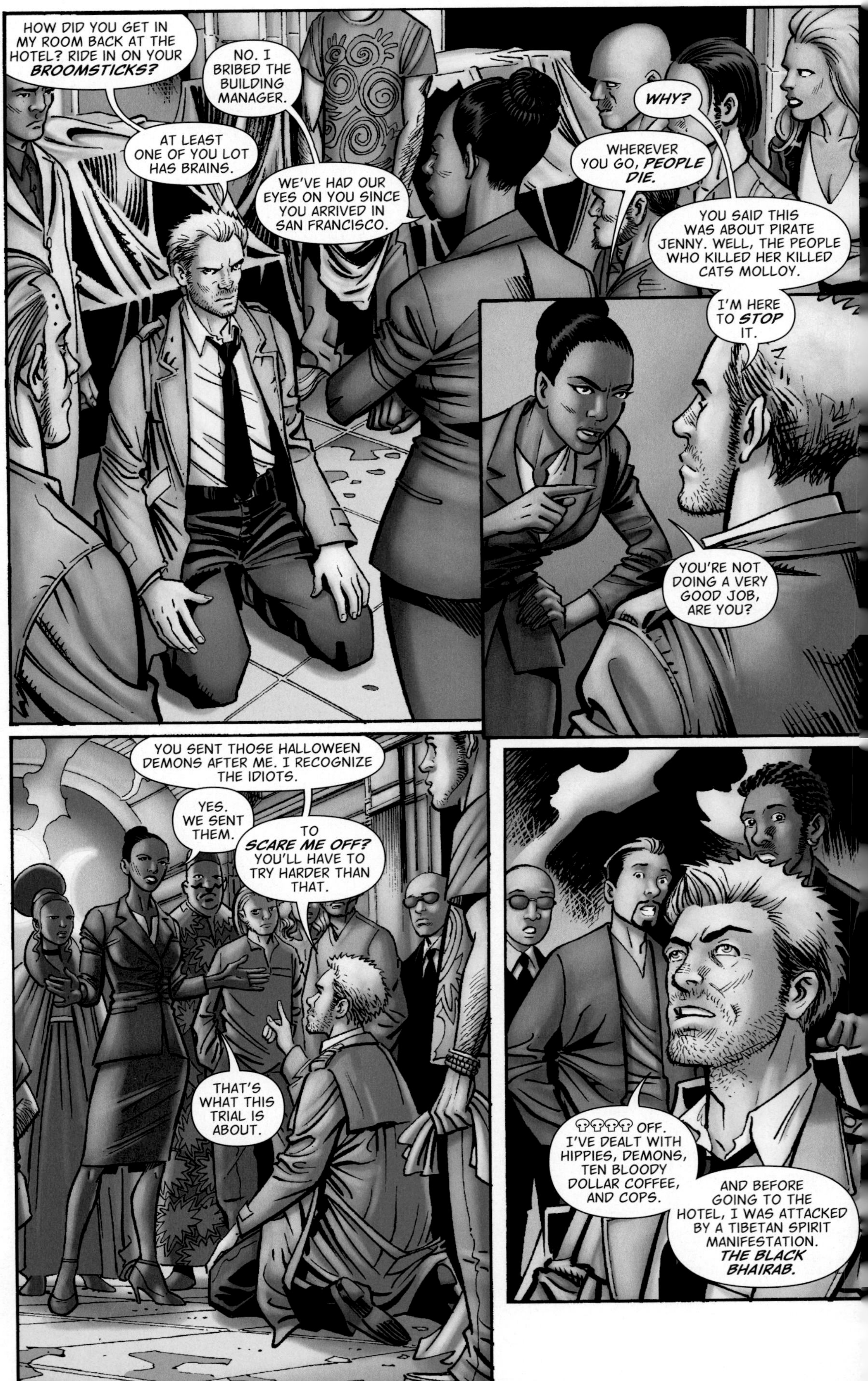
HOW DID YOU GET IN MY ROOM BACK AT THE HOTEL? RIDE IN ON YOUR BROOMSTICKS?
NO. I BRIBED THE BUILDING MANAGER.
AT LEAST ONE OF YOU LOT HAS BRAINS.
WE'VE HAD OUR EYES ON YOU SINCE YOU ARRIVED IN SAN FRANCISCO.
WHY?
WHEREVER YOU GO, PEOPLE DIE.
YOU SAID THIS WAS ABOUT PIRATE JENNY. WELL, THE PEOPLE WHO KILLED HER KILLED CATS MOLLOY.
I'M HERE TO STOP IT.
YOU'RE NOT DOING A VERY GOOD JOB, ARE YOU?
YOU SENT THOSE HALLOWEEN DEMONS AFTER ME. I RECOGNIZE THE IDIOTS.
YES. WE SENT THEM.
TO SCARE ME OFF? YOU'LL HAVE TO TRY HARDER THAN THAT.
THAT'S WHAT THIS TRIAL IS ABOUT.
OFF. I'VE DEALT WITH HIPPIES, DEMONS, TEN BLOODY DOLLAR COFFEE, AND COPS.
AND BEFORE GOING TO THE HOTEL, I WAS ATTACKED BY A TIBETAN SPIRIT MANIFESTATION. THE BLACK BHAIRAB.

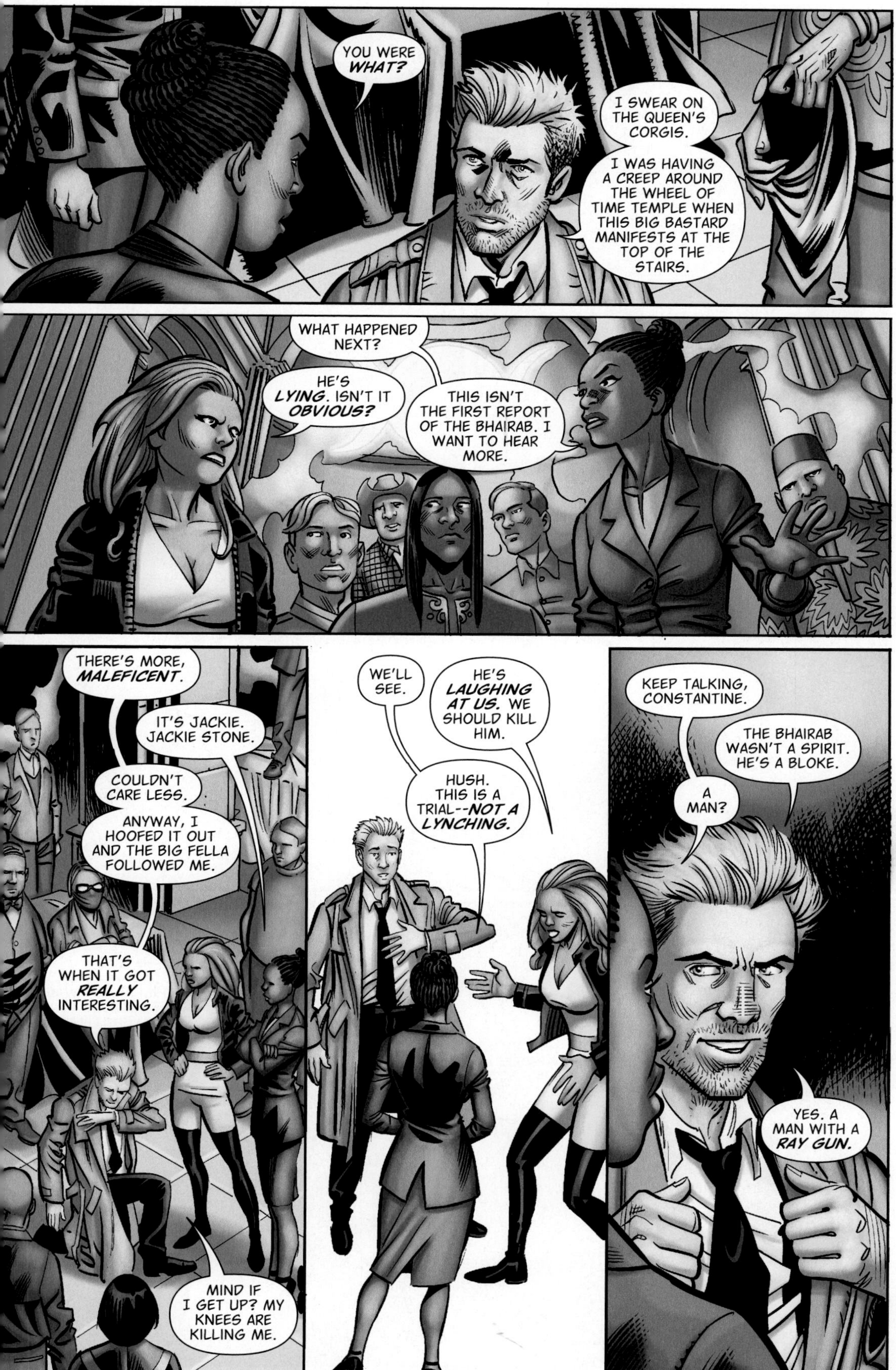
YOU WERE WHAT?
I SWEAR ON THE QUEEN'S CORGIS.
I WAS HAVING A CREEP AROUND THE WHEEL OF TIME TEMPLE WHEN THIS BIG BASTARD MANIFESTS AT THE TOP OF THE STAIRS.
WHAT HAPPENED NEXT?
HE'S LYING. ISN'T IT OBVIOUS?
THIS ISN'T THE FIRST REPORT OF THE BHAIRAB. I WANT TO HEAR MORE.
THERE'S MORE, MALEFICENT.
IT'S JACKIE. JACKIE STONE.
COULDN'T CARE LESS.
ANYWAY, I HOOFED IT OUT AND THE BIG FELLA FOLLOWED ME.
THAT'S WHEN IT GOT REALLY INTERESTING.
MIND IF I GET UP? MY KNEES ARE KILLING ME.
WE'LL SEE.
HE'S LAUGHING AT US. WE SHOULD KILL HIM.
HUSH. THIS IS A TRIAL--NOT A LYNCHING.
KEEP TALKING, CONSTANTINE.
THE BHAIRAB WASN'T A SPIRIT. HE'S A BLOKE.
A MAN?
YES. A MAN WITH A RAY GUN.

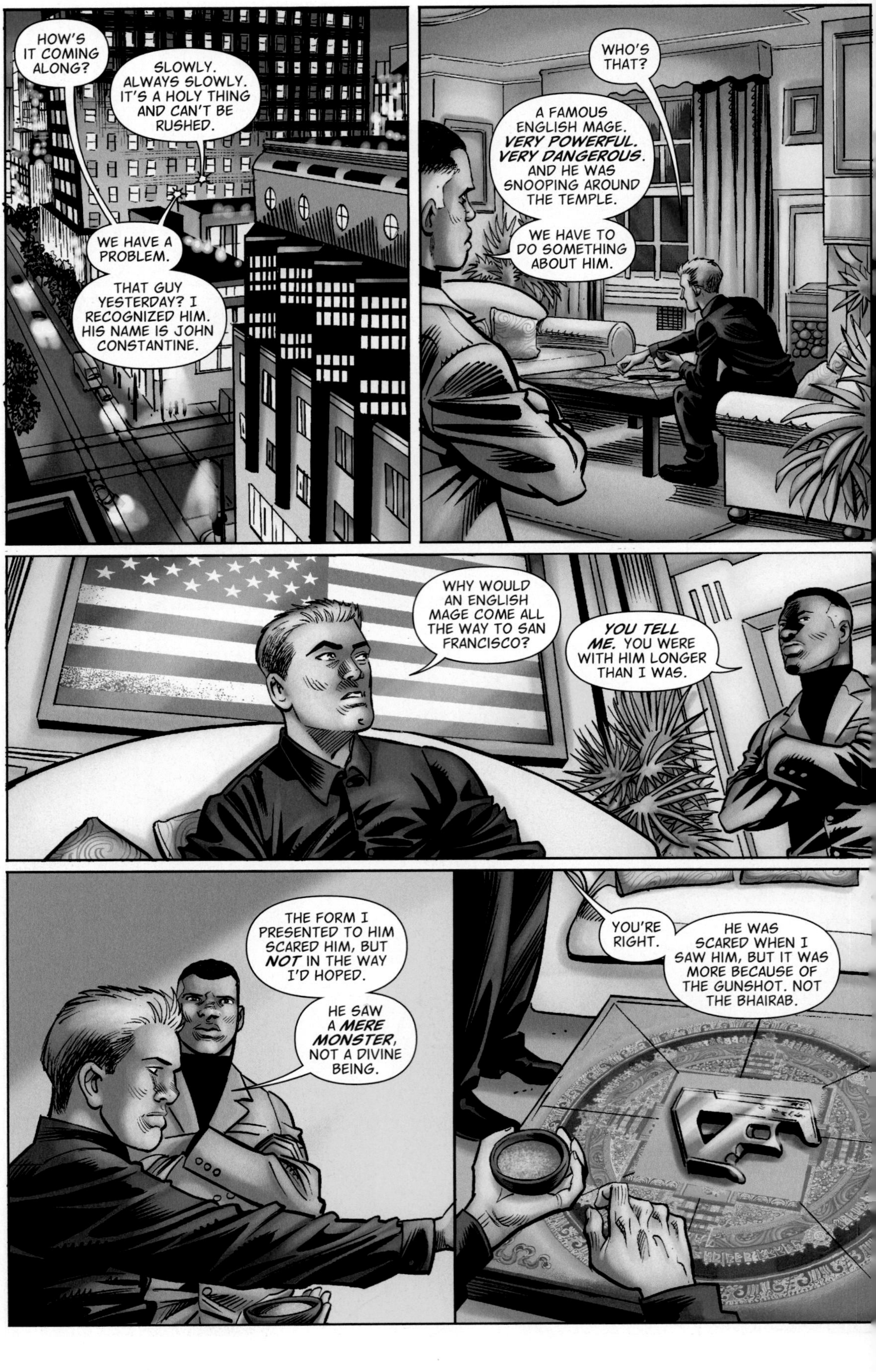
HOW'S IT COMING ALONG?
SLOWLY. ALWAYS SLOWLY. IT'S A HOLY THING AND CAN'T BE RUSHED.
WE HAVE A PROBLEM.
THAT GUY YESTERDAY? I RECOGNIZED HIM. HIS NAME IS JOHN CONSTANTINE.
WHO'S THAT?
A FAMOUS ENGLISH MAGE. VERY POWERFUL. VERY DANGEROUS. AND HE WAS SNOOPING AROUND THE TEMPLE.
WE HAVE TO DO SOMETHING ABOUT HIM.
WHY WOULD AN ENGLISH MAGE COME ALL THE WAY TO SAN FRANCISCO?
YOU TELL ME. YOU WERE WITH HIM LONGER THAN I WAS.
THE FORM I PRESENTED TO HIM SCARED HIM, BUT NOT IN THE WAY I'D HOPED.
HE SAW A MERE MONSTER, NOT A DIVINE BEING.
YOU'RE RIGHT.
HE WAS SCARED WHEN I SAW HIM, BUT IT WAS MORE BECAUSE OF THE GUNSHOT. NOT THE BHAIRAB.

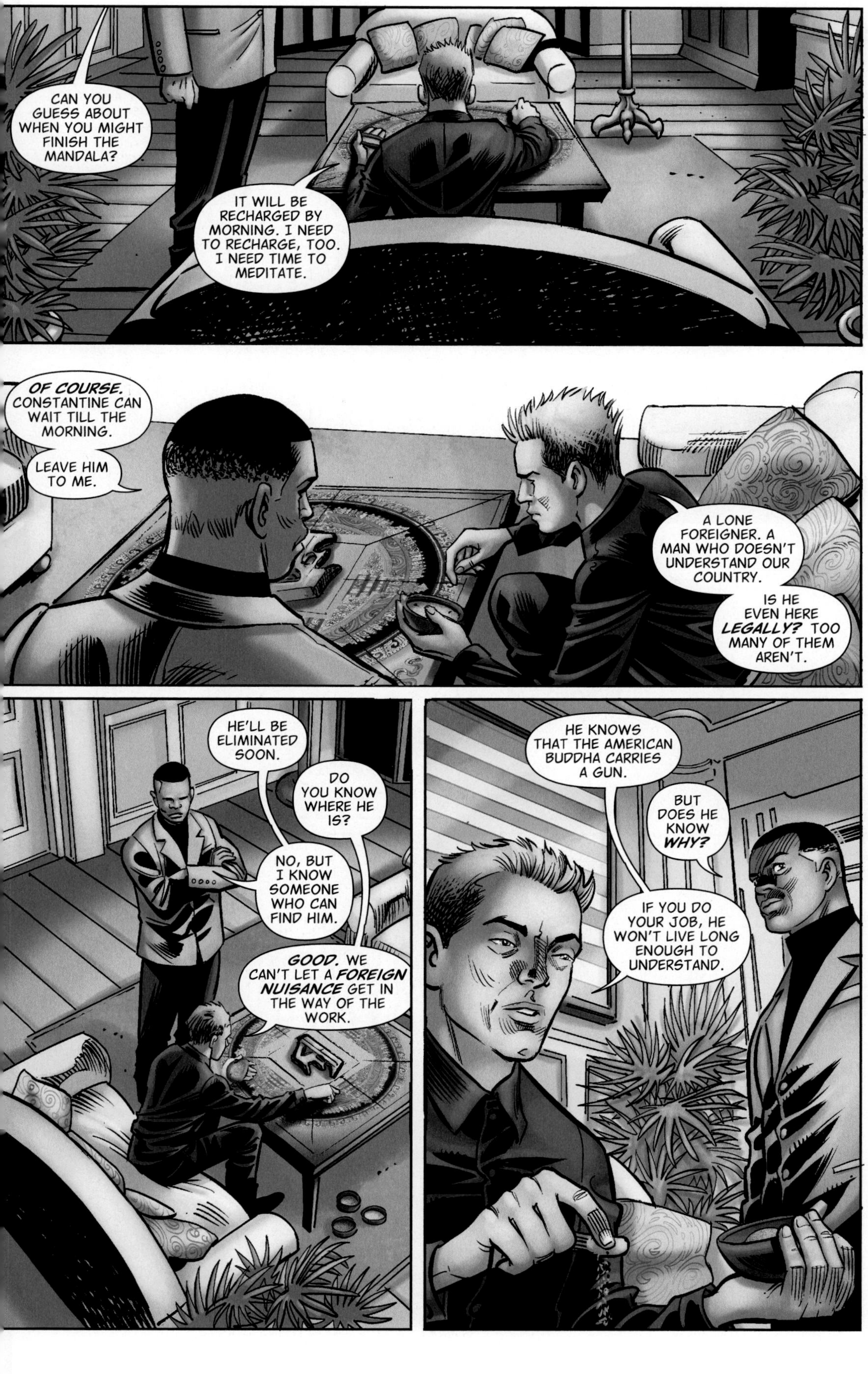
CAN YOU GUESS ABOUT WHEN YOU MIGHT FINISH THE MANDALA?
IT WILL BE RECHARGED BY MORNING. I NEED TO RECHARGE, TOO. I NEED TIME TO MEDITATE.
OF COURSE. CONSTANTINE CAN WAIT TILL THE MORNING.
LEAVE HIM TO ME.
A LONE FOREIGNER. A MAN WHO DOESN'T UNDERSTAND OUR COUNTRY.
IS HE EVEN HERE *LEGALLY?* TOO MANY OF THEM AREN'T.
HE'LL BE ELIMINATED SOON.
DO YOU KNOW WHERE HE IS?
NO, BUT I KNOW SOMEONE WHO CAN FIND HIM.
GOOD. WE CAN'T LET A *FOREIGN NUISANCE* GET IN THE WAY OF THE WORK.
HE KNOWS THAT THE AMERICAN BUDDHA CARRIES A GUN.
BUT DOES HE KNOW *WHY?*
IF YOU DO YOUR JOB, HE WON'T LIVE LONG ENOUGH TO UNDERSTAND.

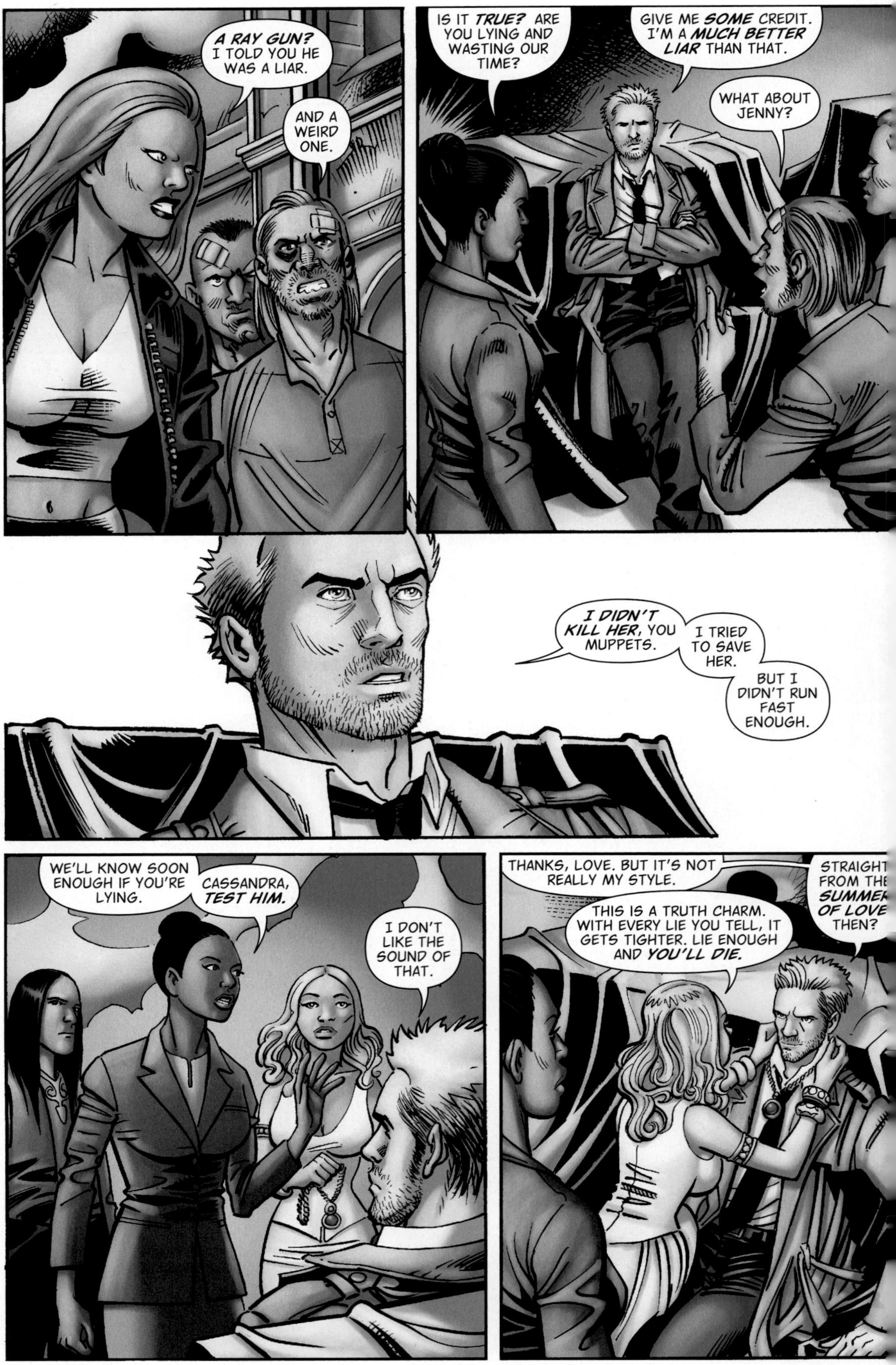
A RAY GUN? I TOLD YOU HE WAS A LIAR.
AND A WEIRD ONE.
IS IT TRUE? ARE YOU LYING AND WASTING OUR TIME?
GIVE ME SOME CREDIT. I'M A MUCH BETTER LIAR THAN THAT.
WHAT ABOUT JENNY?
I DIDN'T KILL HER, YOU MUPPETS.
I TRIED TO SAVE HER.
BUT I DIDN'T RUN FAST ENOUGH.
WE'LL KNOW SOON ENOUGH IF YOU'RE LYING.
CASSANDRA, TEST HIM.
I DON'T LIKE THE SOUND OF THAT.
THANKS, LOVE. BUT IT'S NOT REALLY MY STYLE.
STRAIGHT FROM THE SUMMER OF LOVE THEN?
THIS IS A TRUTH CHARM. WITH EVERY LIE YOU TELL, IT GETS TIGHTER. LIE ENOUGH AND YOU'LL DIE.

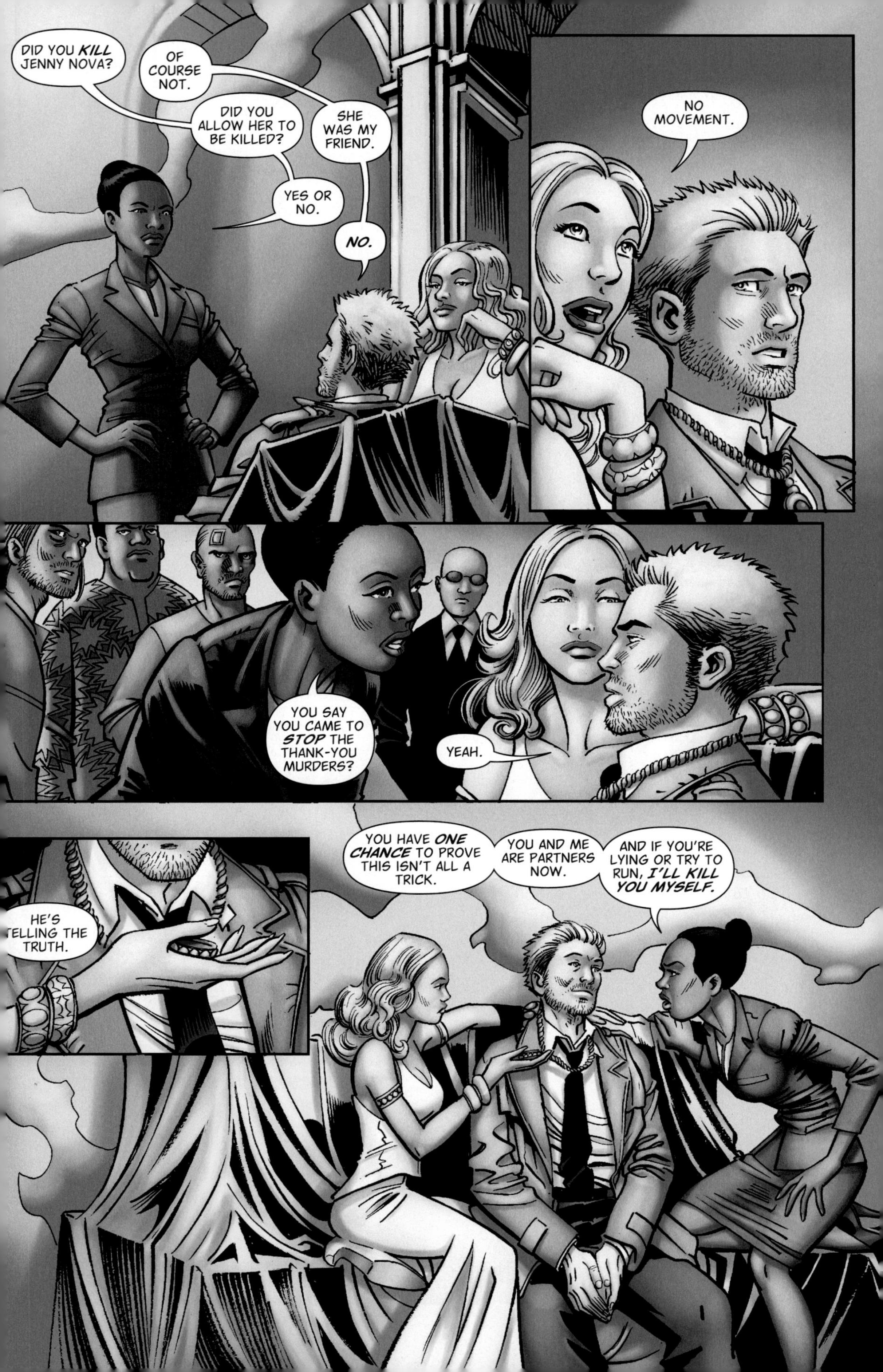
DID YOU KILL JENNY NOVA?
OF COURSE NOT.
DID YOU ALLOW HER TO BE KILLED?
SHE WAS MY FRIEND.
YES OR NO.
NO.
NO MOVEMENT.
YOU SAY YOU CAME TO STOP THE THANK-YOU MURDERS?
YEAH.
HE'S TELLING THE TRUTH.
YOU HAVE ONE CHANCE TO PROVE THIS ISN'T ALL A TRICK.
YOU AND ME ARE PARTNERS NOW.
AND IF YOU'RE LYING OR TRY TO RUN, I'LL KILL YOU MYSELF.

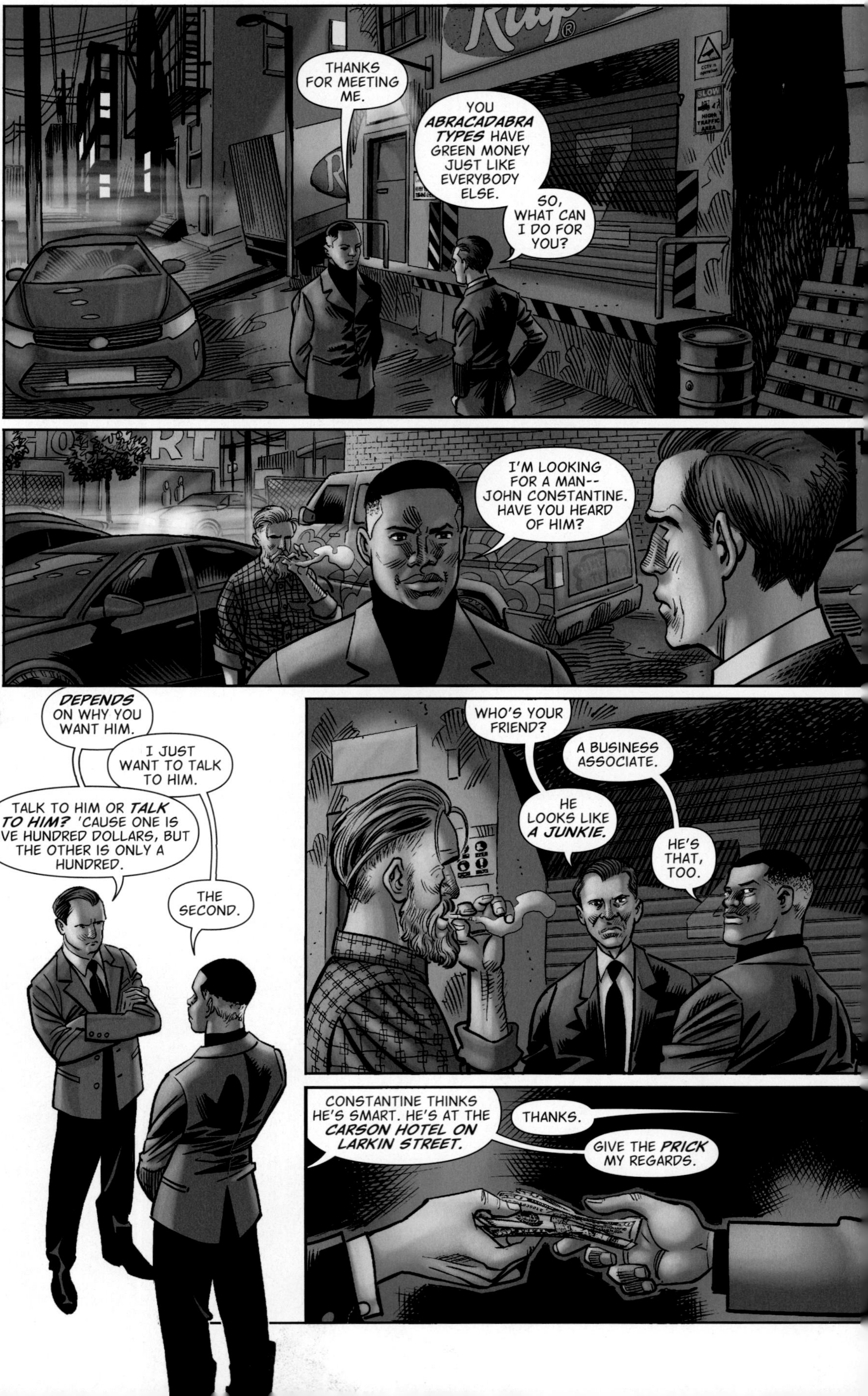
THANKS FOR MEETING ME.
YOU ABRACADABRA TYPES HAVE GREEN MONEY JUST LIKE EVERYBODY ELSE.
SO, WHAT CAN I DO FOR YOU?
I'M LOOKING FOR A MAN-- JOHN CONSTANTINE. HAVE YOU HEARD OF HIM?
DEPENDS ON WHY YOU WANT HIM.
I JUST WANT TO TALK TO HIM.
TALK TO HIM OR TALK TO HIM? 'CAUSE ONE IS FIVE HUNDRED DOLLARS, BUT THE OTHER IS ONLY A HUNDRED.
THE SECOND.
WHO'S YOUR FRIEND?
A BUSINESS ASSOCIATE.
HE LOOKS LIKE A JUNKIE.
HE'S THAT, TOO.
CONSTANTINE THINKS HE'S SMART. HE'S AT THE CARSON HOTEL ON LARKIN STREET.
THANKS.
GIVE THE PRICK MY REGARDS.

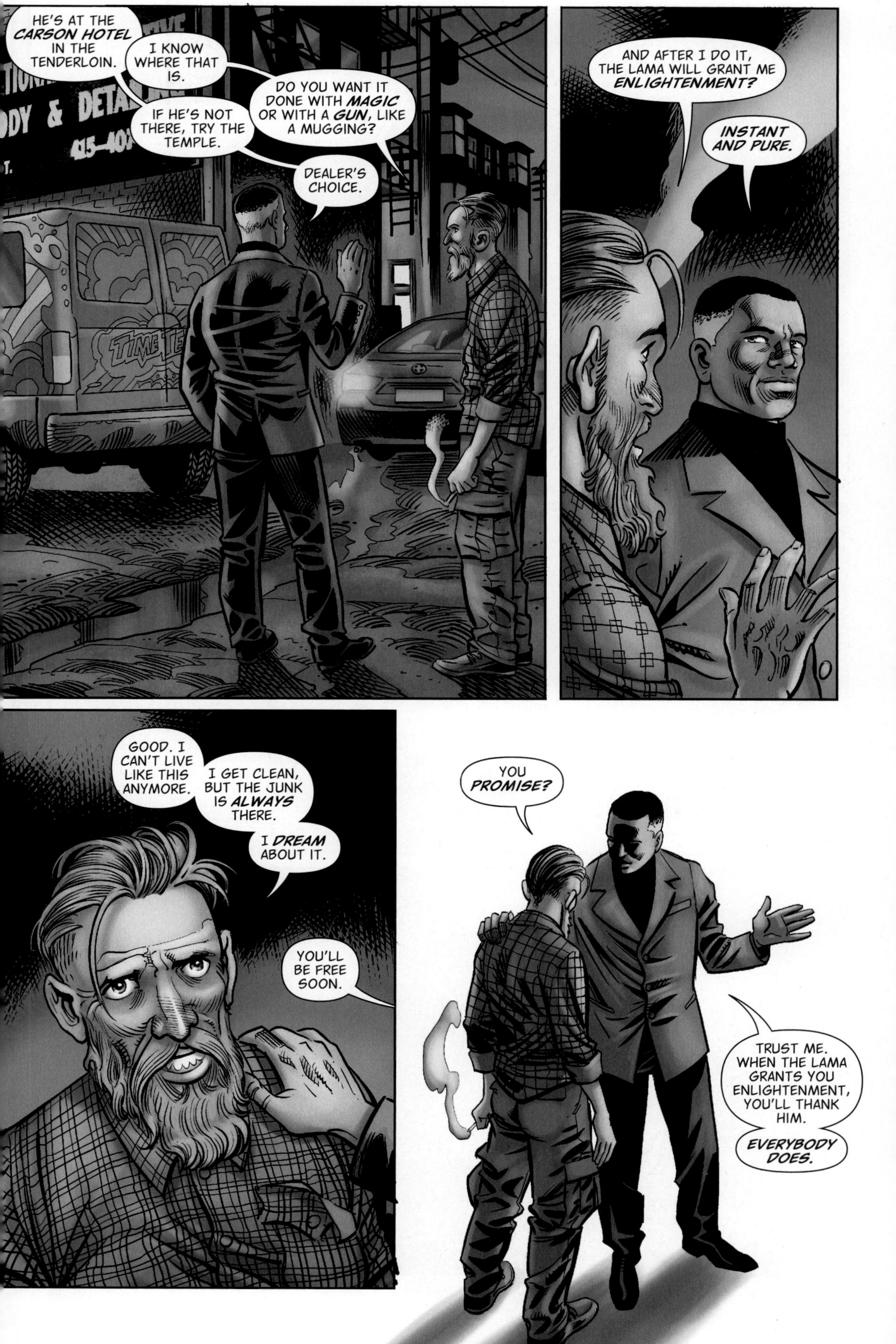
HE'S AT THE *CARSON HOTEL* IN THE TENDERLOIN.
I KNOW WHERE THAT IS.
IF HE'S NOT THERE, TRY THE TEMPLE.
DO YOU WANT IT DONE WITH *MAGIC* OR WITH A *GUN*, LIKE A MUGGING?
DEALER'S CHOICE.
AND AFTER I DO IT, THE LAMA WILL GRANT ME *ENLIGHTENMENT?*
INSTANT AND PURE.
GOOD. I CAN'T LIVE LIKE THIS ANYMORE.
I GET CLEAN, BUT THE JUNK IS *ALWAYS* THERE.
I *DREAM* ABOUT IT.
YOU'LL BE FREE SOON.
YOU *PROMISE?*
TRUST ME. WHEN THE LAMA GRANTS YOU ENLIGHTENMENT, YOU'LL THANK HIM.
EVERYBODY DOES.

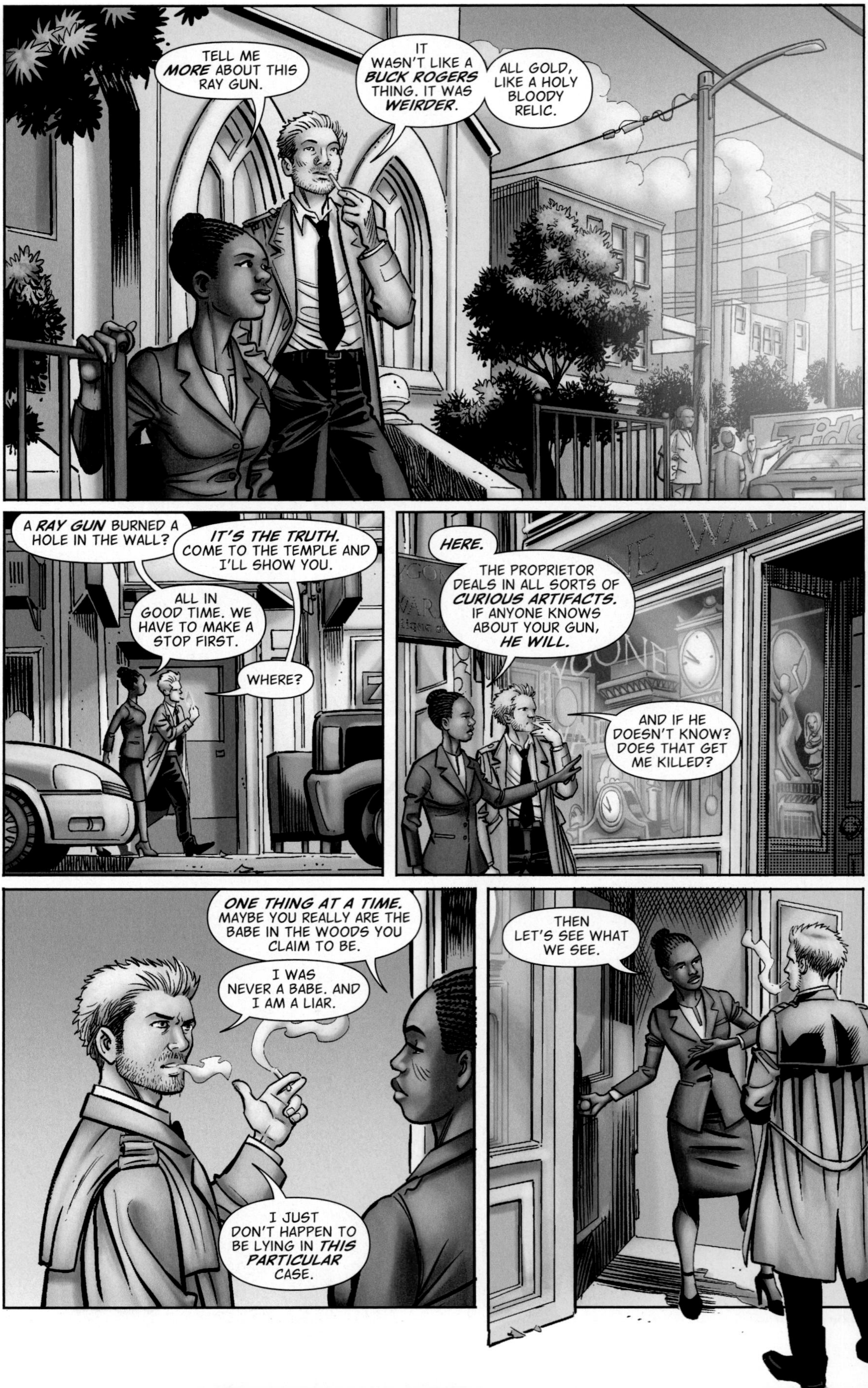
TELL ME MORE ABOUT THIS RAY GUN.
IT WASN'T LIKE A BUCK ROGERS THING. IT WAS WEIRDER.
ALL GOLD, LIKE A HOLY BLOODY RELIC.
A RAY GUN BURNED A HOLE IN THE WALL?
IT'S THE TRUTH. COME TO THE TEMPLE AND I'LL SHOW YOU.
ALL IN GOOD TIME. WE HAVE TO MAKE A STOP FIRST.
WHERE?
HERE.
THE PROPRIETOR DEALS IN ALL SORTS OF CURIOUS ARTIFACTS. IF ANYONE KNOWS ABOUT YOUR GUN, HE WILL.
AND IF HE DOESN'T KNOW? DOES THAT GET ME KILLED?
ONE THING AT A TIME. MAYBE YOU REALLY ARE THE BABE IN THE WOODS YOU CLAIM TO BE.
I WAS NEVER A BABE. AND I AM A LIAR.
I JUST DON'T HAPPEN TO BE LYING IN THIS PARTICULAR CASE.
THEN LET'S SEE WHAT WE SEE.

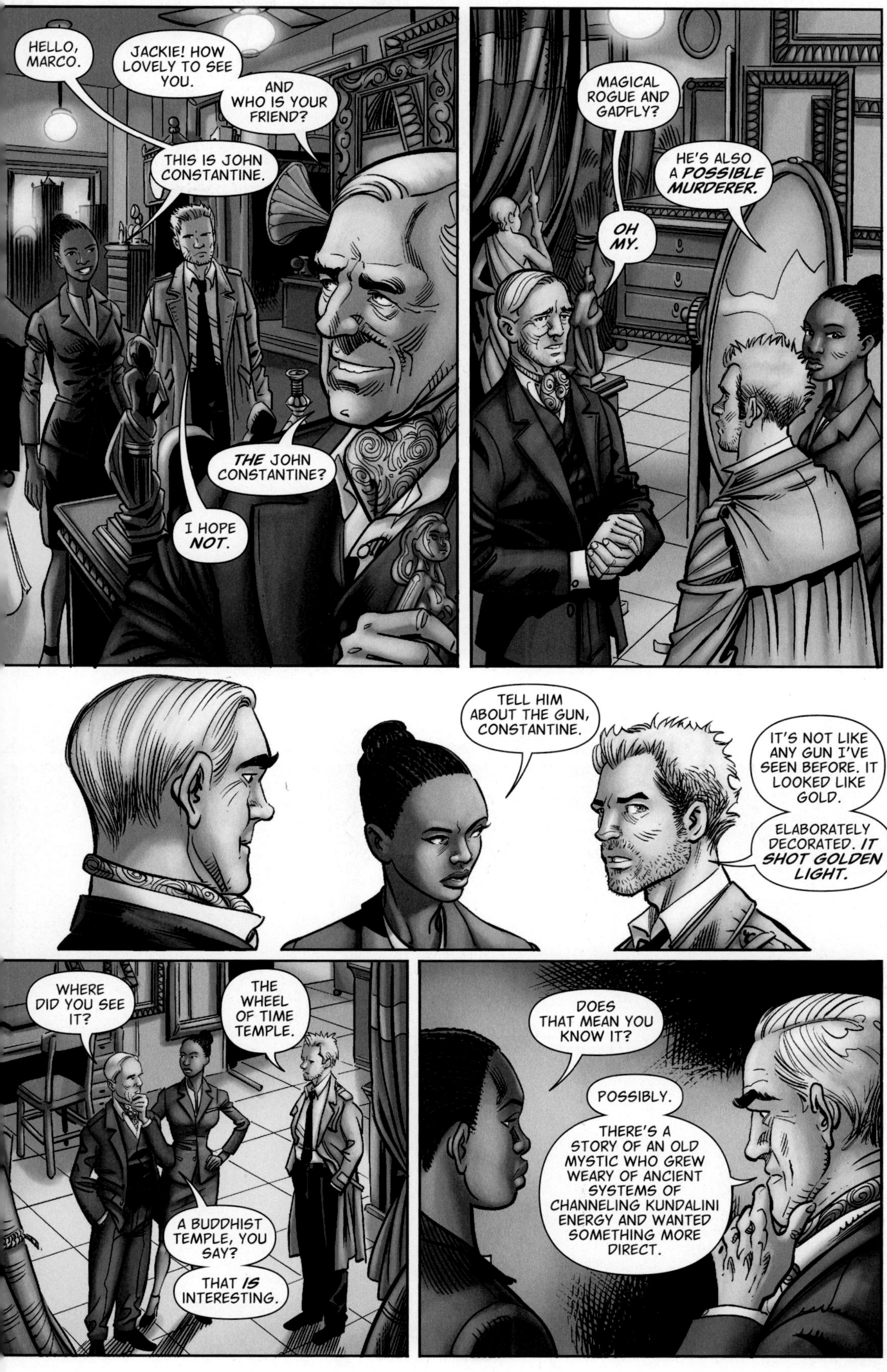
HELLO, MARCO.
JACKIE! HOW LOVELY TO SEE YOU.
AND WHO IS YOUR FRIEND?
THIS IS JOHN CONSTANTINE.
THE JOHN CONSTANTINE?
I HOPE *NOT*.
MAGICAL ROGUE AND GADFLY?
HE'S ALSO A *POSSIBLE MURDERER.*
OH MY.
TELL HIM ABOUT THE GUN, CONSTANTINE.
IT'S NOT LIKE ANY GUN I'VE SEEN BEFORE. IT LOOKED LIKE GOLD.
ELABORATELY DECORATED. *IT SHOT GOLDEN LIGHT.*
WHERE DID YOU SEE IT?
THE WHEEL OF TIME TEMPLE.
A BUDDHIST TEMPLE, YOU SAY?
THAT *IS* INTERESTING.
DOES THAT MEAN YOU KNOW IT?
POSSIBLY.
THERE'S A STORY OF AN OLD MYSTIC WHO GREW WEARY OF ANCIENT SYSTEMS OF CHANNELING KUNDALINI ENERGY AND WANTED SOMETHING MORE DIRECT.

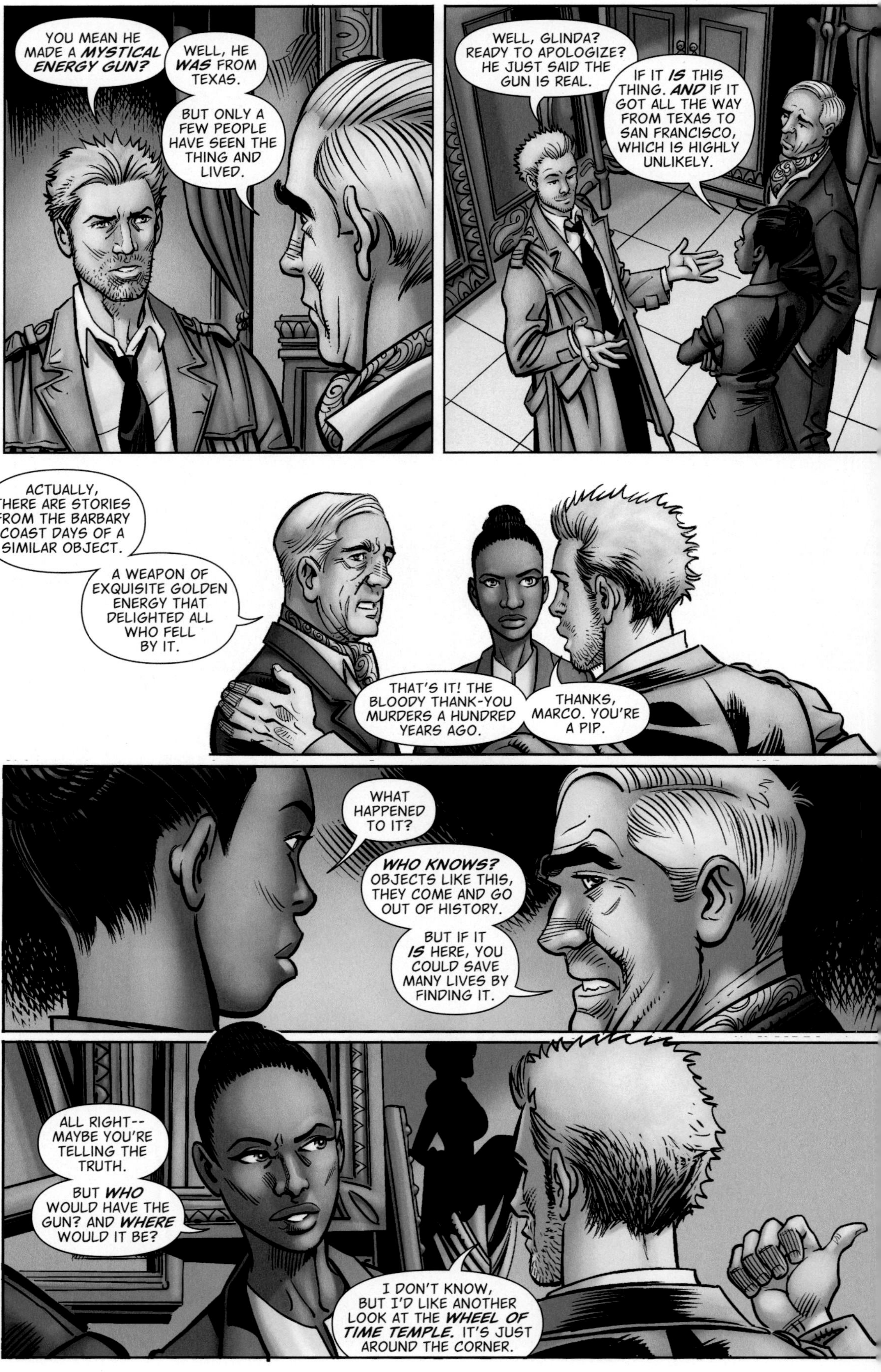
YOU MEAN HE MADE A *MYSTICAL ENERGY GUN?*
WELL, HE *WAS* FROM TEXAS.
BUT ONLY A FEW PEOPLE HAVE SEEN THE THING AND LIVED.
WELL, GLINDA? READY TO APOLOGIZE? HE JUST SAID THE GUN IS REAL.
IF IT *IS* THIS THING. *AND* IF IT GOT ALL THE WAY FROM TEXAS TO SAN FRANCISCO, WHICH IS HIGHLY UNLIKELY.
ACTUALLY, THERE ARE STORIES FROM THE BARBARY COAST DAYS OF A SIMILAR OBJECT.
A WEAPON OF EXQUISITE GOLDEN ENERGY THAT DELIGHTED ALL WHO FELL BY IT.
THAT'S IT! THE BLOODY THANK-YOU MURDERS A HUNDRED YEARS AGO.
THANKS, MARCO. YOU'RE A PIP.
WHAT HAPPENED TO IT?
WHO KNOWS? OBJECTS LIKE THIS, THEY COME AND GO OUT OF HISTORY.
BUT IF IT *IS* HERE, YOU COULD SAVE MANY LIVES BY FINDING IT.
ALL RIGHT-- MAYBE YOU'RE TELLING THE TRUTH.
BUT *WHO* WOULD HAVE THE GUN? AND *WHERE* WOULD IT BE?
I DON'T KNOW, BUT I'D LIKE ANOTHER LOOK AT THE *WHEEL OF TIME TEMPLE.* IT'S JUST AROUND THE CORNER.

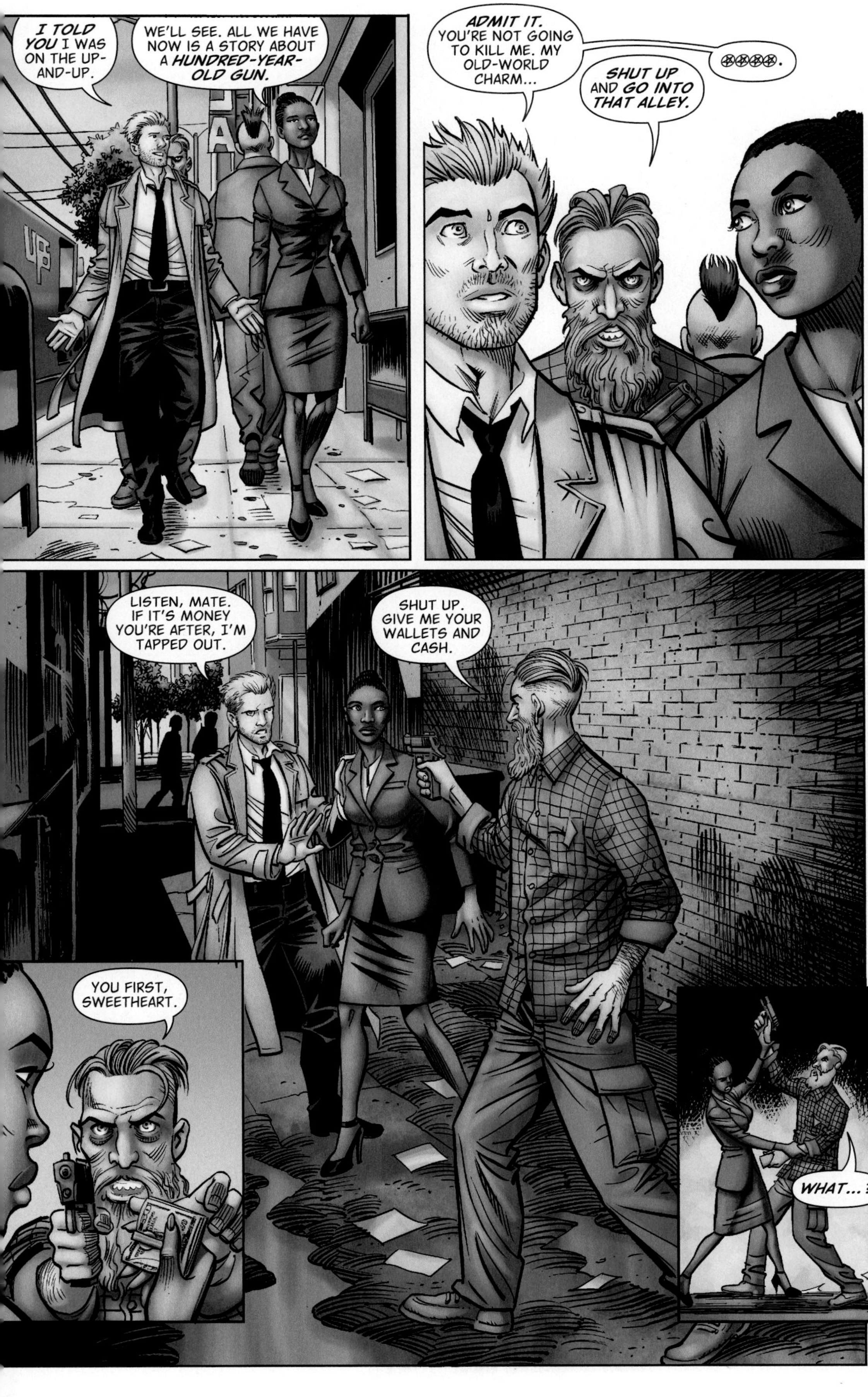

I TOLD YOU I WAS ON THE UP-AND-UP.
WE'LL SEE. ALL WE HAVE NOW IS A STORY ABOUT A HUNDRED-YEAR-OLD GUN.
ADMIT IT. YOU'RE NOT GOING TO KILL ME. MY OLD-WORLD CHARM...
SHUT UP AND GO INTO THAT ALLEY.
LISTEN, MATE. IF IT'S MONEY YOU'RE AFTER, I'M TAPPED OUT.
SHUT UP. GIVE ME YOUR WALLETS AND CASH.
YOU FIRST, SWEETHEART.
WHAT...?

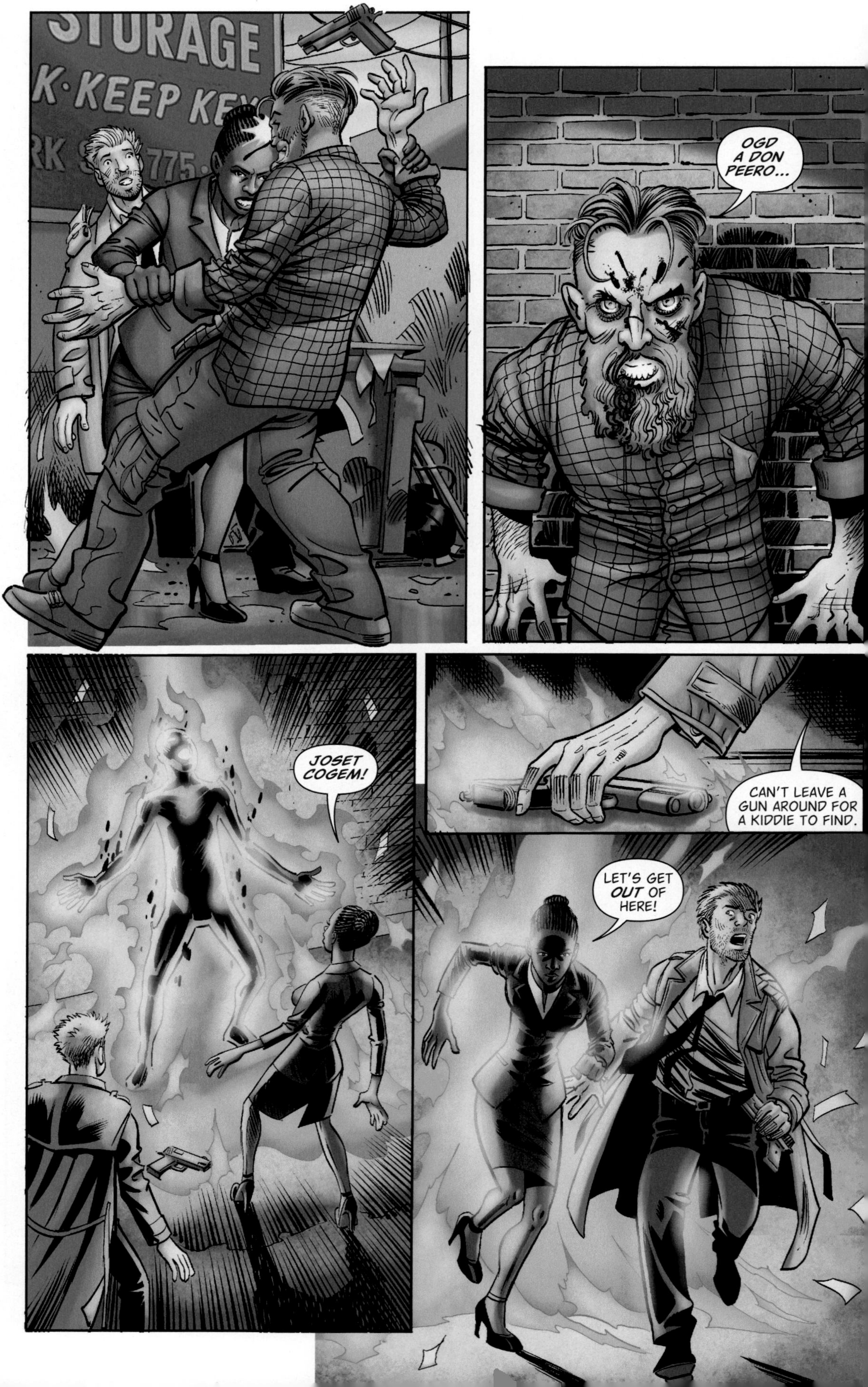
STORAGE
K·KEEP KE
OGD A DON PEERO...
JOSET COGEM!
CAN'T LEAVE A GUN AROUND FOR A KIDDIE TO FIND.
LET'S GET OUT OF HERE!

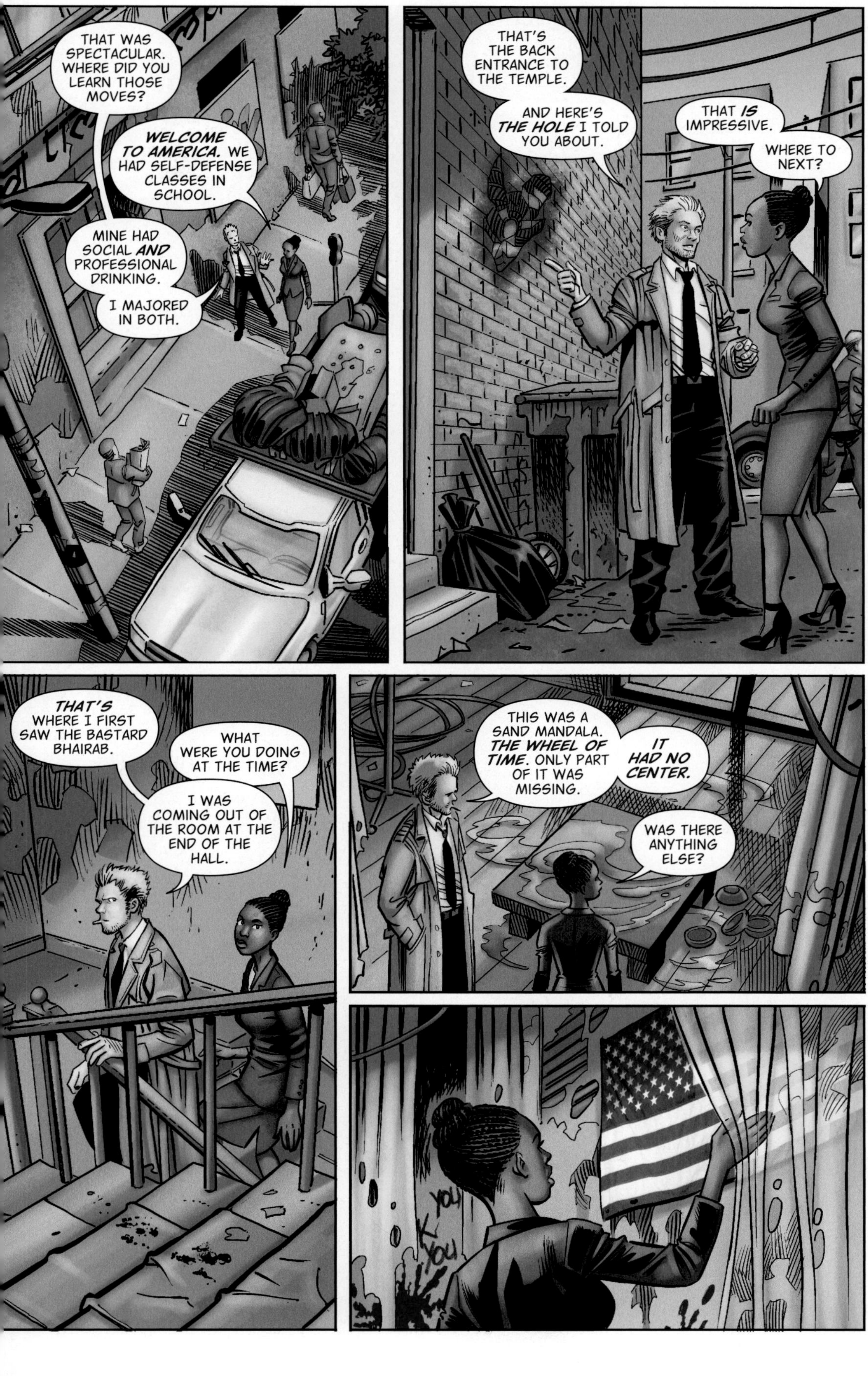
THAT WAS SPECTACULAR. WHERE DID YOU LEARN THOSE MOVES?
WELCOME TO AMERICA. WE HAD SELF-DEFENSE CLASSES IN SCHOOL.
MINE HAD SOCIAL **AND** PROFESSIONAL DRINKING.
I MAJORED IN BOTH.
THAT'S THE BACK ENTRANCE TO THE TEMPLE.
AND HERE'S **THE HOLE** I TOLD YOU ABOUT.
THAT **IS** IMPRESSIVE.
WHERE TO NEXT?
THAT'S WHERE I FIRST SAW THE BASTARD BHAIRAB.
WHAT WERE YOU DOING AT THE TIME?
I WAS COMING OUT OF THE ROOM AT THE END OF THE HALL.
THIS WAS A SAND MANDALA. **THE WHEEL OF TIME.** ONLY PART OF IT WAS MISSING.
IT HAD NO CENTER.
WAS THERE ANYTHING ELSE?

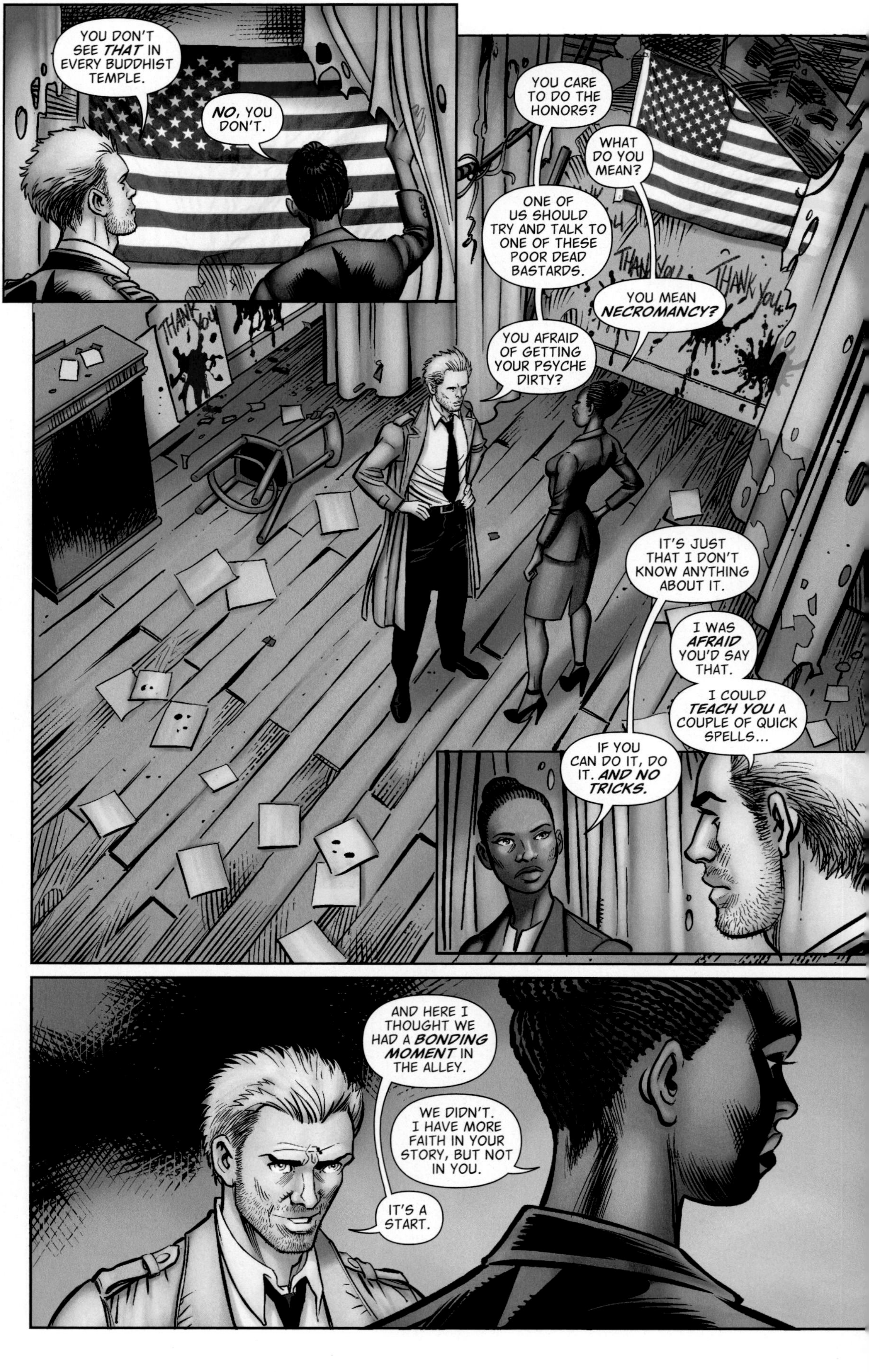
YOU DON'T SEE THAT IN EVERY BUDDHIST TEMPLE.
NO, YOU DON'T.
YOU CARE TO DO THE HONORS?
WHAT DO YOU MEAN?
ONE OF US SHOULD TRY AND TALK TO ONE OF THESE POOR DEAD BASTARDS.
YOU MEAN NECROMANCY?
YOU AFRAID OF GETTING YOUR PSYCHE DIRTY?
THANK YOU
IT'S JUST THAT I DON'T KNOW ANYTHING ABOUT IT.
I WAS AFRAID YOU'D SAY THAT.
I COULD TEACH YOU A COUPLE OF QUICK SPELLS...
IF YOU CAN DO IT, DO IT. AND NO TRICKS.
AND HERE I THOUGHT WE HAD A BONDING MOMENT IN THE ALLEY.
WE DIDN'T. I HAVE MORE FAITH IN YOUR STORY, BUT NOT IN YOU.
IT'S A START.

PING

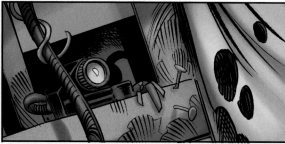

DAMMIT. LEONARD SCREWED UP.

CONSTANTINE IS IN THE TEMPLE. WE HAVE TO STOP HIM.

I HAVE AN *IDEA.*

CALL YOUR POLICEMAN FRIEND. HAVE HIM MEET US THERE.

YOU WANT TO ARREST HIM?

ARE YOU *QUESTIONING* ME?

NO, BUT...

CALL THE POLICEMAN.

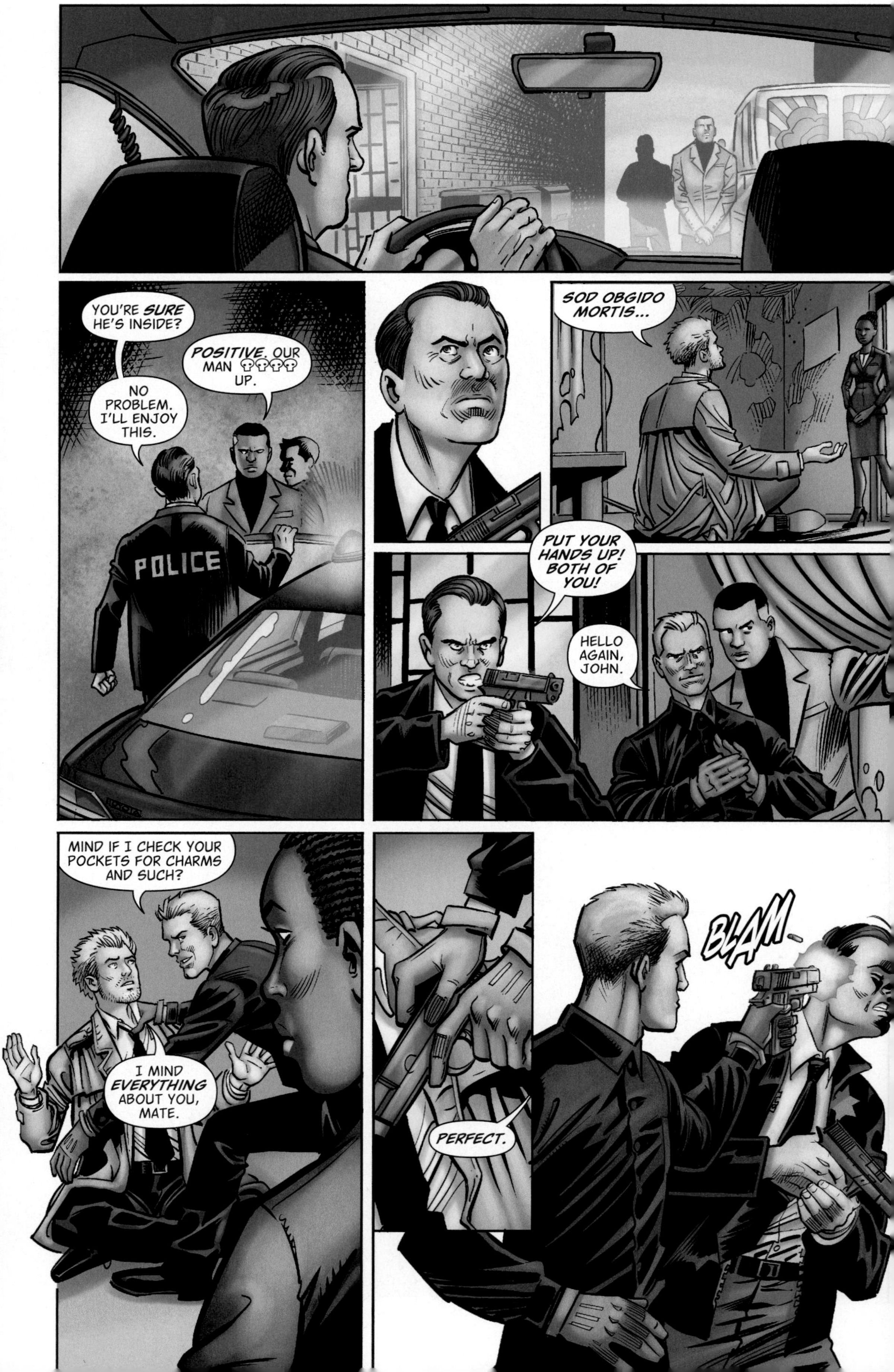

YOU'RE SURE HE'S INSIDE?
POSITIVE. OUR MAN ☠☠☠☠ UP.
NO PROBLEM. I'LL ENJOY THIS.
POLICE
SOD OBGIDO MORTIS...
PUT YOUR HANDS UP! BOTH OF YOU!
HELLO AGAIN, JOHN.
MIND IF I CHECK YOUR POCKETS FOR CHARMS AND SUCH?
I MIND EVERYTHING ABOUT YOU, MATE.
PERFECT.
BLAM

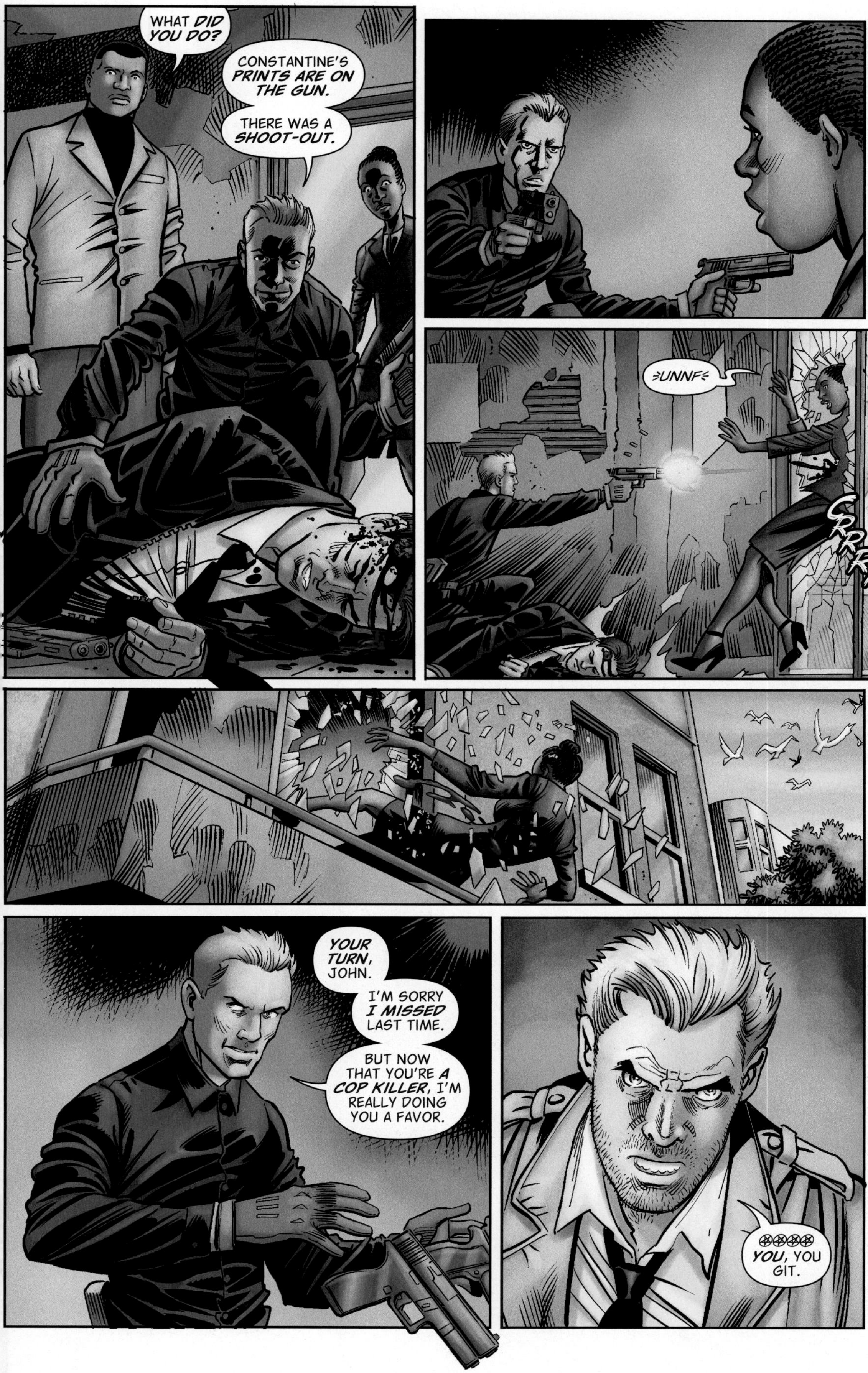
WHAT DID YOU DO?
CONSTANTINE'S PRINTS ARE ON THE GUN.
THERE WAS A SHOOT-OUT.
UNNF
CRRRK
YOUR TURN, JOHN.
I'M SORRY I MISSED LAST TIME.
BUT NOW THAT YOU'RE A COP KILLER, I'M REALLY DOING YOU A FAVOR.
YOU, YOU GIT.

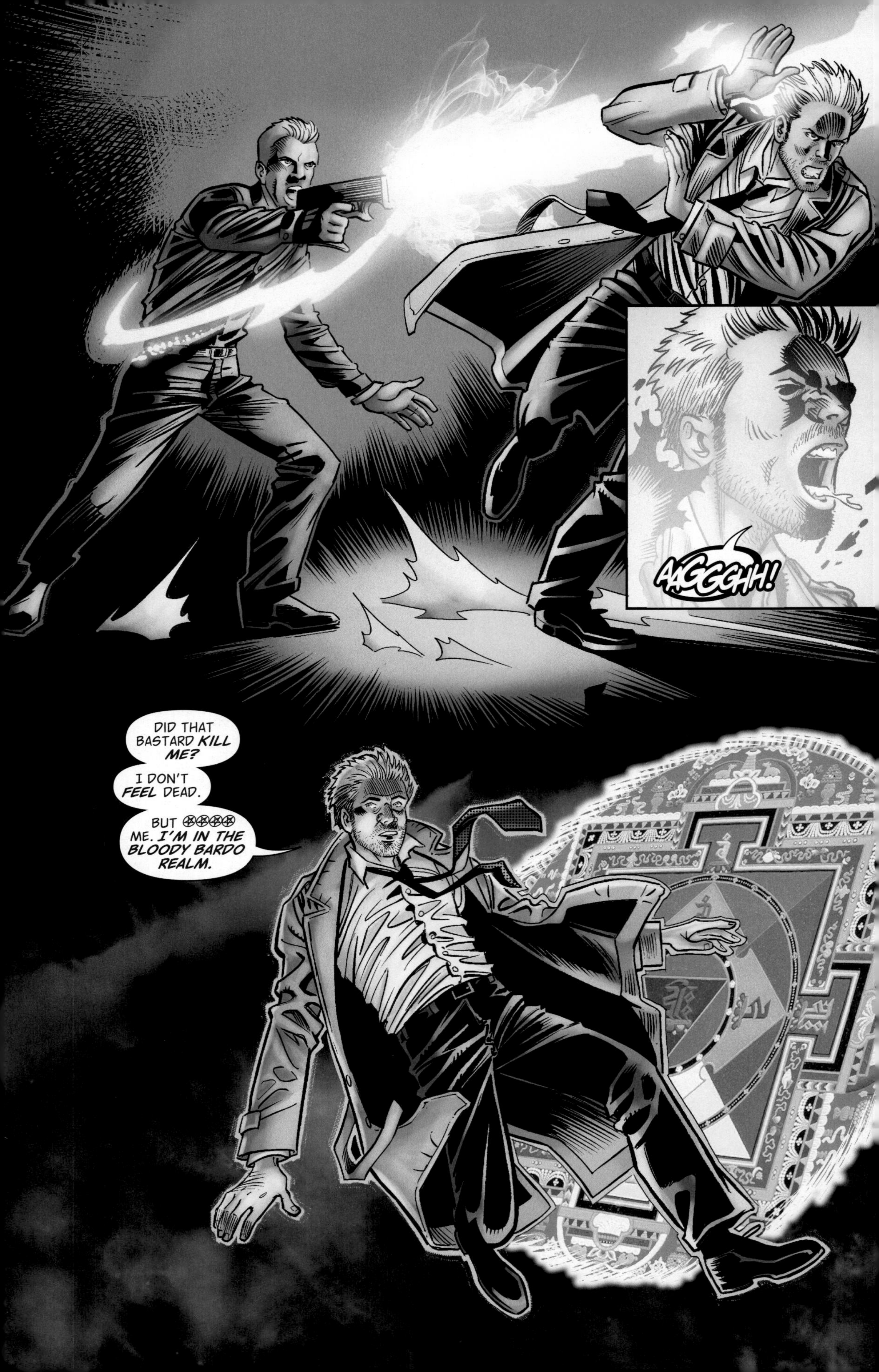
AAGGGHH!
DID THAT BASTARD KILL ME?
I DON'T FEEL DEAD.
BUT ✪✪✪✪ ME. I'M IN THE BLOODY BARDO REALM.

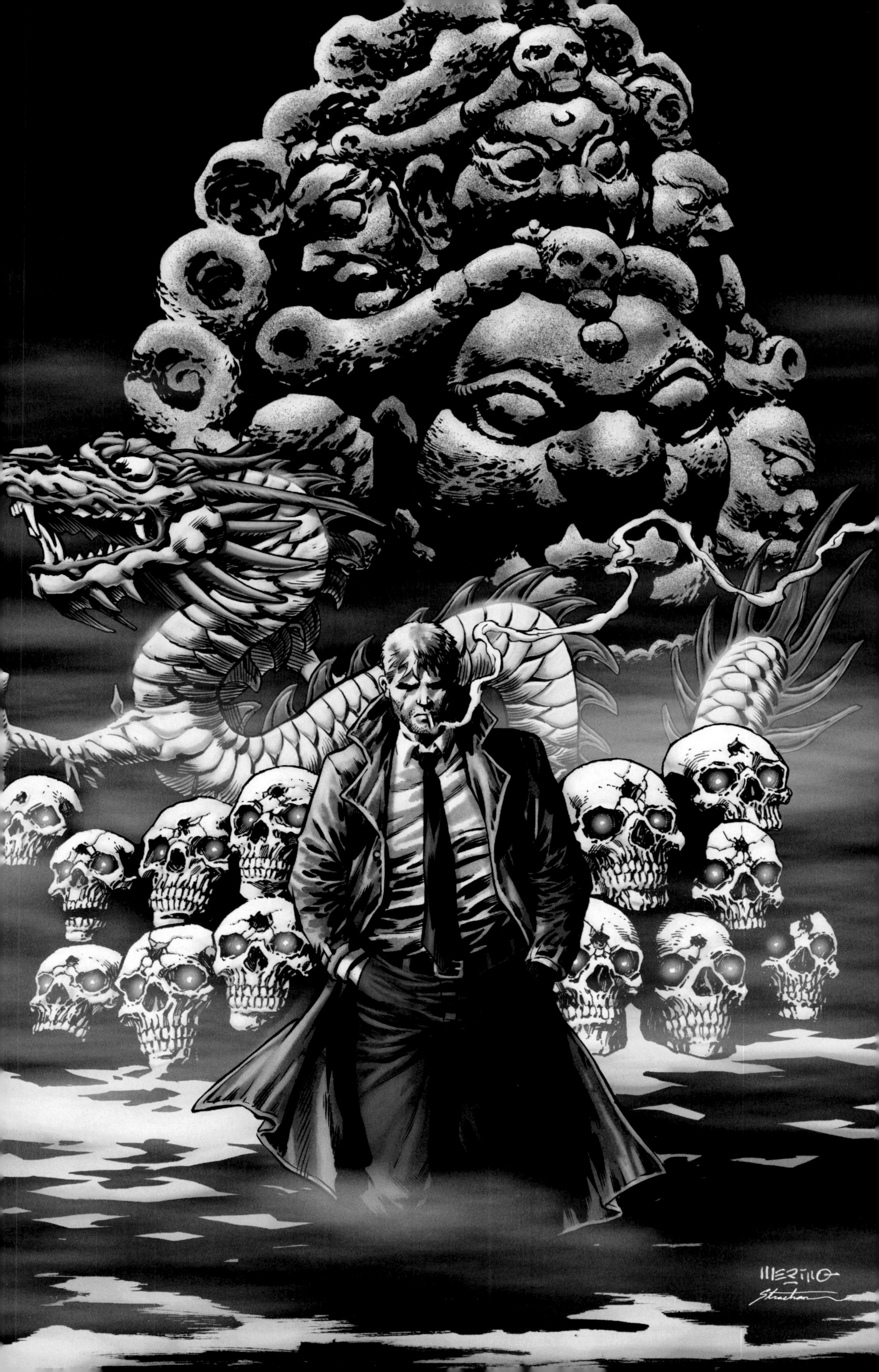

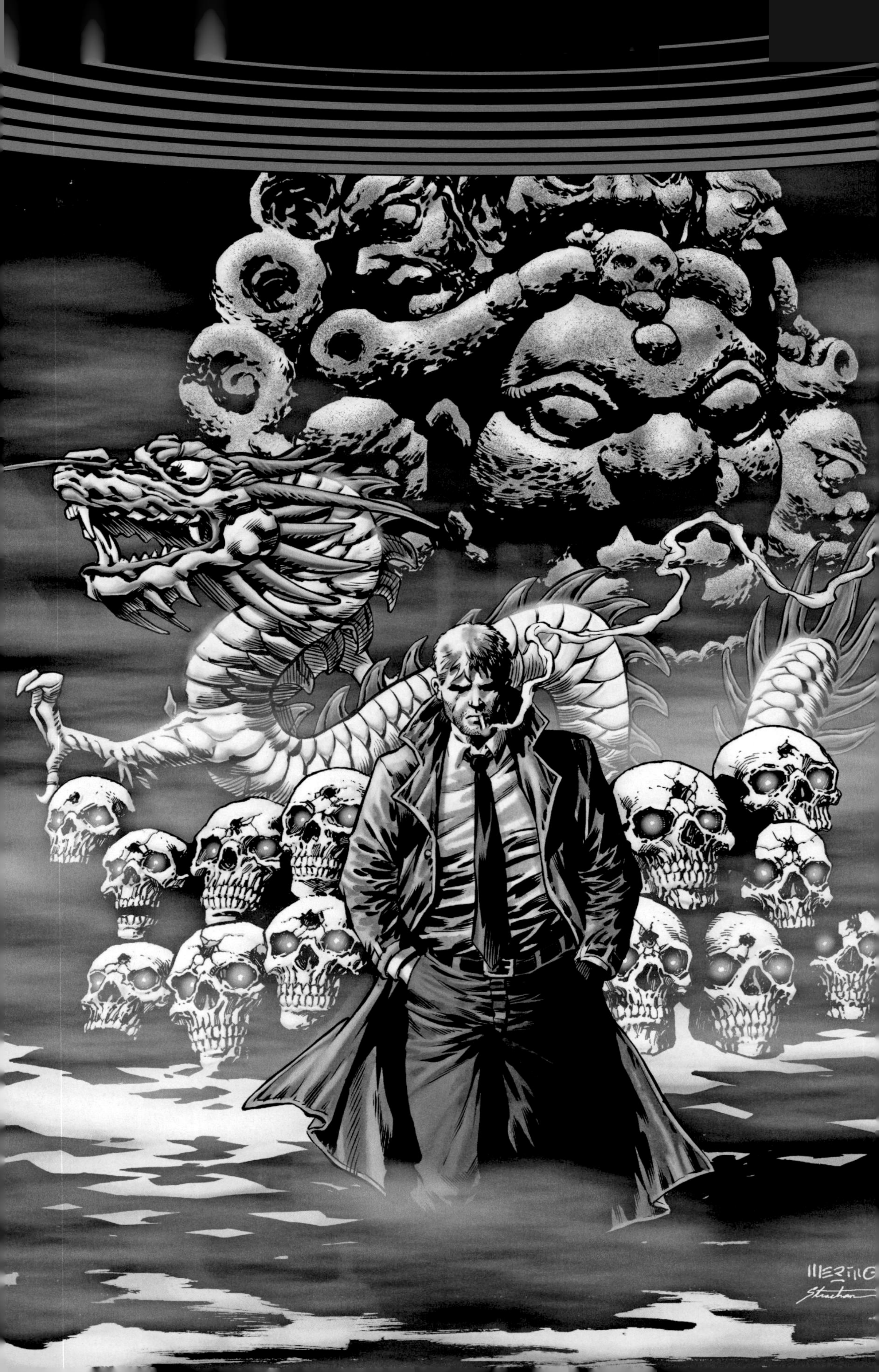

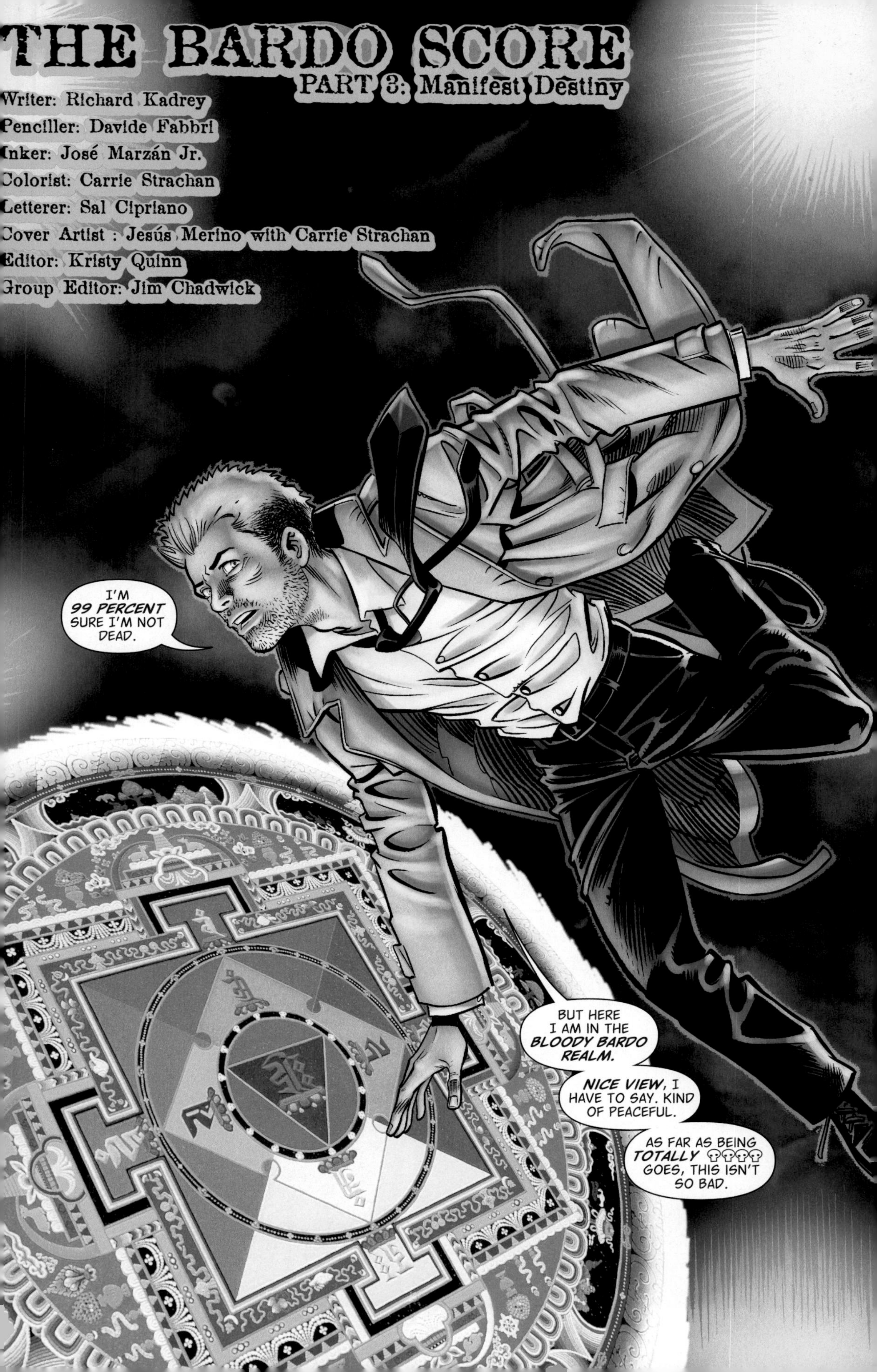
THE BARDO SCORE
PART 3: Manifest Destiny
Writer: Richard Kadrey
Penciller: Davide Fabbri
Inker: José Marzán Jr.
Colorist: Carrie Strachan
Letterer: Sal Cipriano
Cover Artist : Jesús Merino with Carrie Strachan
Editor: Kristy Quinn
Group Editor: Jim Chadwick
I'M 99 PERCENT SURE I'M NOT DEAD.
BUT HERE I AM IN THE BLOODY BARDO REALM.
NICE VIEW, I HAVE TO SAY. KIND OF PEACEFUL.
AS FAR AS BEING TOTALLY GOES, THIS ISN'T SO BAD.

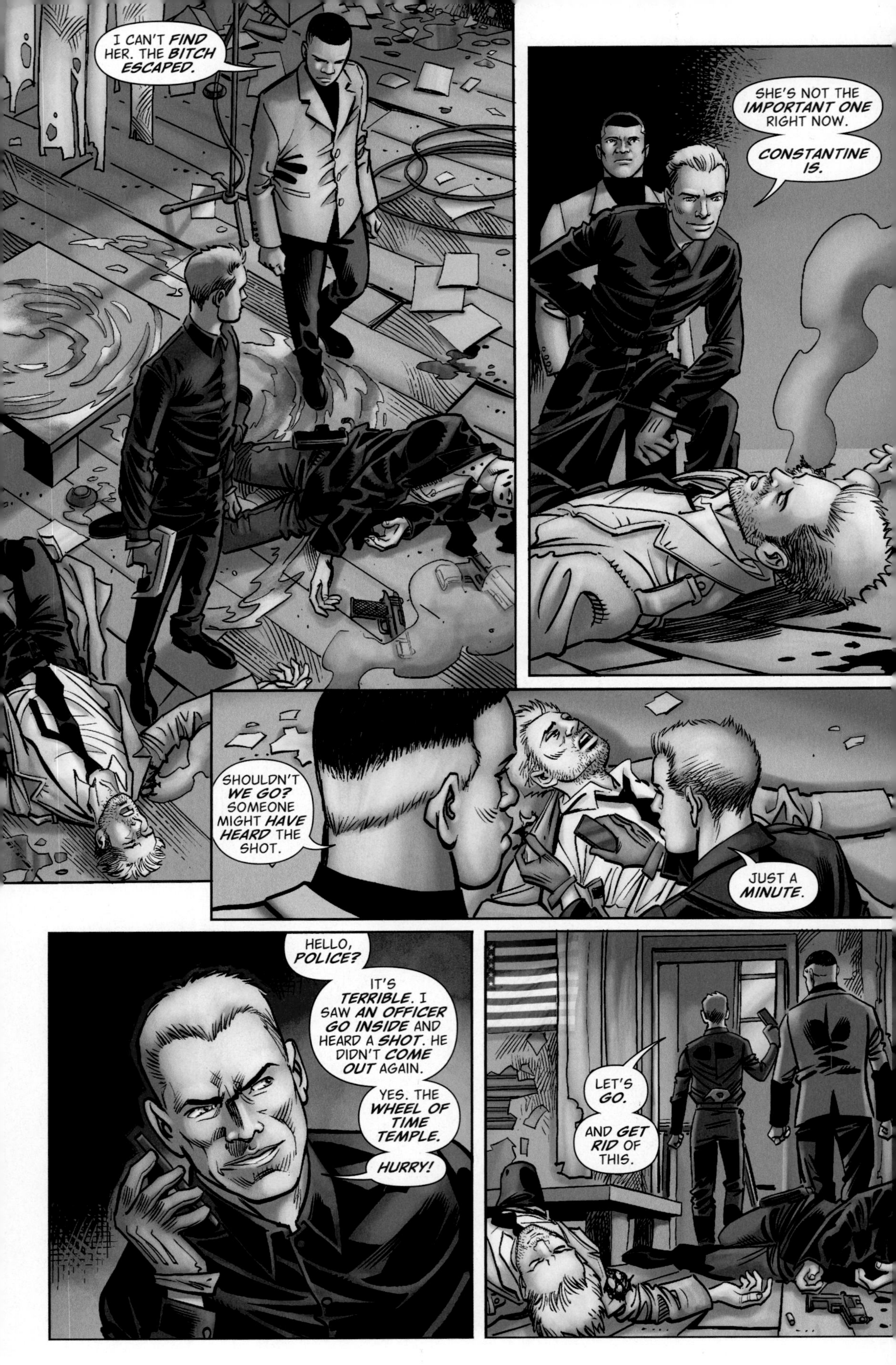

I CAN'T FIND HER. THE BITCH ESCAPED.
SHE'S NOT THE IMPORTANT ONE RIGHT NOW.
CONSTANTINE IS.
SHOULDN'T WE GO? SOMEONE MIGHT HAVE HEARD THE SHOT.
JUST A MINUTE.
HELLO, POLICE?
IT'S TERRIBLE. I SAW AN OFFICER GO INSIDE AND HEARD A SHOT. HE DIDN'T COME OUT AGAIN.
YES. THE WHEEL OF TIME TEMPLE.
HURRY!
LET'S GO.
AND GET RID OF THIS.

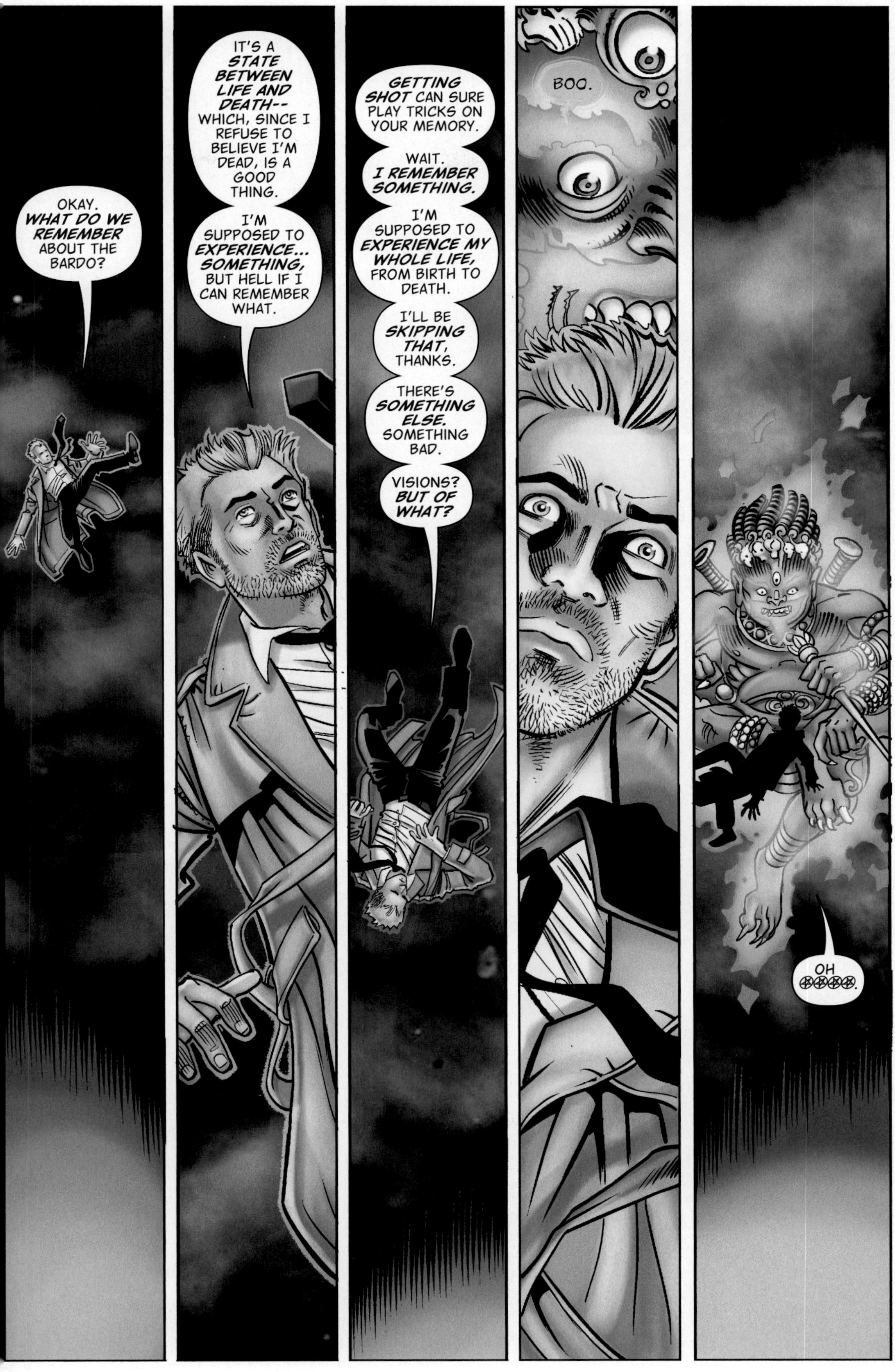

OKAY. WHAT DO WE REMEMBER ABOUT THE BARDO?
IT'S A STATE BETWEEN LIFE AND DEATH-- WHICH, SINCE I REFUSE TO BELIEVE I'M DEAD, IS A GOOD THING.
I'M SUPPOSED TO EXPERIENCE... SOMETHING, BUT HELL IF I CAN REMEMBER WHAT.
GETTING SHOT CAN SURE PLAY TRICKS ON YOUR MEMORY.
WAIT. I REMEMBER SOMETHING.
I'M SUPPOSED TO EXPERIENCE MY WHOLE LIFE, FROM BIRTH TO DEATH.
I'LL BE SKIPPING THAT, THANKS.
THERE'S SOMETHING ELSE. SOMETHING BAD.
VISIONS? BUT OF WHAT?
BOO.
OH ✠✠✠✠.

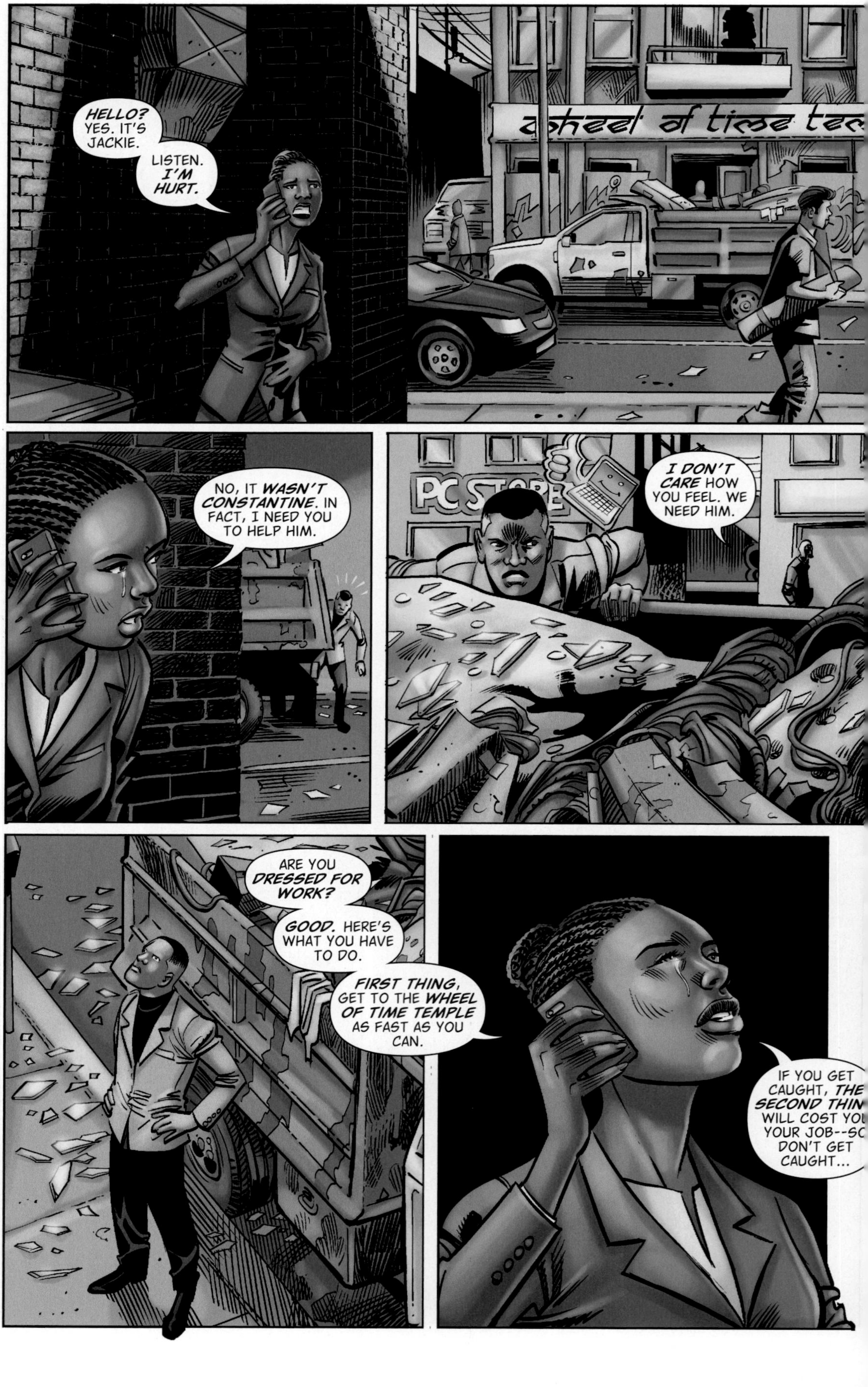
HELLO? YES. IT'S JACKIE.
LISTEN. I'M HURT.
wheel of time te
NO, IT WASN'T CONSTANTINE. IN FACT, I NEED YOU TO HELP HIM.
PC STORE
I DON'T CARE HOW YOU FEEL. WE NEED HIM.
ARE YOU DRESSED FOR WORK?
GOOD. HERE'S WHAT YOU HAVE TO DO.
FIRST THING, GET TO THE WHEEL OF TIME TEMPLE AS FAST AS YOU CAN.
IF YOU GET CAUGHT, THE SECOND THIN WILL COST YO YOUR JOB--SO DON'T GET CAUGHT...

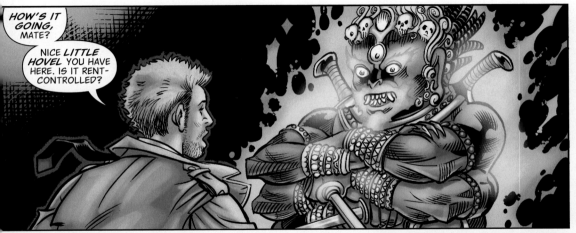

HOW'S IT GOING, MATE?

NICE *LITTLE HOVEL* YOU HAVE HERE. IS IT RENT-CONTROLLED?

GRRRWWL!

LISTEN--I RESPECT THAT YOU HAVE A JOB TO DO, BUT YOU'RE *BARKING UP THE WRONG SOUL.*

I WILL REND THE PUTREFYING FLESH FROM YOUR BONES!

GIVE IT A GO, IF YOU LIKE. I DON'T MIND.

JUST WATCH *ME NETHERS.* I'M A BIT ATTACHED TO THOSE.

YOU'RE TAKING THIS A LOT BETTER THAN MOST PEOPLE.

REALLY? WHERE WAS THAT?

THERE'S A REASON FOR THAT. *YOU AND ME, WE'VE MET BEFORE.*

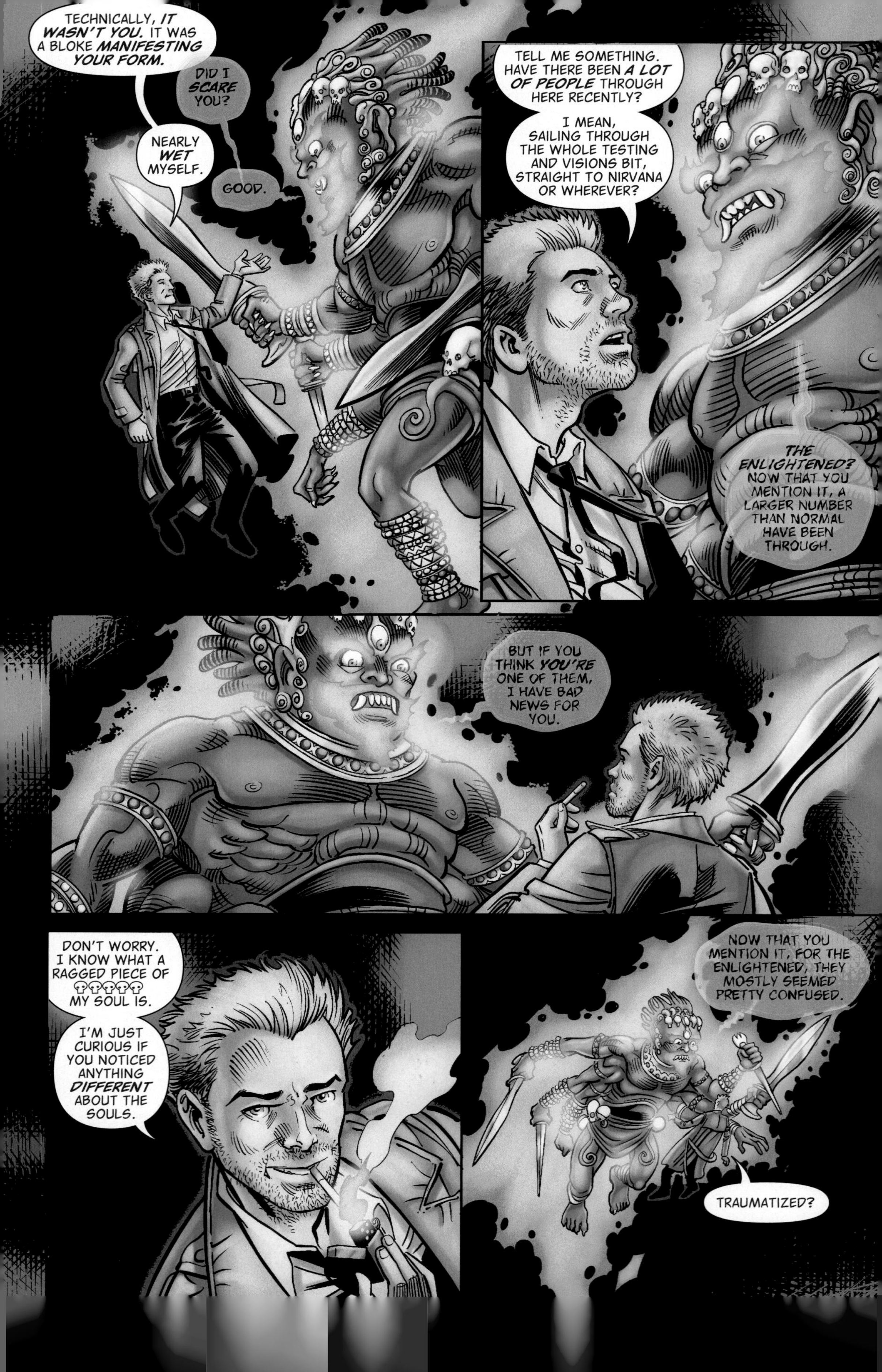
TECHNICALLY, IT WASN'T YOU. IT WAS A BLOKE MANIFESTING YOUR FORM.
DID I SCARE YOU?
NEARLY WET MYSELF.
GOOD.
TELL ME SOMETHING. HAVE THERE BEEN A LOT OF PEOPLE THROUGH HERE RECENTLY?
I MEAN, SAILING THROUGH THE WHOLE TESTING AND VISIONS BIT, STRAIGHT TO NIRVANA OR WHEREVER?
THE ENLIGHTENED? NOW THAT YOU MENTION IT, A LARGER NUMBER THAN NORMAL HAVE BEEN THROUGH.
BUT IF YOU THINK YOU'RE ONE OF THEM, I HAVE BAD NEWS FOR YOU.
DON'T WORRY. I KNOW WHAT A RAGGED PIECE OF MY SOUL IS.
I'M JUST CURIOUS IF YOU NOTICED ANYTHING DIFFERENT ABOUT THE SOULS.
NOW THAT YOU MENTION IT, FOR THE ENLIGHTENED, THEY MOSTLY SEEMED PRETTY CONFUSED.
TRAUMATIZED?

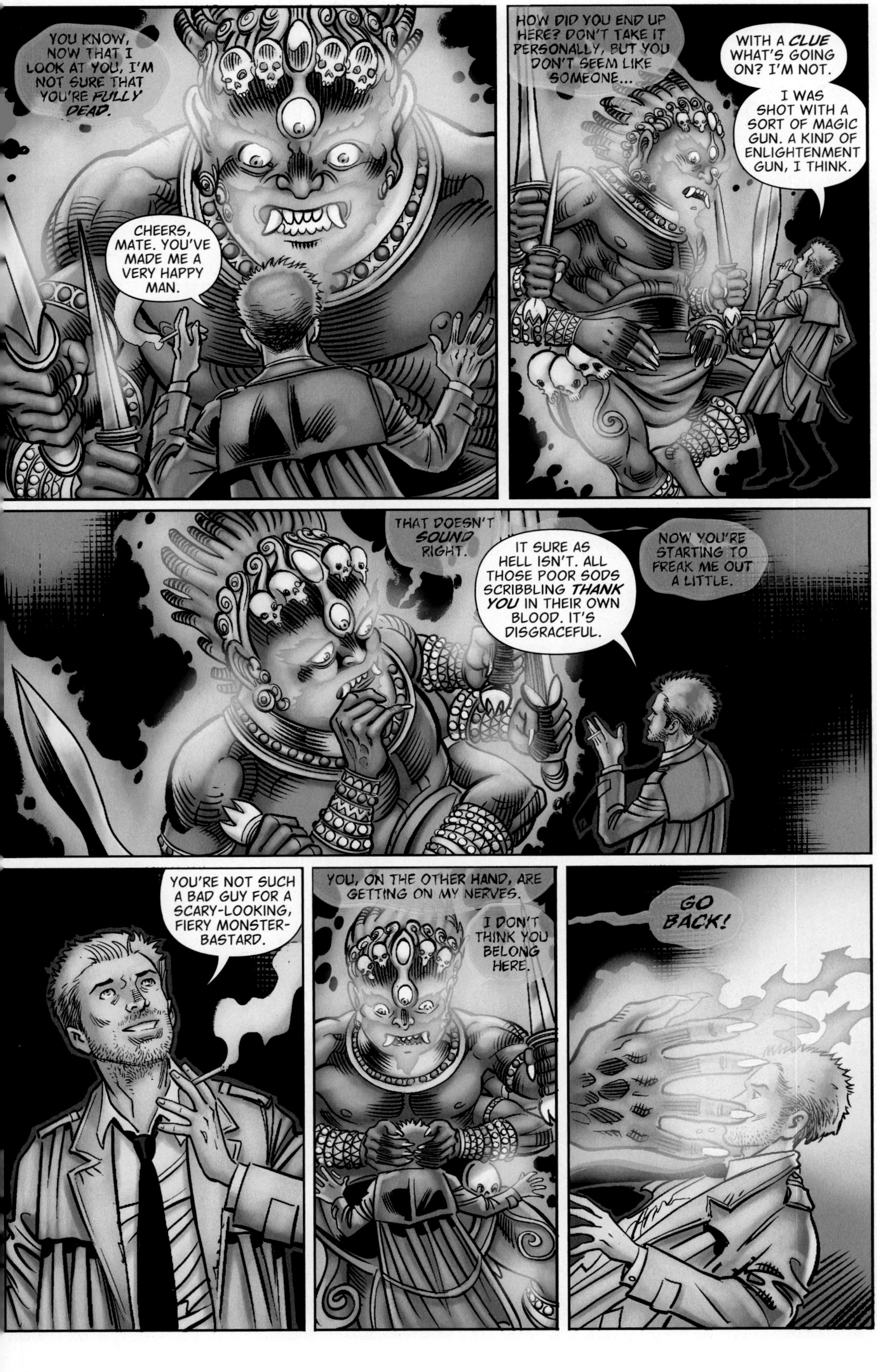
YOU KNOW, NOW THAT I LOOK AT YOU, I'M NOT SURE THAT YOU'RE FULLY DEAD.
CHEERS, MATE. YOU'VE MADE ME A VERY HAPPY MAN.
HOW DID YOU END UP HERE? DON'T TAKE IT PERSONALLY, BUT YOU DON'T SEEM LIKE SOMEONE...
WITH A CLUE WHAT'S GOING ON? I'M NOT.
I WAS SHOT WITH A SORT OF MAGIC GUN. A KIND OF ENLIGHTENMENT GUN, I THINK.
THAT DOESN'T SOUND RIGHT.
IT SURE AS HELL ISN'T. ALL THOSE POOR SODS SCRIBBLING THANK YOU IN THEIR OWN BLOOD. IT'S DISGRACEFUL.
NOW YOU'RE STARTING TO FREAK ME OUT A LITTLE.
YOU'RE NOT SUCH A BAD GUY FOR A SCARY-LOOKING, FIERY MONSTER-BASTARD.
YOU, ON THE OTHER HAND, ARE GETTING ON MY NERVES.
I DON'T THINK YOU BELONG HERE.
GO BACK!

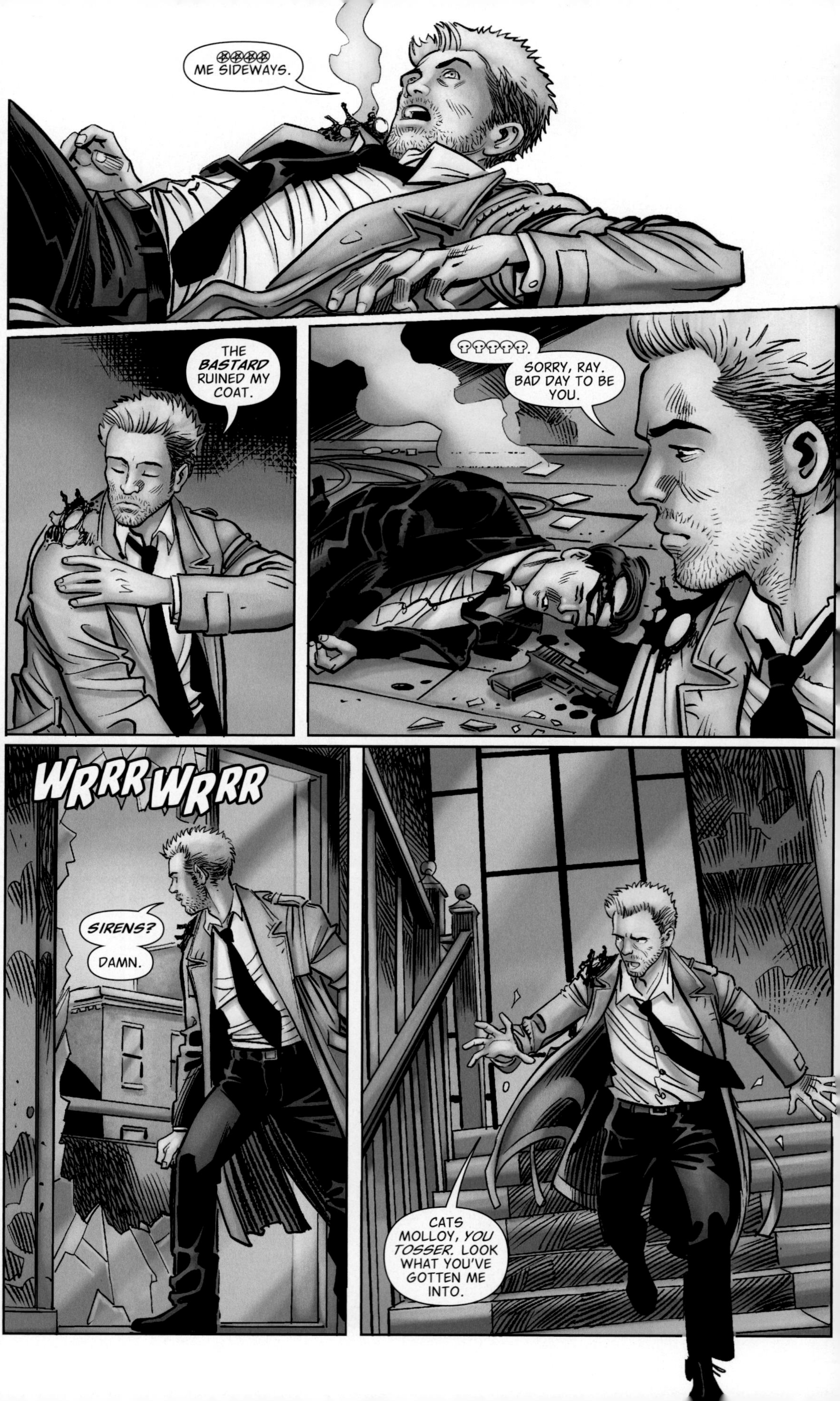
ME SIDEWAYS.
THE BASTARD RUINED MY COAT.
SORRY, RAY. BAD DAY TO BE YOU.
WRRR WRRR
SIRENS?
DAMN.
CATS MOLLOY, YOU TOSSER. LOOK WHAT YOU'VE GOTTEN ME INTO.

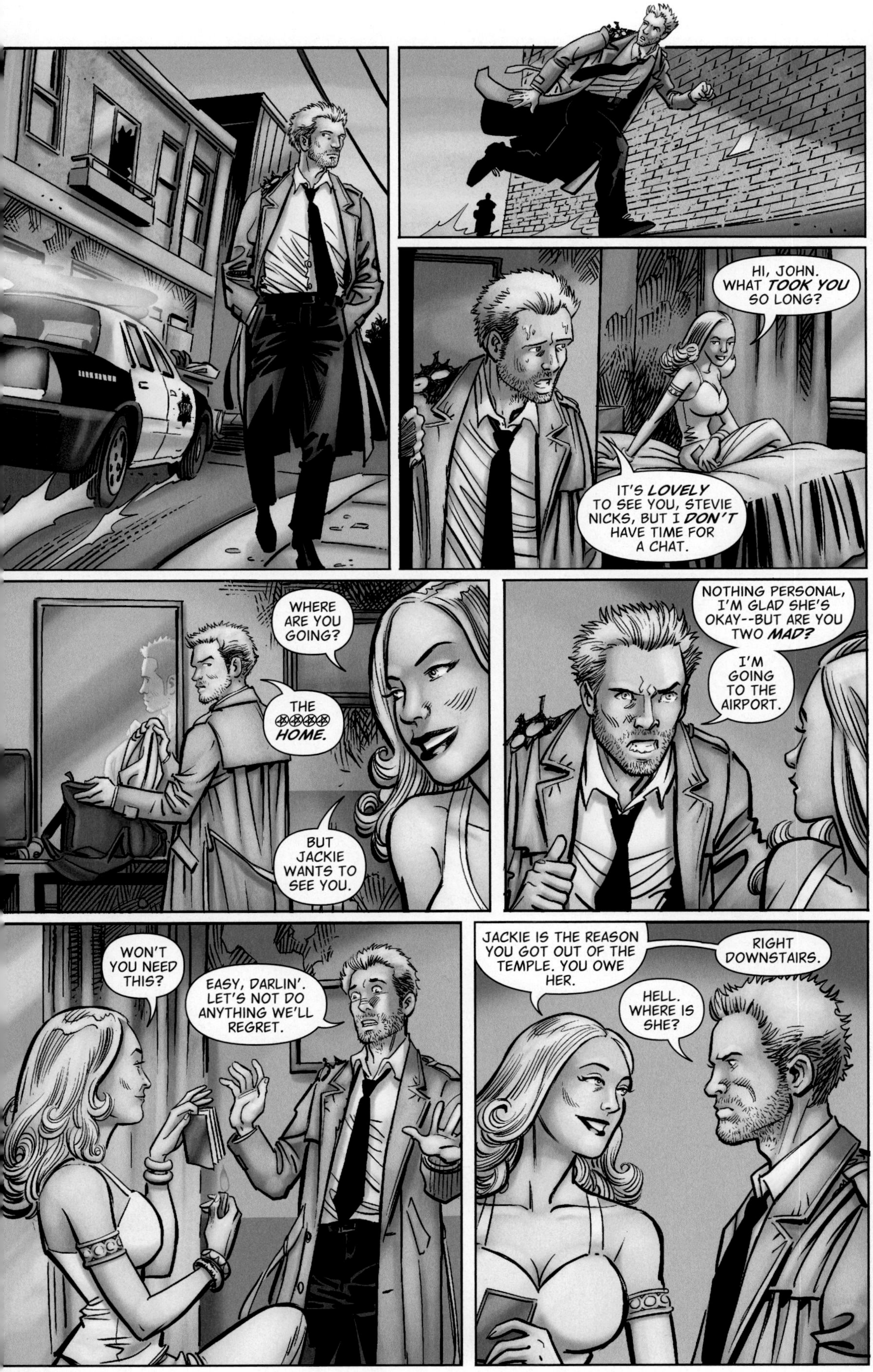

HI, JOHN. WHAT TOOK YOU SO LONG?
IT'S LOVELY TO SEE YOU, STEVIE NICKS, BUT I DON'T HAVE TIME FOR A CHAT.
WHERE ARE YOU GOING?
THE ✪✪✪✪ HOME.
BUT JACKIE WANTS TO SEE YOU.
NOTHING PERSONAL, I'M GLAD SHE'S OKAY--BUT ARE YOU TWO MAD?
I'M GOING TO THE AIRPORT.
WON'T YOU NEED THIS?
EASY, DARLIN'. LET'S NOT DO ANYTHING WE'LL REGRET.
JACKIE IS THE REASON YOU GOT OUT OF THE TEMPLE. YOU OWE HER.
HELL. WHERE IS SHE?
RIGHT DOWNSTAIRS.

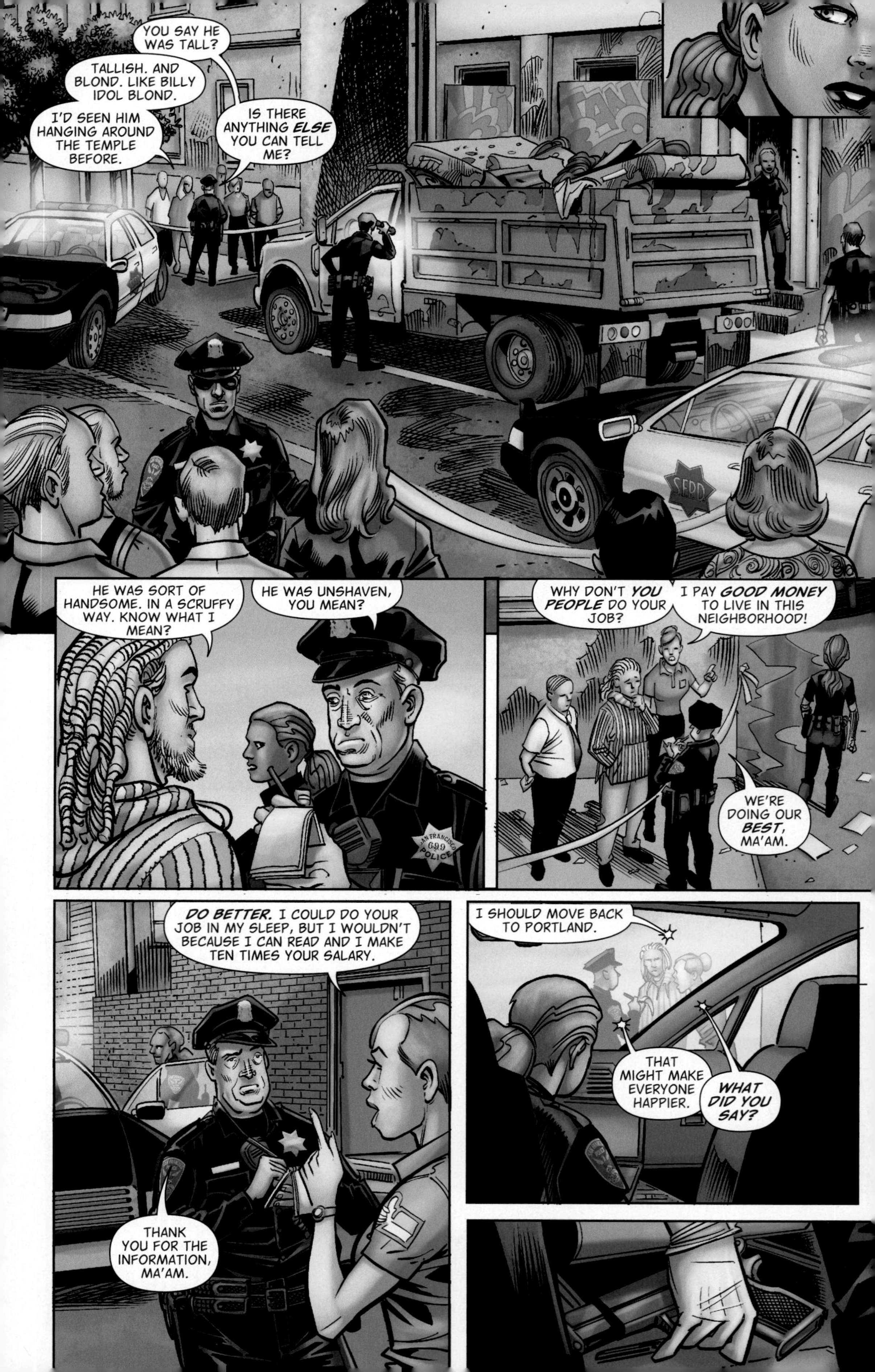
YOU SAY HE WAS TALL?
TALLISH. AND BLOND. LIKE BILLY IDOL BLOND.
I'D SEEN HIM HANGING AROUND THE TEMPLE BEFORE.
IS THERE ANYTHING *ELSE* YOU CAN TELL ME?
S.F.P.D.
HE WAS SORT OF HANDSOME. IN A SCRUFFY WAY. KNOW WHAT I MEAN?
HE WAS UNSHAVEN, YOU MEAN?
SAN FRANCISCO 699 POLICE
WHY DON'T *YOU PEOPLE* DO YOUR JOB?
I PAY *GOOD MONEY* TO LIVE IN THIS NEIGHBORHOOD!
WE'RE DOING OUR *BEST*, MA'AM.
DO BETTER. I COULD DO YOUR JOB IN MY SLEEP, BUT I WOULDN'T BECAUSE I CAN READ AND I MAKE TEN TIMES YOUR SALARY.
THANK YOU FOR THE INFORMATION, MA'AM.
I SHOULD MOVE BACK TO PORTLAND.
THAT MIGHT MAKE EVERYONE HAPPIER.
WHAT DID YOU SAY?

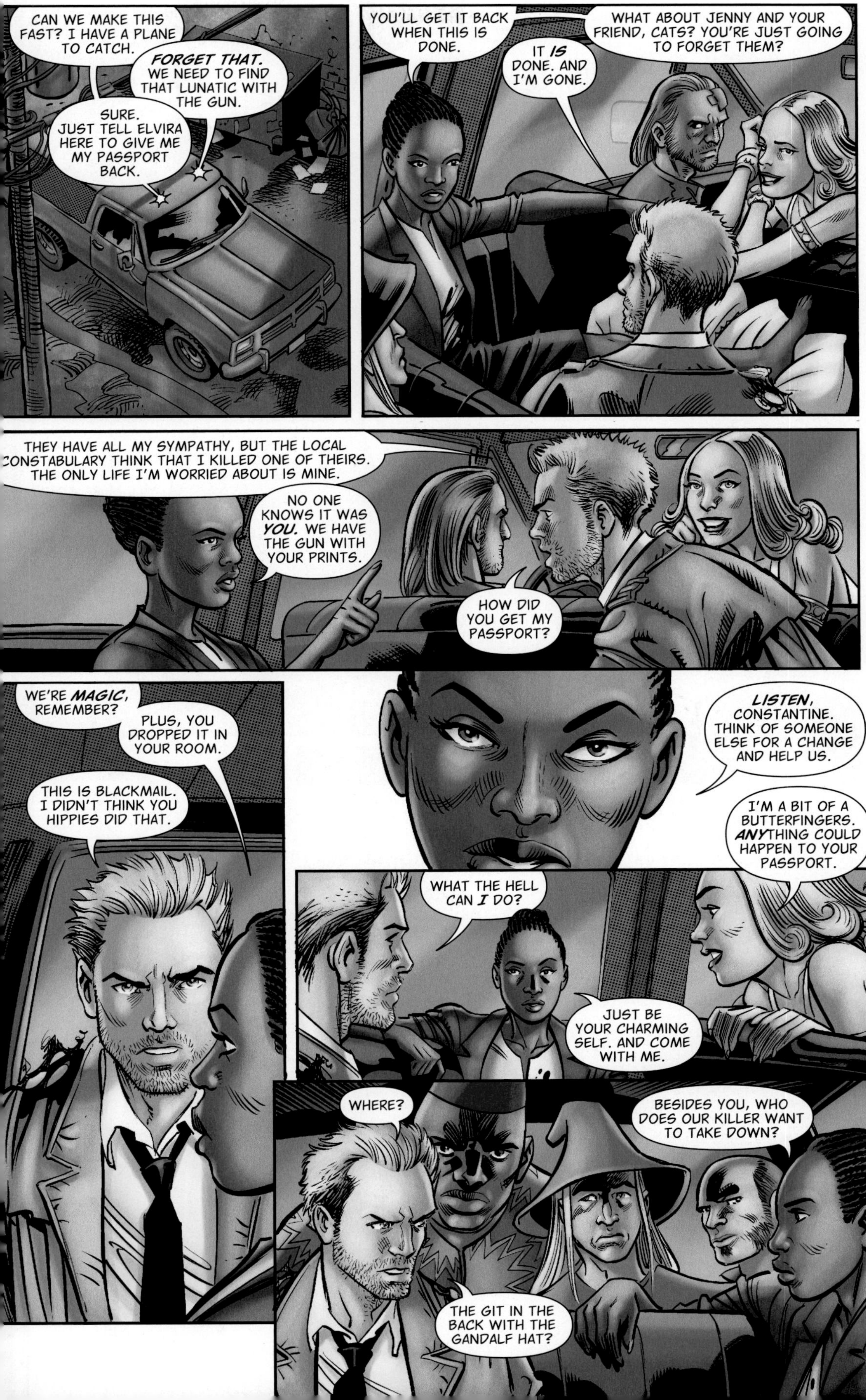
CAN WE MAKE THIS FAST? I HAVE A PLANE TO CATCH.
SURE. JUST TELL ELVIRA HERE TO GIVE ME MY PASSPORT BACK.
FORGET THAT. WE NEED TO FIND THAT LUNATIC WITH THE GUN.
YOU'LL GET IT BACK WHEN THIS IS DONE.
IT IS DONE. AND I'M GONE.
WHAT ABOUT JENNY AND YOUR FRIEND, CATS? YOU'RE JUST GOING TO FORGET THEM?
THEY HAVE ALL MY SYMPATHY, BUT THE LOCAL CONSTABULARY THINK THAT I KILLED ONE OF THEIRS. THE ONLY LIFE I'M WORRIED ABOUT IS MINE.
NO ONE KNOWS IT WAS YOU. WE HAVE THE GUN WITH YOUR PRINTS.
HOW DID YOU GET MY PASSPORT?
WE'RE MAGIC, REMEMBER?
PLUS, YOU DROPPED IT IN YOUR ROOM.
THIS IS BLACKMAIL. I DIDN'T THINK YOU HIPPIES DID THAT.
LISTEN, CONSTANTINE. THINK OF SOMEONE ELSE FOR A CHANGE AND HELP US.
I'M A BIT OF A BUTTERFINGERS. ANYTHING COULD HAPPEN TO YOUR PASSPORT.
WHAT THE HELL CAN I DO?
JUST BE YOUR CHARMING SELF. AND COME WITH ME.
WHERE?
BESIDES YOU, WHO DOES OUR KILLER WANT TO TAKE DOWN?
THE GIT IN THE BACK WITH THE GANDALF HAT?

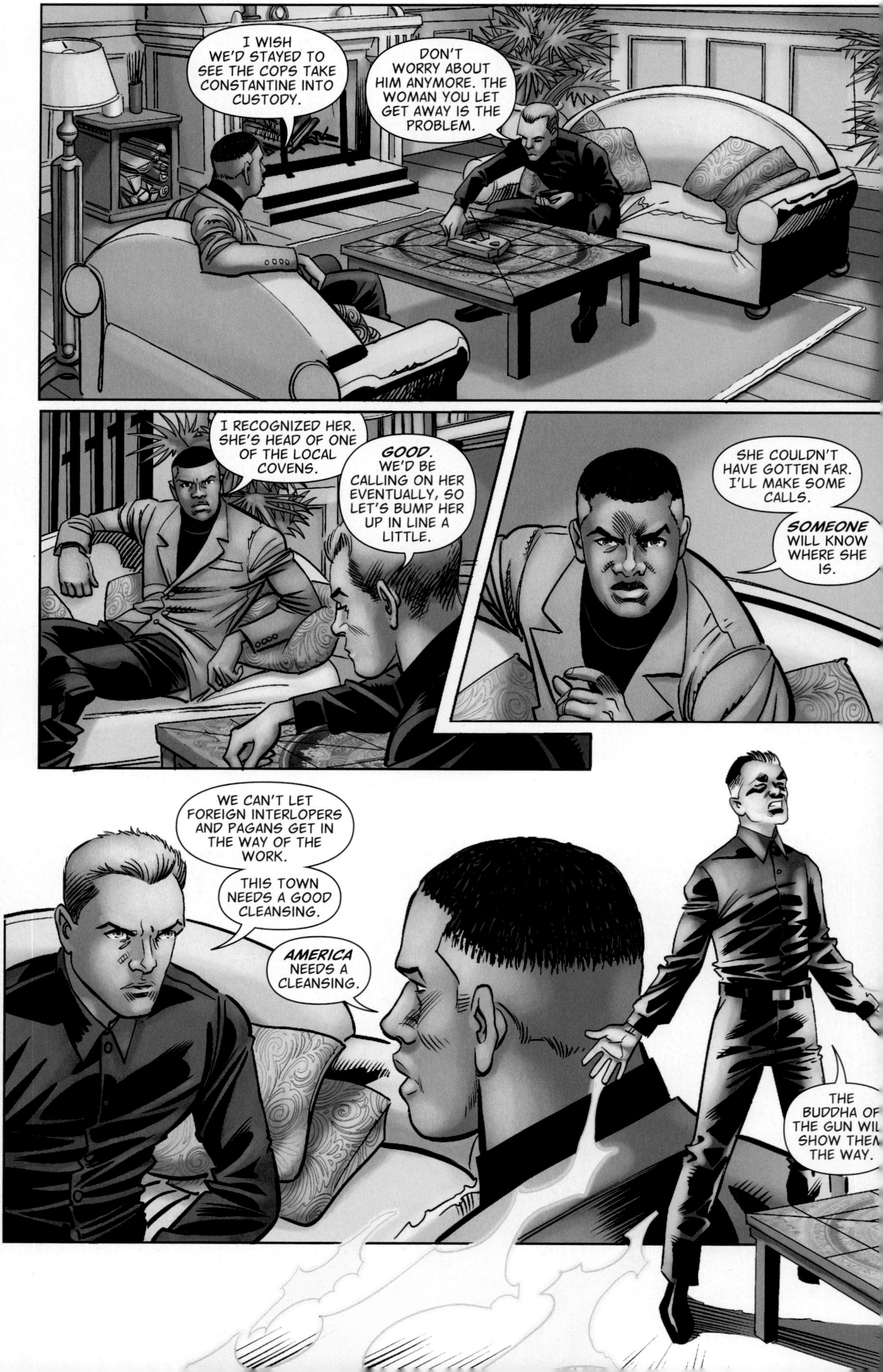
I WISH WE'D STAYED TO SEE THE COPS TAKE CONSTANTINE INTO CUSTODY.
DON'T WORRY ABOUT HIM ANYMORE. THE WOMAN YOU LET GET AWAY IS THE PROBLEM.
I RECOGNIZED HER. SHE'S HEAD OF ONE OF THE LOCAL COVENS.
GOOD. WE'D BE CALLING ON HER EVENTUALLY, SO LET'S BUMP HER UP IN LINE A LITTLE.
SHE COULDN'T HAVE GOTTEN FAR. I'LL MAKE SOME CALLS.
SOMEONE WILL KNOW WHERE SHE IS.
WE CAN'T LET FOREIGN INTERLOPERS AND PAGANS GET IN THE WAY OF THE WORK.
THIS TOWN NEEDS A GOOD CLEANSING.
AMERICA NEEDS A CLEANSING.
THE BUDDHA OF THE GUN WIL SHOW THEM THE WAY.

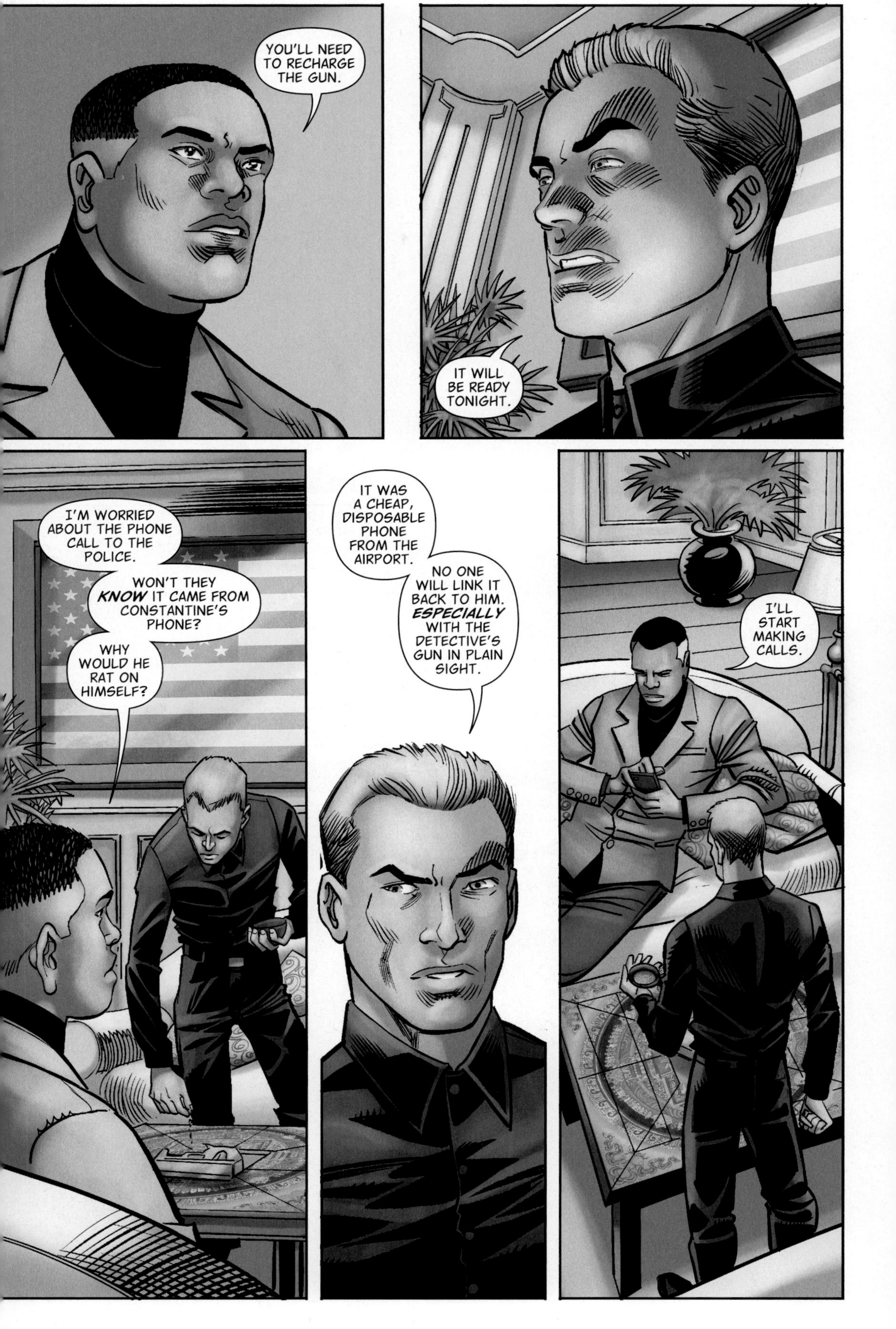
YOU'LL NEED TO RECHARGE THE GUN.
IT WILL BE READY TONIGHT.
I'M WORRIED ABOUT THE PHONE CALL TO THE POLICE.
WON'T THEY **KNOW** IT CAME FROM CONSTANTINE'S PHONE?
WHY WOULD HE RAT ON HIMSELF?
IT WAS A CHEAP, DISPOSABLE PHONE FROM THE AIRPORT.
NO ONE WILL LINK IT BACK TO HIM. **ESPECIALLY** WITH THE DETECTIVE'S GUN IN PLAIN SIGHT.
I'LL START MAKING CALLS.

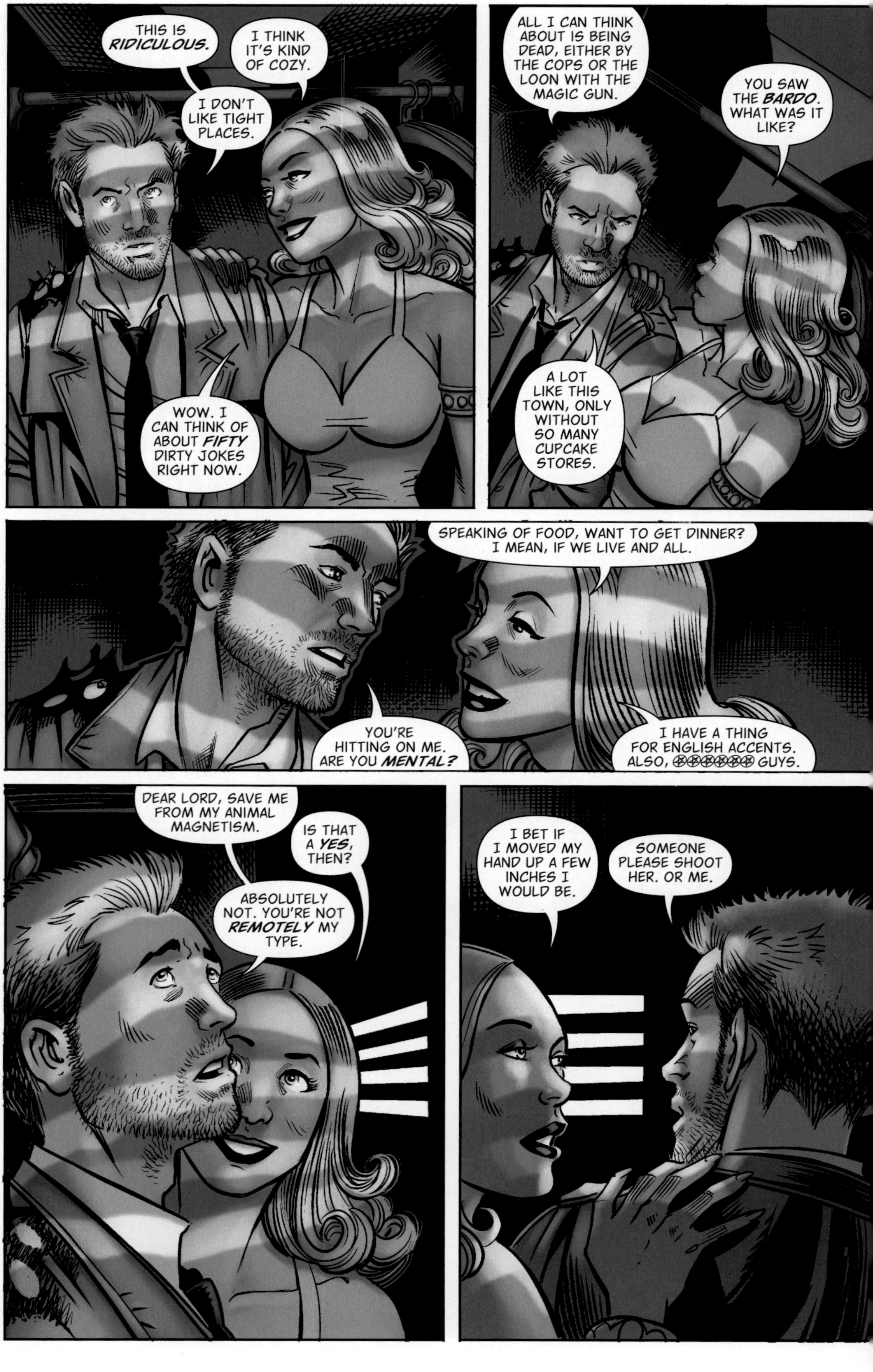
THIS IS RIDICULOUS.
I THINK IT'S KIND OF COZY.
I DON'T LIKE TIGHT PLACES.
WOW. I CAN THINK OF ABOUT FIFTY DIRTY JOKES RIGHT NOW.
ALL I CAN THINK ABOUT IS BEING DEAD, EITHER BY THE COPS OR THE LOON WITH THE MAGIC GUN.
YOU SAW THE BARDO. WHAT WAS IT LIKE?
A LOT LIKE THIS TOWN, ONLY WITHOUT SO MANY CUPCAKE STORES.
SPEAKING OF FOOD, WANT TO GET DINNER? I MEAN, IF WE LIVE AND ALL.
YOU'RE HITTING ON ME. ARE YOU MENTAL?
I HAVE A THING FOR ENGLISH ACCENTS. ALSO, ⛤⛤⛤⛤⛤⛤ GUYS.
DEAR LORD, SAVE ME FROM MY ANIMAL MAGNETISM.
IS THAT A YES, THEN?
ABSOLUTELY NOT. YOU'RE NOT REMOTELY MY TYPE.
I BET IF I MOVED MY HAND UP A FEW INCHES I WOULD BE.
SOMEONE PLEASE SHOOT HER. OR ME.

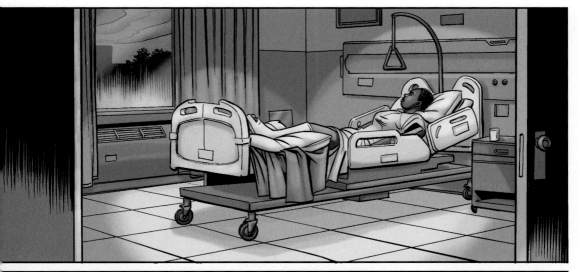

EVENING, GENTS.

WE'VE BEEN EXPECTING YOU.

YOU'LL NOTICE THE ATTRACTIVE ASSORTMENT OF RUNES ON THE DOOR.

IN CASE YOU'RE NOT ACQUAINTED WITH THEM, LET ME TRANSLATE.

THEY MEAN ✦✦✦ ALL GETS *OUT* OF THIS ROOM WITHOUT MY SAY SO.

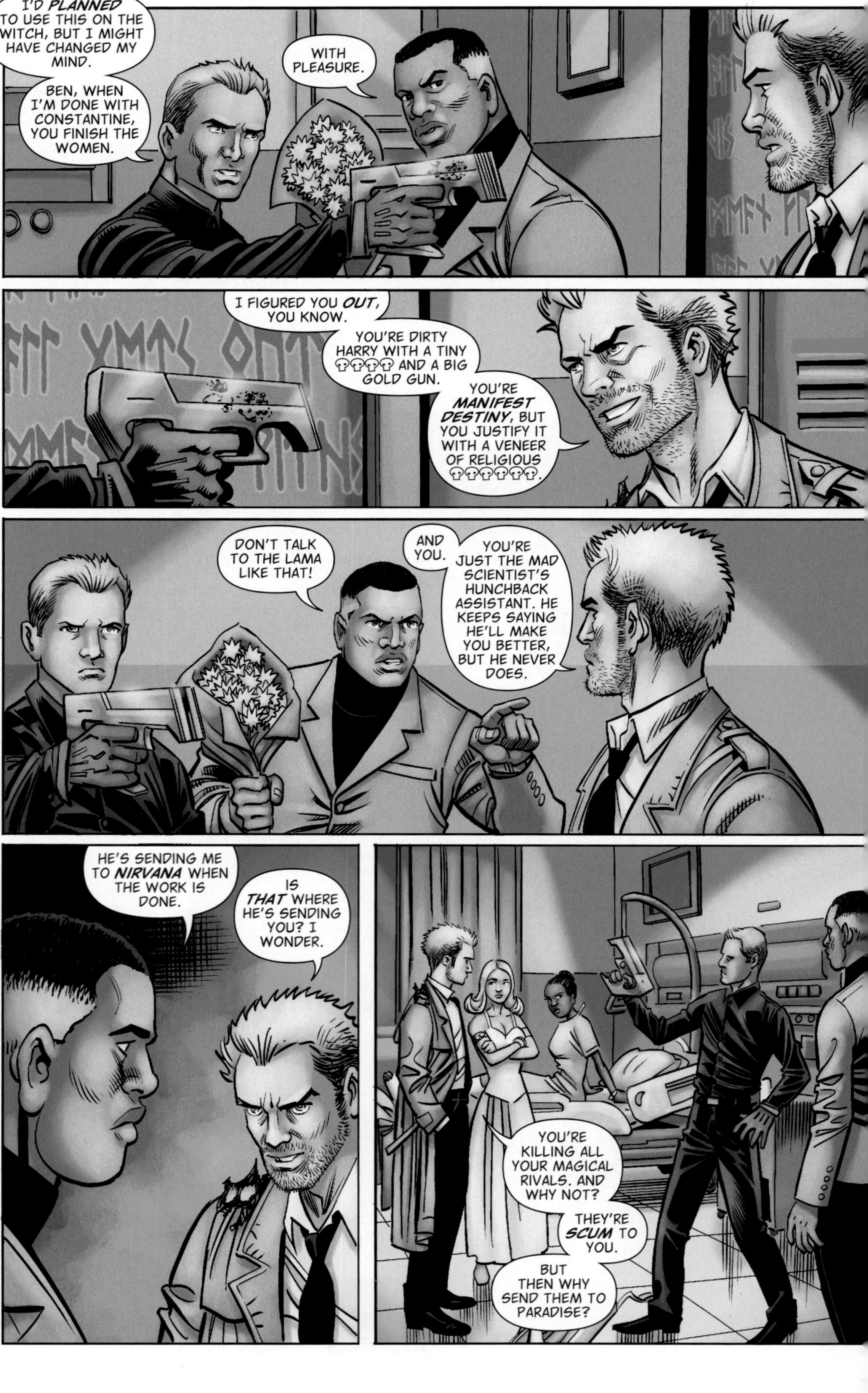
I'D PLANNED TO USE THIS ON THE WITCH, BUT I MIGHT HAVE CHANGED MY MIND.
BEN, WHEN I'M DONE WITH CONSTANTINE, YOU FINISH THE WOMEN.
WITH PLEASURE.
I FIGURED YOU OUT, YOU KNOW.
YOU'RE DIRTY HARRY WITH A TINY AND A BIG GOLD GUN.
YOU'RE MANIFEST DESTINY, BUT YOU JUSTIFY IT WITH A VENEER OF RELIGIOUS .
DON'T TALK TO THE LAMA LIKE THAT!
AND YOU.
YOU'RE JUST THE MAD SCIENTIST'S HUNCHBACK ASSISTANT. HE KEEPS SAYING HE'LL MAKE YOU BETTER, BUT HE NEVER DOES.
HE'S SENDING ME TO NIRVANA WHEN THE WORK IS DONE.
IS THAT WHERE HE'S SENDING YOU? I WONDER.
YOU'RE KILLING ALL YOUR MAGICAL RIVALS. AND WHY NOT?
THEY'RE SCUM TO YOU.
BUT THEN WHY SEND THEM TO PARADISE?

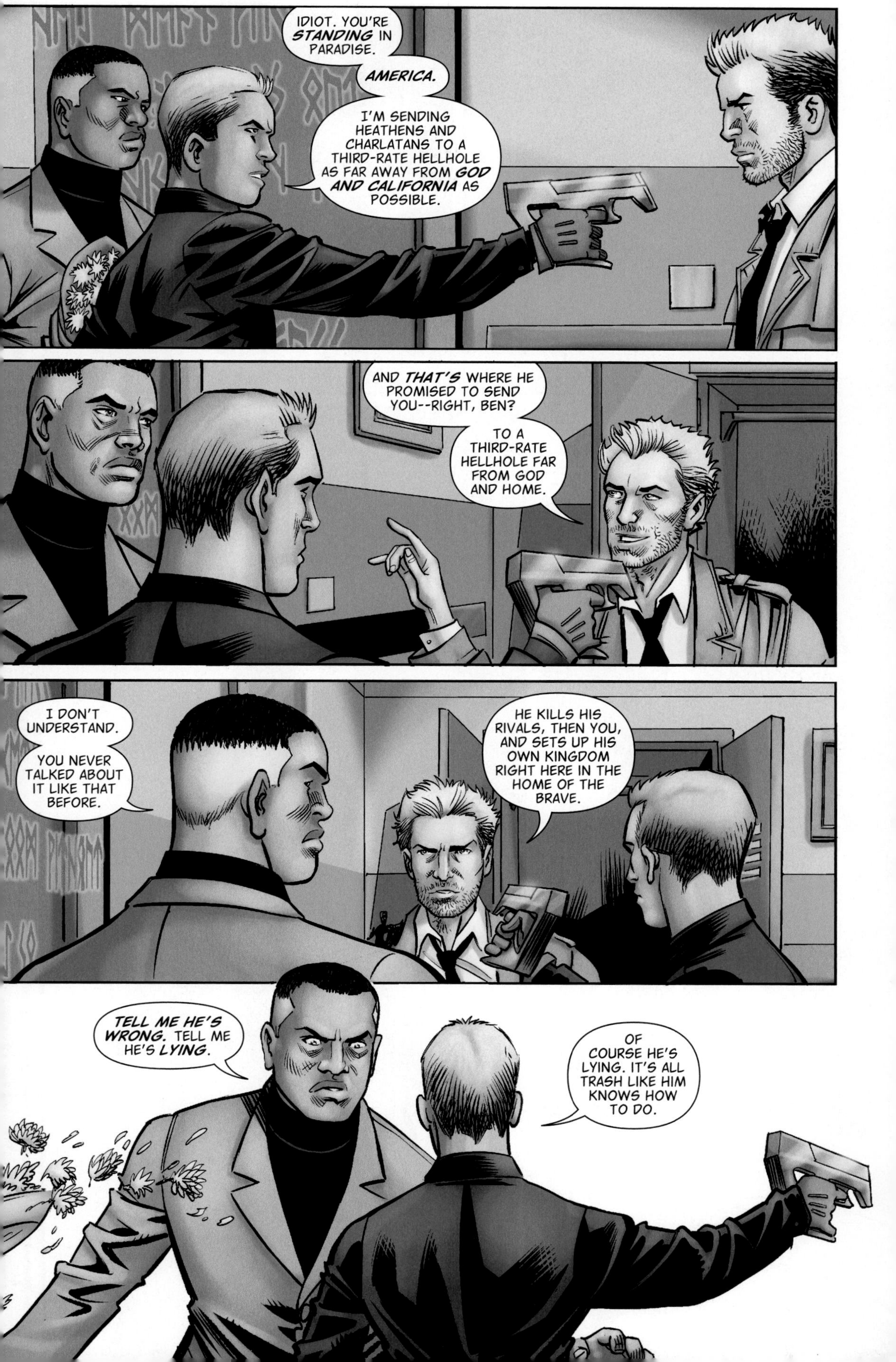
IDIOT. YOU'RE STANDING IN PARADISE.
AMERICA.
I'M SENDING HEATHENS AND CHARLATANS TO A THIRD-RATE HELLHOLE AS FAR AWAY FROM GOD AND CALIFORNIA AS POSSIBLE.
AND THAT'S WHERE HE PROMISED TO SEND YOU--RIGHT, BEN?
TO A THIRD-RATE HELLHOLE FAR FROM GOD AND HOME.
I DON'T UNDERSTAND.
YOU NEVER TALKED ABOUT IT LIKE THAT BEFORE.
HE KILLS HIS RIVALS, THEN YOU, AND SETS UP HIS OWN KINGDOM RIGHT HERE IN THE HOME OF THE BRAVE.
TELL ME HE'S WRONG. TELL ME HE'S LYING.
OF COURSE HE'S LYING. IT'S ALL TRASH LIKE HIM KNOWS HOW TO DO.

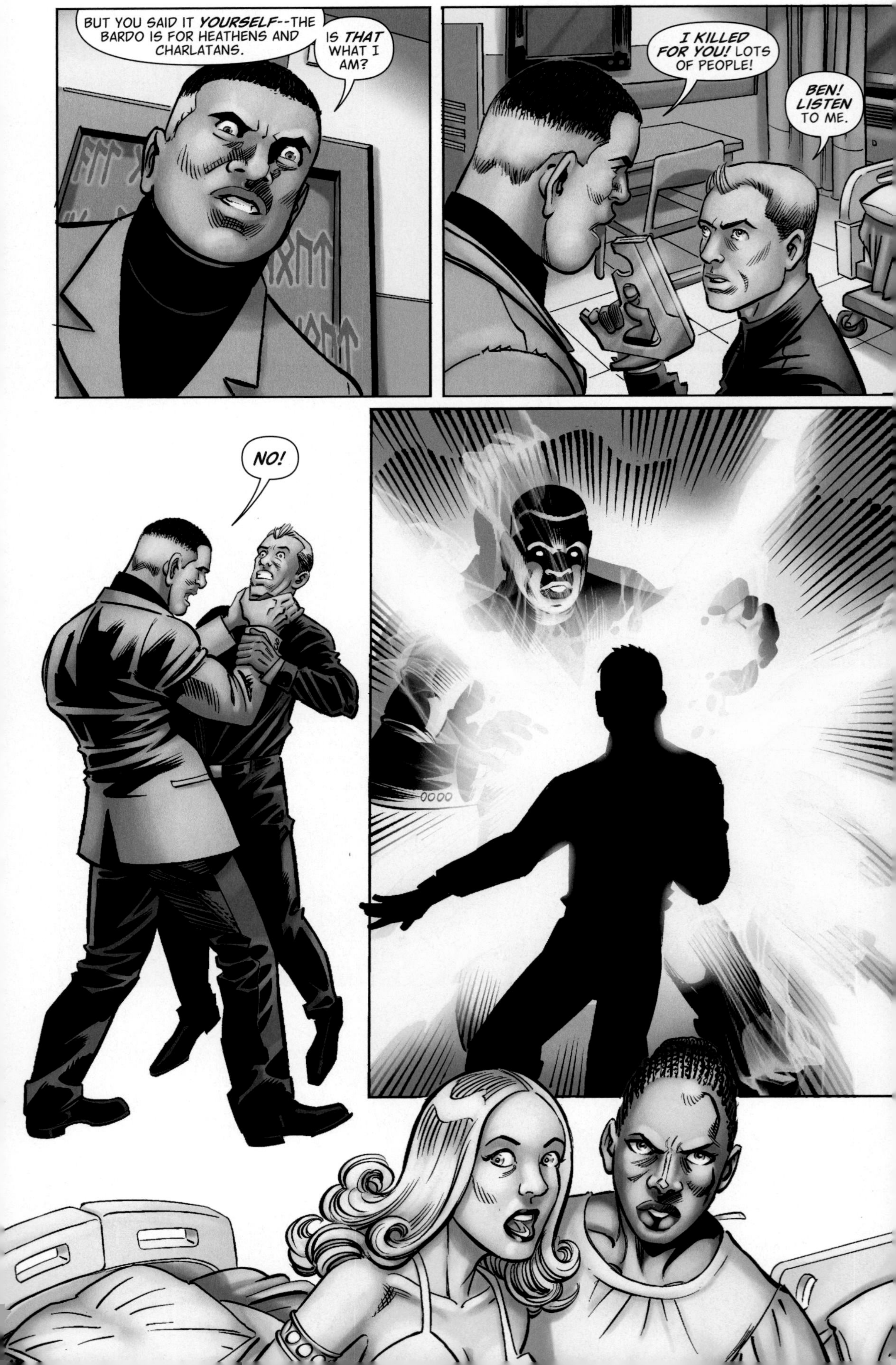
BUT YOU SAID IT YOURSELF--THE BARDO IS FOR HEATHENS AND CHARLATANS.
IS THAT WHAT I AM?
I KILLED FOR YOU! LOTS OF PEOPLE!
BEN! LISTEN TO ME.
NO!

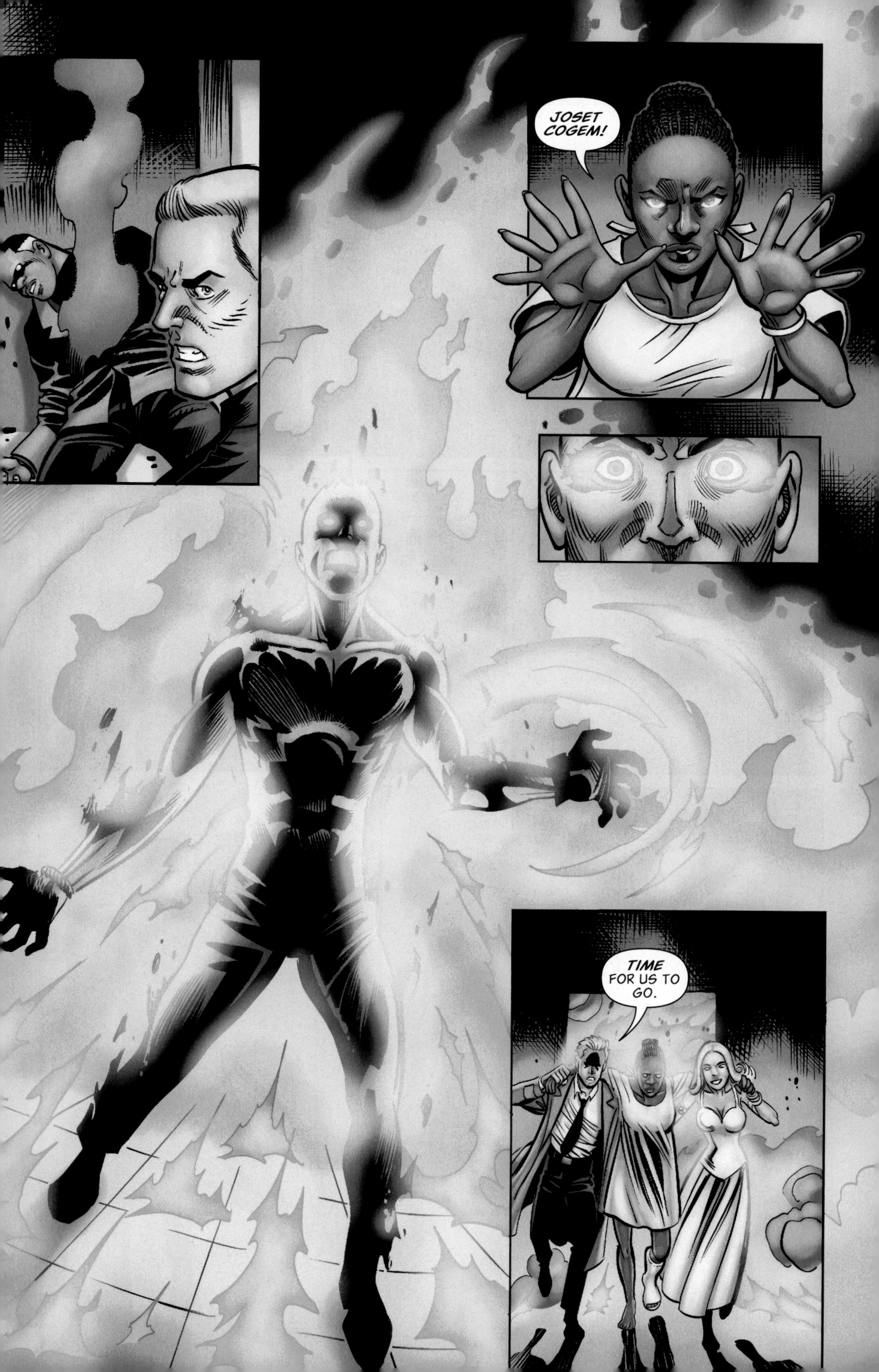
JOSET COGEM!
TIME FOR US TO GO.

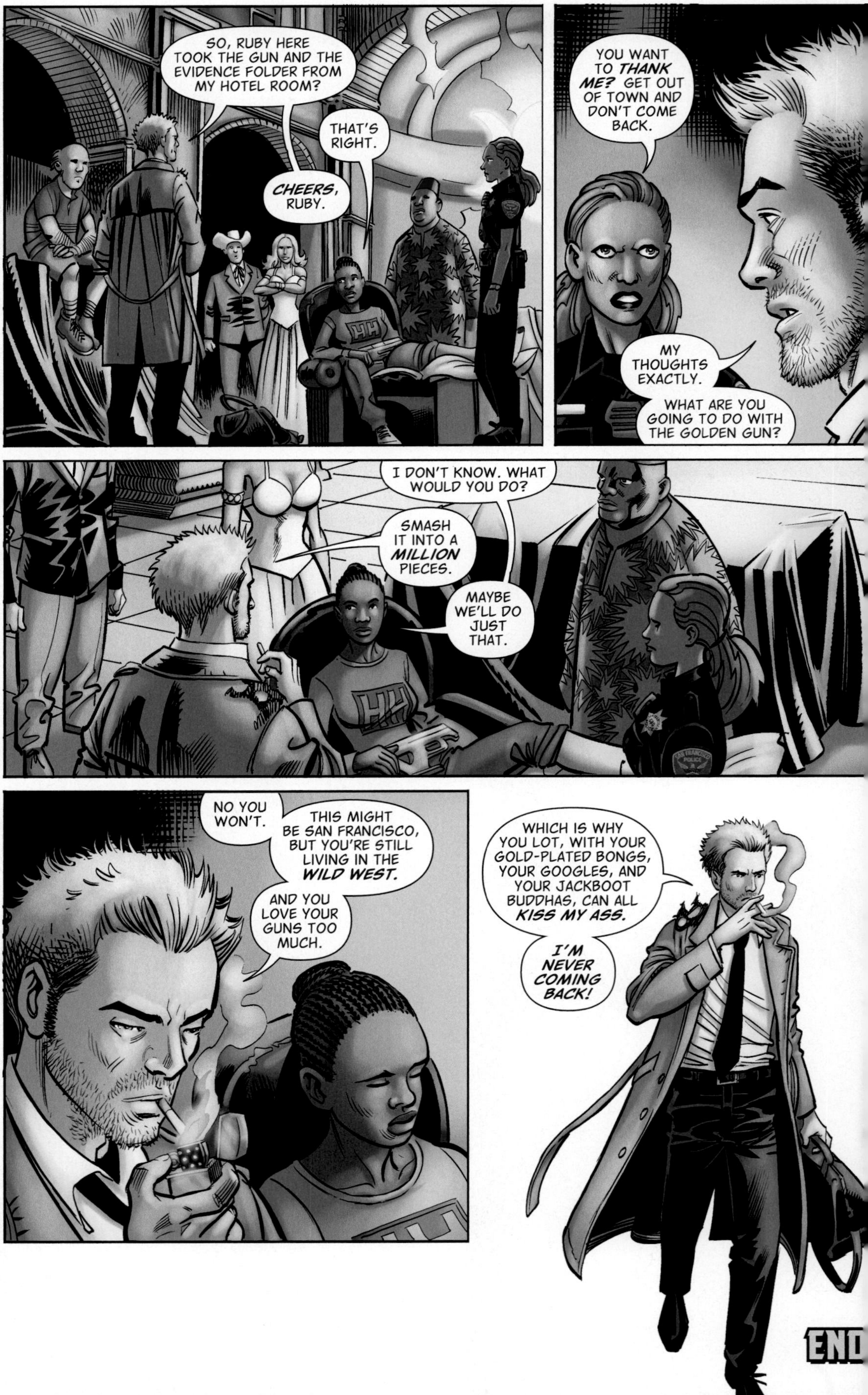
SO, RUBY HERE TOOK THE GUN AND THE EVIDENCE FOLDER FROM MY HOTEL ROOM?
THAT'S RIGHT.
CHEERS, RUBY.
YOU WANT TO THANK ME? GET OUT OF TOWN AND DON'T COME BACK.
MY THOUGHTS EXACTLY.
WHAT ARE YOU GOING TO DO WITH THE GOLDEN GUN?
I DON'T KNOW. WHAT WOULD YOU DO?
SMASH IT INTO A MILLION PIECES.
MAYBE WE'LL DO JUST THAT.
NO YOU WON'T.
THIS MIGHT BE SAN FRANCISCO, BUT YOU'RE STILL LIVING IN THE WILD WEST.
AND YOU LOVE YOUR GUNS TOO MUCH.
WHICH IS WHY YOU LOT, WITH YOUR GOLD-PLATED BONGS, YOUR GOOGLES, AND YOUR JACKBOOT BUDDHAS, CAN ALL KISS MY ASS.
I'M NEVER COMING BACK!
END

THE HELLBLAZER

VARIANT COVER GALLERY

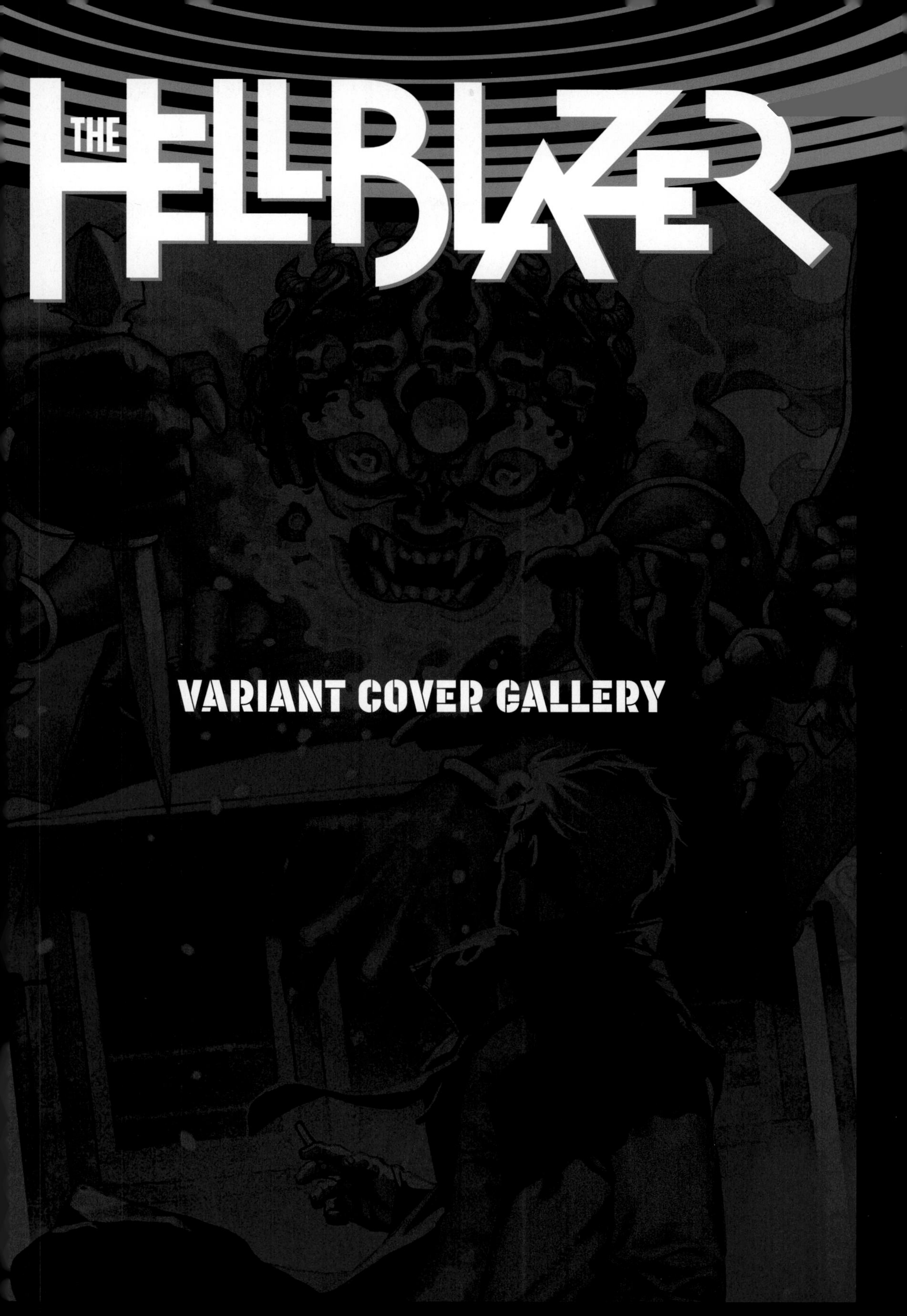

THE HELLBLAZER #13 by YASMINE PUTRI

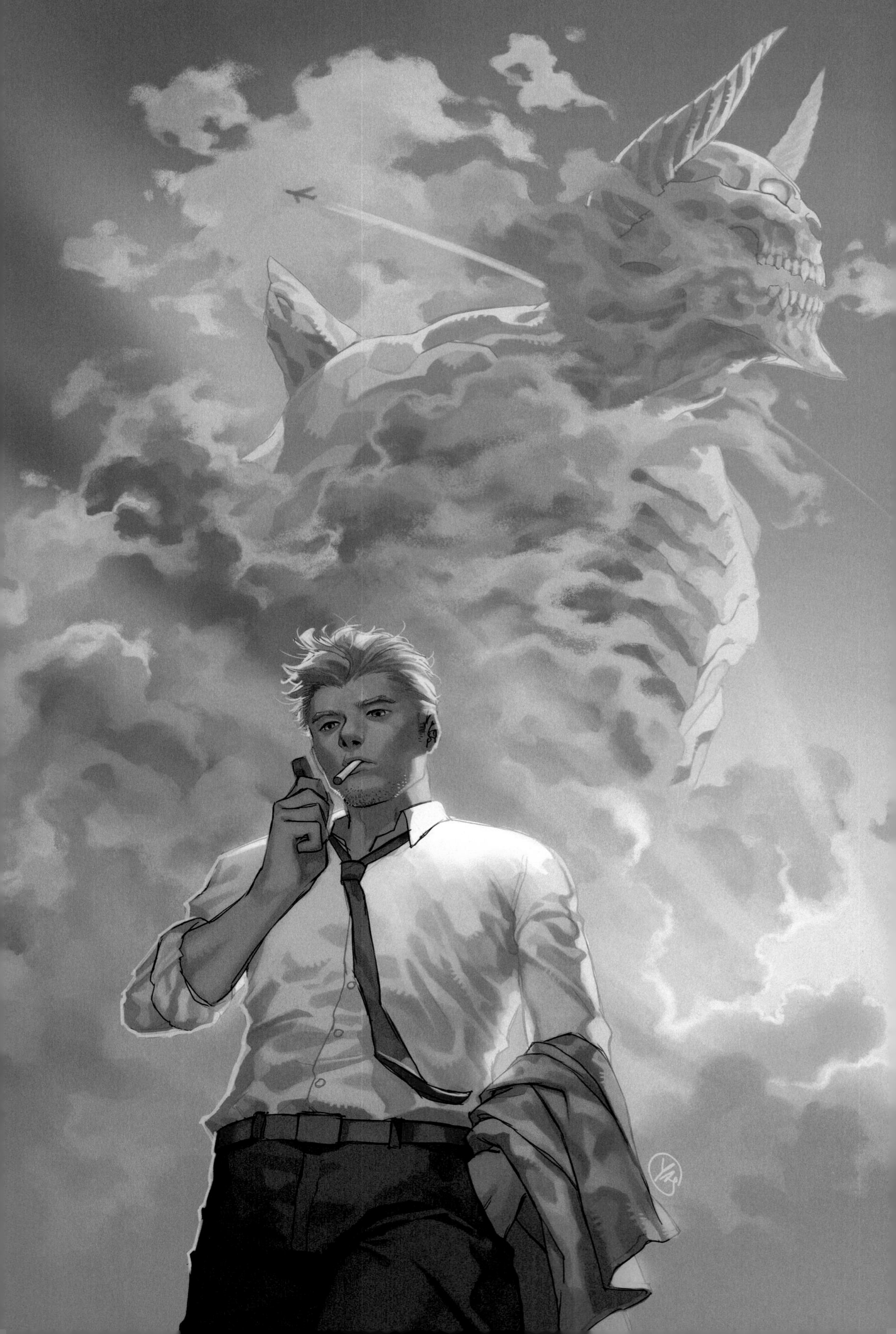

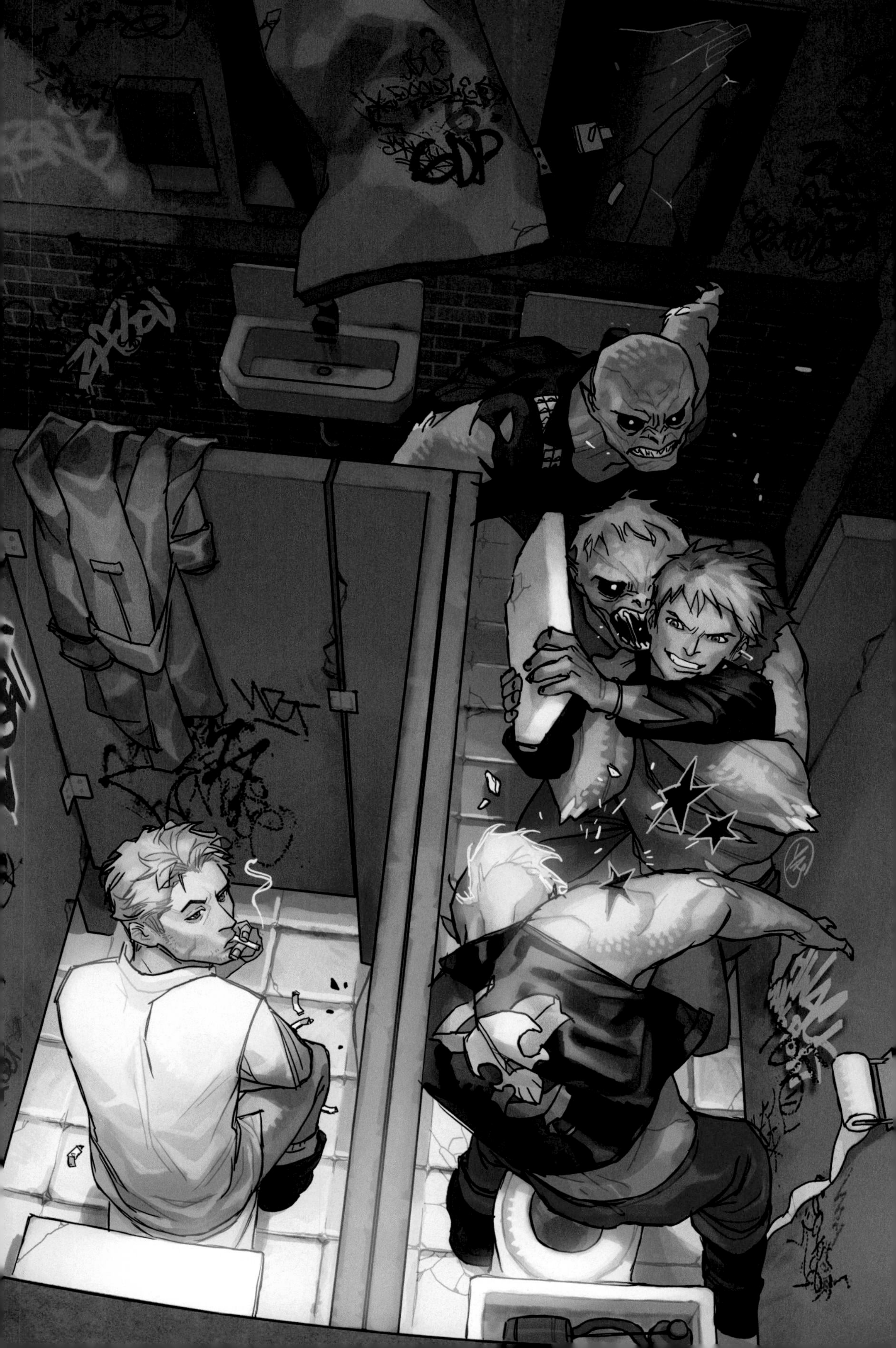

THE HELLBLAZER #14 by YASMINE PUTRI

THE HELLBLAZER #15 by YASMINE PUTR

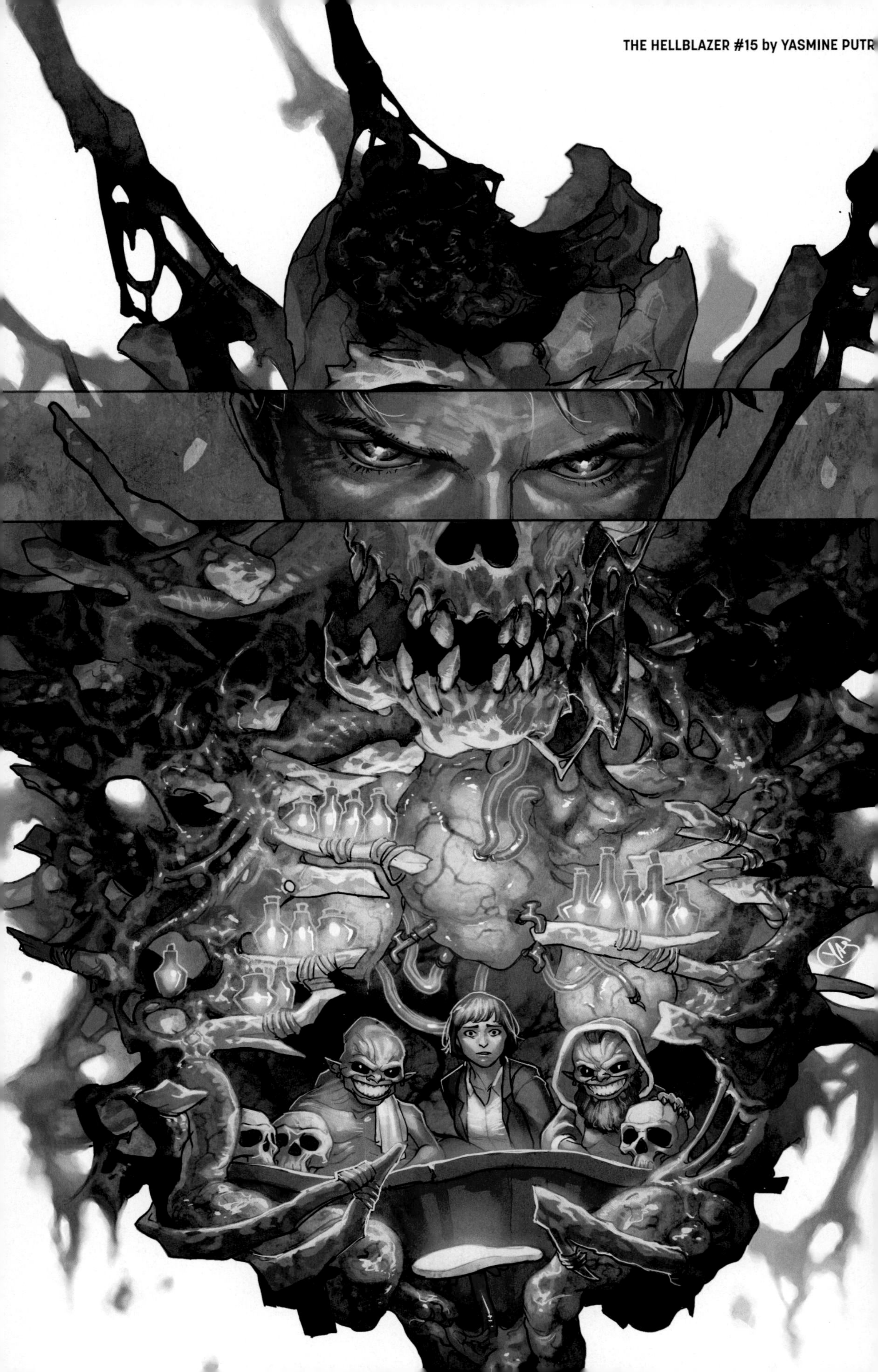

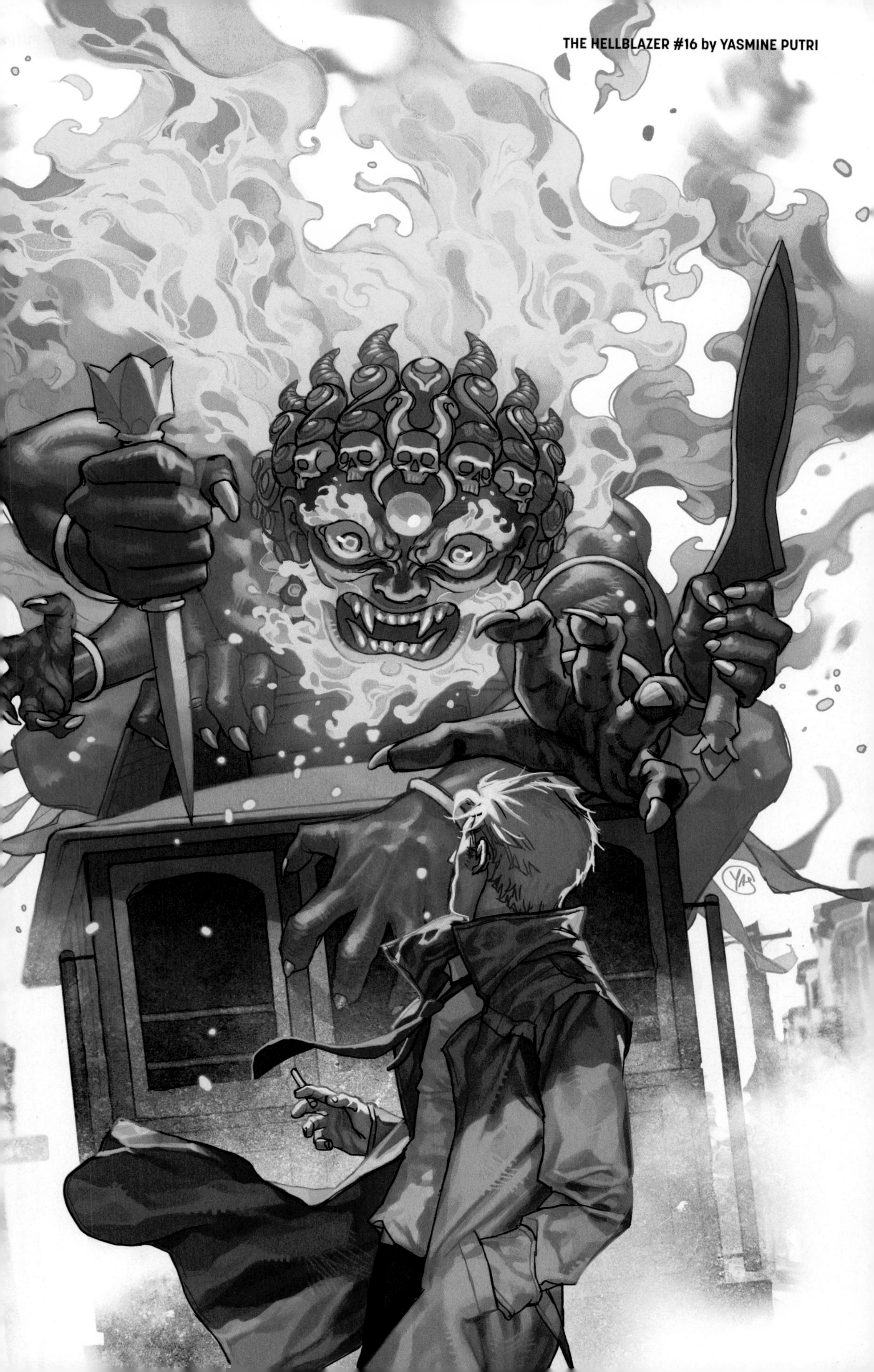

THE HELLBLAZER #16 by YASMINE PUTRI

THE HELLBLAZER #17 by YASMINE PUTR

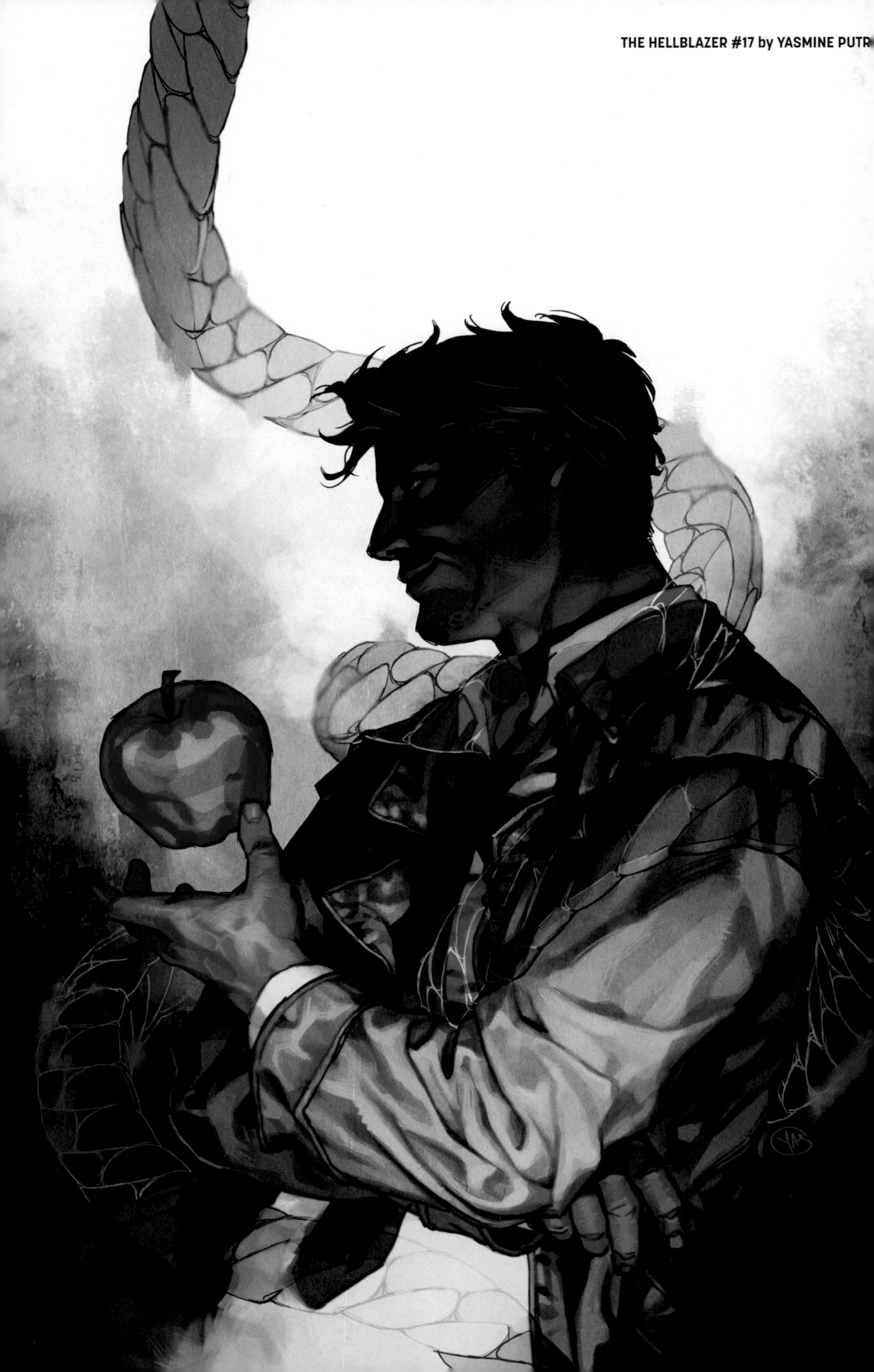

THE HELLBLAZER #18 by SEAN PHILLIPS

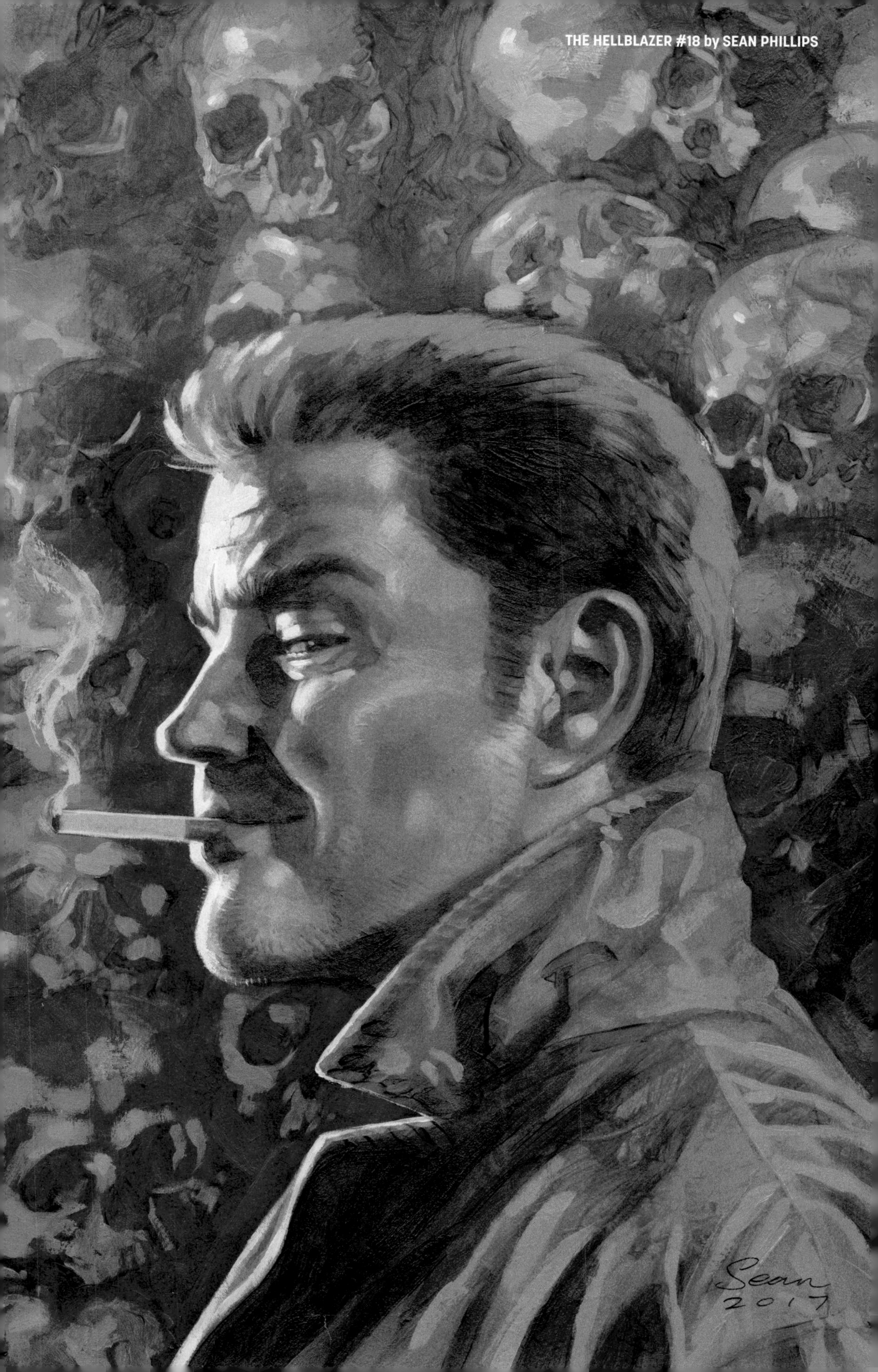
Sean
2017

DC UNIVERSE REBIRTH

SUICIDE SQUAD

VOL. 1: THE BLACK VAULT

ROB WILLIAMS
with JIM LEE and others

VOL.1 THE BLACK VAULT
ROB WILLIAMS • JIM LEE • PHILIP TAN • JASON FABOK • IVAN REIS • GARY FRANK

VOL.1 THE POISON TRUTH
SIMON OLIVER • MORITAT • ANDRE SZYMANOWICZ

**THE HELLBLAZER VOL. 1:
THE POISON TRUTH**

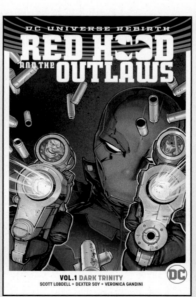

VOL.1 DARK TRINITY
SCOTT LOBDELL • DEXTER SOY • VERONICA GANDINI

**RED HOOD AND THE OUTLAWS VOL. 1:
DARK TRINITY**

VOL.1 DIE LAUGHING
AMANDA CONNER • JIMMY PALMIOTTI • CHAD HARDIN • JOHN TIMMS

**HARLEY QUINN VOL. 1:
DIE LAUGHING**